IDA LUPINO

FORGOTTEN AUTEUR

THE WILLIAM & BETTYE NOWLIN SERIES
in Art, History, and Culture of the Western Hemisphere

IDA LUPINO
FORGOTTEN AUTEUR

From Film Noir to the Director's Chair

ALEXANDRA SEROS

University of Texas Press *Austin*

Frontispiece: Director Ida Lupino thinking about a shot, ca. 1951.

Printed in the United States of America
First edition, 2024
First reprint, 2025

♾ The paper used in this book meets the minimum requirements of ANSI/NISO Z39.48–1992 (R1997) (Permanence of Paper).

Library of Congress Cataloging-in-Publication Data

Names: Seros, Alexandra, author.
Title: Ida Lupino, forgotten auteur : from film noir to the director's chair / Alexandra Seros.
Description: First edition. | Austin : University of Texas Press, 2024. | Includes bibliographical references and index.
Identifiers: LCCN 2024012308
ISBN 978-1-4773-3065-4 (hardcover)
ISBN 978-1-4773-3066-1 (pdf)
ISBN 978-1-4773-3067-8 (epub)
Subjects: LCSH: Lupino, Ida, 1918-1995. | Filmakers, Inc. (Hollywood, Calif.) | Women motion picture producers and directors—United States—Biography. | Women television producers and directors—United States—Biography. | Motion picture actors and actresses—United States—Biography. | Film noir—Production and direction—Case studies. | Thrillers (Television programs)—Production and direction—Case studies.
Classification: LCC PN1998.3.L89 S47 2024 | DDC 791.4302/8092 [B]—dc23/eng/20240325
LC record available at https://lccn.loc.gov/2024012308
doi:10.7560/330654

To Walter Francis Ulloa and our magical son, Bruno Seros-Ulloa, and to Edith and George Seros, my parents, who may have known her.

CONTENTS

Preface

THE AUTHENTICITY OF A FRAGMENT

I held my own in the toughest kind of man's world.

Ida Lupino in Ruthe Stein, "How Ida Lupino Broke into Man's World of Directing"

Some time ago, I saw a poster for a movie called *Outrage*, a low-budget, independent film made in 1950 about rape, unbelievable for that time. Even more surprising, Ida Lupino, who I knew was an actress, had directed it. Actually, between 1949 and 1953, Lupino had directed six movies. But a story about rape—how had she managed that during the Production Code Administration's censorial lock on the film industry? That poster was the beginning of my archival search across the country and ultimately to the film library Renzo Renzi of the Cineteca di Bologna, Italy.

I thought I knew Ida Lupino, but I didn't. Research changes the outcome. Unfortunately, and surprisingly, few books have been written about Ida Lupino. Notable are *Ida Lupino as Film Director, 1949–1953: An Auteur Approach* (1980), Lucy Ann Liggett Stewart's early, prescient book based on her dissertation; *Queen of the 'B's: Ida Lupino behind the Camera* (1995), edited by Annette Kuhn; *Ida Lupino: A Biography* (1996), by William Donati; *Ida Lupino, Director: Her Art and Resilience in Times of Transition* (2017), by Therese Grisham and Julie Grossman; and *The Bigamist* (2009), Amelie Hastie's monograph about Lupino's last independent film, in which she costarred and directed.

Grisham and Grossman's book came out the very day I defended my dissertation prospectus, unbelievable as that sounds, so instead of writing a critical study, as those two authors have done so well, I refocused my thoughts on the silencing of Lupino's talent and skill—which is largely the reason for her anomalous position within the Hollywood film industry—and on writing from a more cinematic or industrial point of view. To do this properly, I turned to the work of Carlo Ginzburg, an Italian historian whose work focuses on microhistory—specifically, his writing of absence in the archive. His brand of historiography is the standard for recovering and identifying creative links between artists and their archival fragments.

Recovering Lupino's story required detective work. It was essential to see around corners by examining "the most trivial details," as Ginzburg advises, and to read between the lines, to "grasp the voices."[1] Ginzburg quotes Bertolt Brecht to make his point: "In reality, only a fragment carries the mark of authenticity."[2] Ginzburg's work in Modena, Italy, on the witch trials—1505 to 1510 and again from 1518 to 1521, when 110 women were murdered—is a model for recovering the voices of marginalized women who have been silenced.[3] Ginzburg's research is a primer on how to locate what is missing from the record by piecing together archival fragments that are found by following authentic traces and footprints and, in Lupino's case, the miscellany of film history. Amelie Hastie makes the point that "miscellany" is a kind of methodological model, that women's histories are inevitably dispersed across genres, forms, and space.[4] Ginzburg states it well: "Though reality may seem to be opaque, there are privileged zones—signs, clues—which allow us to penetrate."[5]

The search for clues in Lupino's historical record uncovered fragments that were overlooked but could be animated and objects that were bypassed but remained available for close inspection. Upon inspection, they yielded a deeper level of understanding of how the concerns of class, gender, and post–World War II culture have influenced the critical reception of Lupino's underexamined work and life.

In the case of Lupino, glamour and domesticity merge. Fragments from scrapbooks in the University of Southern California's Cinematic Library, the Constance McCormick Collection, gathered with the help of Ned Comstock, suggest a link between Lupino's years as a young mother and her television work. As a mother and a working screenwriter, I was curious about how Lupino structured her life. I wondered if motherhood altered her mode and choices of work. Did she make career adjustments to take care of her daughter, Bridget, born to Lupino and her husband Howard Duff in 1952? I found clues in documents related, especially, to the vast extent of the work she did for television and in the more mundane evidence that attaches to any celebrity. Because of the tremendous chasms in the television archive, my approach to Lupino's labor became artisanal. I considered the ephemera that constitute a supportive yet peripheral history of Lupino's career, and to better understand her legacy as a director, I undertook a detailed, frame-by-frame analysis of portions of her independent films and selected television episodes. With such an archival study, it was vital to find as many original documents as I could. Seeing the documents is as important as reading about them, so I have included images of many of these in the hope that through them, Lupino's voice will become clearer. These archival documents allow her to speak out over the silences that affected the reception of her work.[6]

Countless female screenwriters and directors, set designers, art directors, and costumers think about motherhood daily on set; these are the women who have raised children while holding demanding jobs in theater, film, and television. In 2019, these issues were finally being addressed. Leigh Silverman, who directed *The Lifespan of a Fact*, asked her mostly female theater cast and crew what they would need "to manage the long hours required for preparing a new stage production."[7] The question of how childcare is accommodated is important because it is the primary reason that women are underrepresented as writers, directors, and designers, especially at the industry's highest pay levels. Artists often are self-employed freelancers without parental leave. Long hours make the life-work balance difficult. Playwright Sarah Ruhl has noted the "huge invisible attrition for parents in the field," pointing out that it is "a problem people are just starting to become aware of."[8] Women often feel trapped after pregnancy, experiencing, for example, postpartum anxiety and depression. This brings up three questions: "What does it mean to be female? What does it mean to be a mother? And what does it mean to be creative?"[9] How to balance work and family was an ever-present concern for Lupino. Susan Sontag writes that the cohesiveness of the family rests on the exploitation of women's domestic labor.[10] In *Wages against Housework*, Italian activist Silvia Federici discusses the billions of dollars lost to the world's GDP from unpaid domestic labor.[11]

Lupino insisted that because she was a wife and mother, she could not leave the state or the country to direct without a great sacrifice to family life. Finding a balance between career and home was extremely challenging for women in the 1950s and 1960s. Working in television was Lupino's answer. She could remain near home and family and, as she said often, pay the bills at the same time.

Lupino was known to be both collaborative and authorial, attributes now considered to be marks of the contemporary auteur, and she shaped her career so that she could care for her husband and daughter while maintaining her author's touch. The more I studied Lupino, examining her films, television movies, and television episodes, the more I felt that I had to intervene in the limited, and often faulty, historiography that had been constructed for her, to redress the distortion and even erasure in the record. In this book, I challenge the notion that Ida Lupino was—or should remain—a marginalized, illegible figure. Indeed, the conspicuous gap in the literature about Lupino's directing work, particularly her television corpus, indicates that we have much to learn about her creative contributions on set. Far from impenetrable, Lupino's work incorporates distinctive patterns and systems meant to form a cohesive visual and industrial design. Amelie Hastie states that "the scuffle for greatness" in the film industry insists on studio categorization. Lupino, though, is not easily categorized; she is far more faceted, resistant to grouping and any sort of placement, and therefore she has remained overlooked.[12] Lupino was right at the hub of independent filmmaking, for which she has not been given the credit she deserves. Although critics greatly admired her acting, once she stepped behind the camera and was no longer the object of the viewer's gaze, she became an anomaly, even a threat—and then she was marginalized.

This book was written over a two-year period. Much of that time was spent working in archival collections, searching for photographs and documents that contain information about the aspect of Lupino's life and work that most intrigued me: the intersection of the transitional moment of the 1950s and Lupino's provocative and sometimes transgressive character. The arrangement of the book is a response to this focus.

The introduction focuses on Lupino's ambiguous endings and the paradox that is Lupino herself. It offers an overview of her life and career and an assessment of what I call the Lupinian brand. Part I follows Lupino's dramatic transition from being one of Hollywood's busiest femmes fatales during the classic period of American cinema to producing, writing, and directing six independently produced movies in five years (1949–1953). Lupino's early years, her career in front of the camera, and a review of her directorial work are the subjects of chapter 1. This chapter also touches on the response of feminist critics to Lupino's work. Chapter 2 considers the gendered expectations that women faced following World War II and how Lupino navigated between motherhood and a demanding career in the film and television industries. This chapter also looks at the connections she had with other noted filmmakers. In chapter 3, Lupino's career as director and producer are explored, beginning with the formation of her independent production company, the Filmakers (spelled with one *m*, perhaps to further distinguish their specific kind of handmade work). The question of auteurship, which is raised in the introduction, is also discussed in this chapter. Comparisons with the work of acknowledged male auteurs of the day—among them Nicholas Ray, Robert Aldrich, and Alfred Hitchcock—show how ambitious Lupino was and how remarkable her accomplishments were, not only in film but also as the sought-after director of many dozens of television episodes. She is a model for today's new collaborative theory of auteurism, even though she was not acknowledged.

Part II proves the point. Chapters 4 through 6 present case studies of three of Lupino's directed films, respectively: *Not Wanted* (1949), *Never Fear* (1949), and *The Hitch-Hiker* (1953). *Not Wanted*, Lupino's first film, and *Never Fear* (also titled *Young Lovers*), her second, are probably the least well known of her independent films. *Not Wanted*, the empathetic story of an unwed mother, was a financial and critical hit, but *Never Fear*, in which a young dancer recovers from polio, was not. A standard marker of a director's legitimacy is a second film that does at least as well as the first. *Never Fear*, Lupino's movie about the psychological and physical effects of polio, was a box office failure. This was a critical failure from which Lupino had to recuperate, and she began again with *Outrage* (1950), for which Mala Powers received rave reviews, followed by *Hard, Fast and Beautiful* (1951), another critical success, particularly for her directing work. *The Hitch-Hiker* was Lupino's favorite of the films she wrote, produced, and directed. The film tackles another disturbing subject: the story of Billy Cook, a real-life serial killer who transfixed the nation in the early 1950s. Lupino's film presents the killer as a three-dimensional character with the empathy that is central to her directorial work and is one of the defining elements of the Lupinian brand. The Library of Congress has preserved and archived *The Hitch-Hiker* as the first noir film directed by a woman, certifying its importance to the cultural heritage of the United States.

Part III explores the astounding number and variety of television shows that Lupino directed during the classic period of television in the United States. She could work within every genre and was in demand by both actors and producers for her skill with the camera and the actors. Not only did she achieve great performances, but she also produced episodes with creative quickness and efficiency, remaining under budget and always wrapping on time. Lupino directed the most famous shows of the period, many of which were pure action: *Have Gun—Will Travel*, with Richard Boone, a known tough actor to direct in a show, iconic as a period piece of unusual modernity; *Hong Kong*, starring Rod Taylor, set on what was then a unique Asian location, using several early Asian actors; *The Untouchables*, starring Robert Stack and Paul Picerni, with a crime voice-over and narrative every week by Walter Winchell, a touch of documentary style; Rod Serling's *Twilight Zone*, which she was the only woman ever to direct, her directed episode the fifth most popular of all the episodes; and comedies like *Gilligan's Island* and "Lucy's Summer Vacation" (an episode of *The Lucy-Desi Comedy Hour*), where Lupino's genetic comic timing compares well to the great Lucille Ball's.

Each of the book's three parts begins with a Snapshots section. These vignettes include photos and short narratives that illustrate different aspects of Lupino's life and career, providing additional insights into her roles as a mother, actress, and filmmaker.

In the conclusion, I discuss the recovery of Lupino's achievements in film and television. She told true stories about real people in a social realistic style that was greatly influenced by Roberto Rossellini. Her films, teleplays, and TV shows are one of a kind, directed by a rare artist the likes of whom comes along only once in several decades.

See Idalupino.com for more photos, archival documents, career charts with her dates, links to Lupino's colleagues in the industry, and lists of all known television episodes directed by Lupino.

IDA LUPINO

FORGOTTEN AUTEUR

Introduction

AMBIGUITY AND PARADOX IN IDA LUPINO

Doesn't it ever enter a man's head that a woman can do without him?

Ida Lupino as Lily Stevens in *Road House*

Ralph Edwards's series *This Is Your Life* was one of the most popular shows on American television in the 1950s.[1] The show's premise was to catch a noteworthy person—often a Hollywood celebrity—off guard, using elaborate advance planning to keep the subject-to-be in the dark, and purportedly showcase the "real" person by delving into the guest's private life. Friends, relatives, and colleagues, often from the subject's past, appeared on the show to tell embarrassing or even traumatic stories about the subject in front of a studio audience. On January 15, 1958, the special guest in front of the camera was Ida Lupino. At that time, she was starring in the second season of her own television series, *Mr. Adams and Eve*, in which she and her real-life husband Howard Duff satirized the notions of Hollywood and celebrity. A year earlier, on February 1, 1957, Lupino's series had aired an episode titled "This Is Your Life," in which Eve is the surprised guest. Written by Sol Saks, it spoofs not only Edwards's series but the host as well. As Eve excitedly greets family and friends who arrive on set, the host completely loses control of his show. Edwards gleefully paid Lupino back by doing a show all about her.

Lupino, although accustomed to being in front of a camera, was horrified by the surprise. Edwards generously compares the Lupino family to the Barrymores and the Redgraves—all accomplished English theatrical families—yet Lupino never quite recovers, even by the end of the show. She stumbles gracefully through the episode, trying to smile but repeating "No, no, no, no" and

Host Ralph Edwards shocking the director on January 15, 1958: "Ida Lupino, this is your life!"

"I don't believe this" for an agonizing thirty minutes. She moves erratically between shock and anxiety, all with a fidgety nervousness. When Duff finally walks onto the set, she says to Edwards, with carefully disguised anger, "I'll never forgive him for this." Then she laughs with a smile that is more grotesque than sweet. In the *This Is Your Life* episode, we see hints of the real Lupino—which was, of course, Edwards's goal.

So who is the real Ida Lupino? What is her truth?

Lupino's truth is that her contributions to the film and television industries tell a vital, realistic, feminist story in American media history. Before postwar feminism found its voice, most opportunities for women in America's entertainment industry were restricted largely to acting. Even given J. E. Smyth's detailed study *Nobody's Girl Friday*, in which the author discusses the many women who worked in various areas of the entertainment industry, from heads of unions and guilds to story consultants, writers, and producers, Lupino's directorial achievements and her seamless transitions—from actor to director, from film to television—remain a rarity. To achieve what she did, Lupino branded herself carefully and variously by downplaying and domesticating her vast intellect and creative power. Multitalented, she produced, wrote, directed, and acted, sometimes all at once.[2] Her many-faceted identity and fragmented image as wife, mother, star, and writer-director-producer resulted in a pixelated legacy, but she never insisted on protecting her work for a future legacy. This complex strategy allowed her to work without pause in film and television from the 1930s well into the 1960s, not only as an actor but, by 1948, as a writer, producer, and director. Ultimately, though, this strategy sometimes minimized her authorship and her legacy. Consequently, she has been confused in histories and analyses of her films and her work in general. An assessment of Lupino's labor practices, particularly her work as a director in the early television industry, reveals that her powerful talent was misjudged and misunderstood. Because of this, she remains relatively unknown despite her vast and eclectic accomplishments. The recovery of Lupino's contributions to film and television is part of a new, alternative history of women's filmmaking.

Lupino has been criticized by some feminists, critics, and reviewers for being anti-feminist. Perhaps they thought they knew who she was, with their expectations having been formed by her image as a hard-boiled actress, but her directorial accomplishments speak for themselves, telling a different story.[3] She operated within a locked-down male system every day, creating films that *are* women's stories. They are documents from the post–World War II era, yet they are still relevant today. The strength of these "feminine" films is found in Lupino's realistic portrayals of women's daily life after the war, portrayals that are clothed in the raw power of the director's provocative narrative style and that end with an unsettling ambiguity that reconfirms the vulnerabilities and flaws of her characters. Lupino recorded the scandal of a forbidden teen pregnancy, the existential fear of a polio contagion, the shame of rape, crime in women's sports, rampant serial murder on the new, open highways, and a fragile postwar masculine psychology that deteriorates pathetically into bigamy. Despite her detractors, Lupino's unique contributions to the industry tell a story that is critical to American media history. It is a feminist story because it narrates the woman's point of view as distinct from the man's, revealing the real, underlying cultural differences in how women and men were perceived in the world.

Lupino was the only female director working inside the Hollywood studio system, as well as the only woman in the Screen Directors Guild of America beginning in 1950, and subsequently the newly named Director's Guild of America (DGA) to 1971.[4] Each of her six independent films—*Not Wanted* (1949), *Never Fear* (1950), *Outrage* (1950), *Hard, Fast and Beautiful* (1951), *The Hitch-Hiker* (1953), and *The Bigamist* (1953)—is executed in a taut, spare, and refined style. Socially realistic and relevant, these were the narratives that she yearned to produce. One of her films, *The Hitch-Hiker*, is a cult classic that has earned a positive rating of 94 percent as of this writing from critics on Rotten Tomatoes and shares film noir status in the Library of Congress

A Westmore cosmetics ad exploiting Lupino's feminine allure. The ad had a possible double meaning, alluding to Senator Joe McCarthy's Red Scare in Hollywood.

with other landmark films, such as Edgar Ulmer's *Detour* (1945).[5] Lupino's directorial career, however, came along at a time when the industry was not interested in Poverty Row fare, and this indifference may have kept her out of the auteur pantheon. Commentators failed to acknowledge that she secured her success by focusing on the popular genre of film noir—and that, as an early female director, she was held to a different standard. Lupino became a sort of auteur-in-waiting.[6]

To find the real Lupino, I have woven together a number of sources: not only articles written about her but also those she was tasked to write, close readings of her directed work in film and television, archival documents, and analyses of unscripted television shows that can expose the real lives of stars. Research on Lupino's career in the television industry is hampered by major gaps in the preservation of early programming, but shooting scripts, prop lists, actors' memoirs, and narratives can help reengineer daytime programs and female viewership patterns. Paratexts such as posters, ads, and commercials are particularly revealing because of their historicizing function. Located at "an intersection between visual and written texts, between ethereal and material

A 1958 feature story offering a domestic anecdote about Lupino bringing the family's patio furniture to the Mr. Adams and Eve *set.*

objects," as film historian Amelie Hastie notes, they offer unique insights into the relationships between the industry and its audiences.[7] Commercials and ads in particular can tie the spectator's life to that of a star. Lupino smoked Camel cigarettes, used Lustre-Creme shampoo, and trusted American Express traveler's checks. She wore red lipstick manufactured by the House of Westmore, Hollywood's makeup royalty.

Other, more mundane forms of documentation can also be invaluable: recipes, mother-daughter dress-up displays, and family photo ops all address issues related to gender and global sociopolitics.[8]

Giuliana Bruno acknowledges the epistemological problem of relying on alternative sources in her biography of forgotten filmmaker Elvira Notari, stating that "in the absence of texts, lost or destroyed, one can only speculate on the mode of production and reception."[9] Yet paratexts, ephemera, and archival fragments do have a story to tell. They offer insights not only about Lupino's fans and family but also about her habits and beliefs, as well as other aspects of her private persona. A feeling of intimacy emerges when spectators are given access to fragments of a star's domestic life. Glimpses inside a star's home can reveal a great deal, as actress Isabella Rossellini acknowledges: "Objects that decorate my house have a history; they aren't just there to look pretty."[10] When insights into a star's private life are shared, they become a narrative that proliferates in the public sphere, connecting the celebrity to the larger culture. In fact, when Lupino brought items from her house to her home on the set, she demonstrated that stars are ordinary and extraordinary at the same time.

Ida's Double Transition

Ida Lupino, a British American actress, was born on February 4, 1918, in the London suburb of Brixton, under a table during a zeppelin raid in the Great War.[11] She came from an English theatrical dynasty that included comedians, dancers, and singers.[12] Her parents were silent screen comedian Stanley Lupino (1893/4–1942) and musical comedy performer Connie Emerald (1892–1959).

Stanley Lupino's father, George (1853–1932), was ballet master at the Royal Theatre, Drury Lane. George married Florence Ann Webster, a ballerina who danced at Drury Lane. Ida knew her grandfather and loved him immensely. She linked the accomplishments of her grandfather to Joseph Grimaldi (1778–1837), the beloved English clown and pantomimist, because Grimaldi set high standards for the next generations of comedians.[13] Lupino Lane, Stanley Lupino's cousin, was one of the best acrobatic comedians in the history of film, second only to Buster Keaton, and even more famous as a silent screen comedian than was Lupino's father.[14] As Elia Kazan noted, an understanding of the comedic skills of acrobatics, juggling, and tumbling are part of a director's repertoire.[15] All require precise timing, and Ida Lupino's mastery of timing is apparent not only in comedy—for example, in the *Lucy-Desi Comedy Hour* episode "Lucy's Summer Vacation"—but also in her suspense-filled television episodes, including those for *The Twilight Zone*, *The Untouchables*, *The Fugitive*, *Thriller*, and *Alfred Hitchcock Presents*.

Lupino studied at Clarence House, a prep school in Hove, Sussex, and then at the prestigious Royal Academy of Dramatic Art (RADA) in London. When she was featured on Ralph Edwards's *This Is Your Life*, Lupino stated that she received only a pass at RADA, then added with a chuckle that Vivien Leigh did no better. Before Lupino's eventual move to the United States in the early 1930s, George Bernard Shaw cast her as Ellie in *Heartbreak House*, her first professional theatrical performance, after he saw her acting at RADA. In 1932, British film director Allan Dwan cast the fourteen-year-old Lupino in *Her First Affaire*, playing opposite George Curzon.[16] Dwan thought that Lupino seemed older than her years, and he may have hired her over her mother, who was supposed to have auditioned for the role.[17]

Lupino made two career transitions in Hollywood, moving first from acting

Stanley Lupino (top), with daughters Ida (right), dressed as a clown, and sister Rita (left), ca. 1928.

to directing in film and then from acting to directing in television. Between 1932 and 1977, she starred or costarred in about 60 films, starred or costarred in 105 television episodes and TV movies, and directed 7 films and about 68 television movies or episodes.[18] She was thirty years old when she founded her independent production company, the Filmakers, in 1948 with her second husband, Collier Young, and writer Malvin Wald. *Not Wanted* began Lupino's move from acting to directing in the film industry.

With the exception of *The Trouble with Angels*, which Lupino directed for Columbia, all her films were made for the Filmakers. These six films were made with small budgets, mostly unknown actors, and—apart from some negotiated concessions to the censors at the Production Code Administration—complete creative freedom.

Lupino named her company the Filmakers because it connoted youth, independence, and collaboration. It was like a family, with many of the same actors, writers, and crews working together from 1948 to 1953.[19] RKO Pictures, headed by Lupino's old chum Howard Hughes, whom she had met as a teenager, distributed three of Lupino's films.

When Hughes pulled distribution from *The Bigamist*, the Filmakers stepped in, but the financial strain was too great, and the company folded in 1955.[20] Lupino has said if the Filmakers had not tried to get into the distribution business, the company would have been able to continue turning out genre hybrids. She wrote that she had made "one fatal mistake": "I opposed

The Filmakers: Lupino, Collier Young, and Malvin Wald, 1949.

the move every step of the way. 'We're creative people, we're picture makers,' I argued. 'We know nothing about distribution. Let's stay away from it.' But I was outvoted and pretty soon we were out of business."[21]

Lupino made her transition from acting in television to directing television episodes and movies in 1956. At the time, the only other filmmaker and actor who made that same double transition was Orson Welles, who is widely regarded as the ur-auteur and one of the most influential film directors of all time.[22] Though they were very different filmmakers, both began in the theater as actors, both worked in radio, both were political activists, both worked in

A very young Lupino with Howard Hughes, ca. 1934. Hughes later financed three of Lupino's films at RKO.

television commercials, and both eventually struggled with marginalization. This dual transition was an extraordinary feat during the early years of television.[23] Nevertheless, although Welles is the subject of hundreds of books and articles that carefully assess him and his work, Lupino, despite the quality and the quantity of her work, has been relatively ignored. The Library of Congress lists 644 records for Welles and 105 for Lupino.[24] The titles of the works on Welles are ultramasculinist in tone; Lupino had to be feminized to avoid undue attention to the fact that she was a woman working in a man's world.[25]

Lupino's attitudes and opinions shifted over the course of her long career as she reacted to the circumstances of her life. She had once loved to act, only to realize that she found work behind the camera more satisfying. She said often that she just wanted to direct, but she later said that directing was physically too difficult and that she preferred writing: "I would like to be quietly, happily married and be able to stay home and write."[26] It took courage for her to make her dramatic career transitions, but Hollywood punished actors for not staying in the lane created for them. Lupino was said to be "an extremely talented maverick" who "frustrated stereotype-demanding Hollywood."[27] Essentially, she made movies while working within the confines and complexities of women's lives in the United States after World War II. This era was characterized by the return of prewar gender-based hierarchies that sent women from the workplace back into the home, the modernization of cities and white migration to the suburbs, new freedoms granted by the shiny automobile in tandem with the rise of the nuclear family, the domestic intimacy of the television set, and the onset of the baby boom. As media critic Ronnie Scheib points out so insightfully, "Lupino was more of a product of her time rather than a product of her sex."[28]

The Lupinian Brand

Lupino has been compared to silent film director Lois Weber, as both focused on controversial and socially relevant topics. The endings of Lupino's films, which never offer simple solutions—but instead are ambiguous, bittersweet, ironic, and often paradoxical—are similar to those in the work of New Wave directors such as Margarethe von Trotta, who explored the notion of abortion, a sister theme to unwed motherhood, some thirty years after Lupino's *Not Wanted*. Lupino can also be compared in some respects to her talented cohort of male directors, all of whom labored alongside her and who respected her work. Nicholas Ray and Lupino both foregrounded disaffected youth in their films, and both saw the redemptive qualities in the pastoral, which is showcased in Ray's *Rebel without a Cause* (1955) and Lupino's *Outrage*. Michel Mourlet, writing in 1956 for France's premier film journal, *Cahiers du Cinéma*, compared Lupino's work to that of Kenji Mizoguchi and Joseph Losey for their underlying violence.[29] Mourlet was referring to a specific type of violence, filled with tension to a bursting point, and it is in that potential eruption where Mourlet included Lupino. For Lupino, violence was, as Jacques Rivette wrote, "never an end, but the most effective means of access." It is "born out of the need for an immediacy of expression that can yield up, and allow the viewer to share in, the original emotions of the *auteur*."[30] Although Lupino was often left out of critical assessments, sometimes she was included, as in Mourlet's analysis. In these instances, a consideration of her talent overcame her looks, her gender, and her time.

Lupino did not curate a legacy for herself, unlike other women in Hollywood such as Dorothy Arzner, whom Lupino admired. Instead, Lupino seemed to be more interested in the day-to-day work of making movies. In 1973, Lupino, who was fifty-five at the time, sat down with writer and director Francine Parker for a rare candid interview that was published in the Directors Guild of America's *Action* magazine. Parker asked Lupino how she produced so much excellent work in film and television on such limited budgets and how she was able to complete all her episodes on time and under budget while ensuring that each one was stylistically complex. Lupino, always direct, replied, "You just do it."[31] This unhesitant flat answer is the response of a quintessential film industry veteran, one who took control of her image as well as her narratives. Lupino's blunt answer reveals her as wholly dedicated to hard work—she was a *pro*.

Director Martin Scorsese acknowledged Lupino as a hardcore professional, equating her skills with Fuller's, in an interview with critic Richard Schickel: "You know Michael Curtiz could do a picture in four weeks, five weeks, Sam Fuller could do it, Ida Lupino did it. But these were real pros, besides being, I think, some of the most extraordinary artists. Every day they'd be there at a certain time, they'd be there before the crew, they'd be there before the actors, fighting through whatever problems a shot or scene presented. I found I couldn't do that."[32] Fuller, together with Ray, was idolized by the influential critics who were published in *Cahiers du Cinéma*. These writers gave Lupino little recognition, even though she and Fuller were producing the same kind of genre films, both influenced by the neorealism of Roberto Rossellini.

Lupino's television and cinema brands were consistent. She produced empathetic stories that addressed gender confusion for women in a dangerous, masculinist world and incorporated artistic experimentation with genre hybrids on very small budgets. Her exemplarity and the way her aesthetic was shaped by industrial, professional, and historical paradoxes make her a fascinating topic for study. I examine her work from screenplay to screen, using archival sources including unpublished research, production notes, studio records, personal papers, photos, and press and publicity materials, which until now have not been widely studied. The screenplays that Lupino wrote and directed often differed from her final cuts.[33] This in itself is not unusual, but the changes she made from page to screen reflect a sophisticated skill with camera angles, a workable method for subverting the censors, a logic for scene deletions, an organized editing philosophy, and an authorial presence. Stanford Tischler, an acclaimed editor of big-budget musicals and action films, noted that Lupino "wasn't the kind of director who would shoot something, then hope any flaws could be fixed in the cutting room. The acting was always there, to her credit."[34]

Lupino used her experience with performance to scaffold her moving images, which were expertly paced to complement her genre hybrids. Keeping the frame spare, Lupino included only what was necessary, without flourish or stylization. Legendary cinematographer Archie Stout—who received an Academy Award for John Ford's *The Quiet Man* (1952) just after working with Lupino on *Never Fear*, *Outrage*, and *Hard, Fast and Beautiful*—praised her work, stating, "Ida has more knowledge of camera angles and lenses than almost any director I've ever worked with."[35] Lupino's films move quickly, without excess, and her final cut always served the writing and the performances. As I watched her directed films and myriad television show episodes, these elements supplied ample visual proof of Lupino's unique style. Scorsese recognized it, as he wrote in his contribution to Lupino's legacy after her death: "I never met Ida Lupino, but I always wanted to. Her tough, emotional acting is well remembered, but her considerable accomplishments as a film maker are largely forgotten. . . . Her work is resilient, with a remarkable empathy for the fragile and the heart-broken. It is essential."[36]

Early critics who wrote about her directorial work gave her credit only for making a few low-budget films before they briefly surveyed her television episodes. Her work behind the camera was sidelined as lacking authorial intent. It was only after her death in 1995, at age seventy-seven, that she began to attract the attention of critics operating within a feminist critical framework. Today her history is slowly being recovered. The essays in *Queen of the 'B's*, edited by Annette Kuhn, begin to discuss Lupino's themes, styles, and writer-director dimension. Amelie Hastie's monograph on Lupino's final independent feature, *The Bigamist*, and Lucy Stewart's original argument that Lupino's work satisfies every tenet of the *politique des auteurs* are both instructive and persuasive.[37]

Consistency and collaboration are the basis of a reconceptualization of auteurship recently proposed by C. Paul Sellors. Sellors's notion of auteurism is more modern and more precise than what was prescribed in the 1960s. He argues essentially that filmmaking is a collective endeavor and that films are made for a reason, bringing authorial intention and the conditions of production into the consideration of "Who is the author?" He discusses the importance of film's "capacity for communication."[38] The subsequent chapters follow this logic, showing that Lupino's work is thematically consistent and reflects intense collaboration.[39]

I identify Lupino as an auteur because her thematic consistency, involvement in every aspect of her film and television work, and intense and repeated

Lupino pointing out a detail regarding Sally Forrest's makeup to a crew member, perhaps the cinematographer or makeup artist, on the set of Never Fear. *Lupino was involved in every aspect of production.*

collaborations with her above-the-line cohort were essential elements of her work. She was involved with every aspect of directing, developing strategies and producing creative patterns that can be identified as hers alone, just as did the male directors in her cohort—those who are considered dominant auteurs, such as Nicholas Ray and Alfred Hitchcock. In addition to discussing her skills and knowledge, I explore the varied genres and provocative themes she chose as a director. This new look at Lupino is an intermedial author study that attends to Lupino's vision while appreciating her as an author among other authors. I examine how Lupino allocated her time and budgets, including such details as how much money she spent on her crews. I have tried to synthesize the paradoxes—aesthetic, industrial, professional, and historical—that structured Lupino's long and diverse career.

Although Lupino questioned Hollywood's established moral code, she refused to define herself as a feminist or anti-feminist or to assume any other cultural identity. Nevertheless, her story is interconnected with the concerns of the feminist movement. Her themes reflect relevant attitudes toward women during the postwar period, attitudes that factored into her transition from actress to director and produced what seems like a paradoxical legacy. Evolving norms of censorship and changing regulations in the industry both enabled and constrained a new vision of femininity, just as the industry enabled and constrained Lupino's position within the Hollywood studio system.

Lupino's directing career began as important industrial changes were being made in Hollywood. She was ahead of her time, successfully navigating a film career and motherhood by making choices that are more relevant today than they were during the 1950s and 1960s. Her career is a road map to understanding the overlapping production worlds in which she worked. Her collaborations with directors, writers, cinematographers, editors, and musicians crisscrossed the industries of film in the 1940s and 1950s and television in the 1950s and 1960s.[40] The genres she employed encompassed the many shades of noir, realism and social realism, documentary and docudrama, western, action, psychological thriller, horror, and the grotesque. Her story is unique, offering fresh insights into the realignment of the film industry as it experimented with new content and as Production Code Administration regulations and local standards of decency began to change.[41]

The emphasis on realism as it related to social issues and representation, the push to expand acceptable depictions of female sexuality, the emergence of contested gender norms, and the increasing competition between film and television all were changes in the industrial context that Lupino helped shape through her work in film and television. A look at the confusion surrounding Lupino's image helps us understand her particular form of gendered, collaborative, and authorial labor and redresses the attempted erasure of her directing work from cinema and television history. These Lupinian intersections—her unique, intense collaboration on set; her involvement with every aspect of filmmaking, identified as hers alone; her hybrid genres, which flared into exploitative narratives; her neorealistic, semidocumentary themes—all occurred during an upending of the industrial complex. In the creation of her own paradoxical image, neither masculine nor feminine, but always "mother," is where I believe Lupino is best understood and reconsidered.

In 1960, a spread in *TV Guide* featured four actresses and their daughters in "look-alike fashions." Barbara Hale, who costarred in the iconic *Perry Mason* series, poses with her two daughters. They wear matching dresses by Lanz, a manufacturer who had a lock on the wardrobes of preteen girls living in the white upper-middle-class environs of Los Angeles. Also pictured with their daughters are Gloria Henry, who played the mother in *Dennis the Menace*, and June Lockhart, the mother in the *Lassie* television series. Lupino poses with her daughter, Bridget Duff, wearing designer "Linda Lo's pink checked gingham trimmed with embroidery." The article notes in parentheses, "Ida recently directed the test film of *Dante*, a projected NBC TV series starring husband Howard Duff."[42] The domestic merged with the industrial for women in television, and like Lucille Ball, Lupino used opportunities such as this mother-daughter photo shoot to promote both her work and her husband's. Masculinist directors weren't expected to be domesticated—only women need apply.

Part I

AUTEUR-IN-WAITING

SNAPSHOTS

Like other film stars in the 1930s and 1940s, Lupino supplemented her income with radio, a powerful medium found in virtually every home. On December 13, 1937, the Lux Radio Theater, in conjunction with Alfred Hitchcock and Gaumont-British Picture Corporation, presented *The 39 Steps*, starring Robert Montgomery and newcomer Ida Lupino. In his introduction to the broadcast, Cecil B. DeMille described Lupino's many talents:

> Ida Lupino is a girl I watch very closely and suggest that you do the same—for every Lupino seems destined to greatness in the theater. To American film audiences, she's the best-known representative of perhaps the oldest stage family in the world. Three hundred and fifty years ago, when acting was considered a crime in Italy, Alfred Luppino, acrobat and troubadour, fled from Naples, turned gypsy, and eventually found welcome and fame in England. . . . Ida's father is Stanley Lupino, among London's most popular comedians. . . . Ida has inherited a turned-up nose, violet eyes and blonde hair. She's an excellent musician and painter, can speak the language of the deaf and dumb, whistles as well as a farmboy, likes to wear sneakers and is a prize mimic. A highly entertaining miss, you'll meet her tonight in the role of Pamela.[1]

DeMille made it clear that Lupino's presence was already an anomaly: she was unique. Not as feminine as expected, yet not too masculine either, she was obviously multitalented. This paradoxical commentary, coded as female *and* male, has consistently marked Lupino's accomplishments over the years.

This photo of Lupino captures her often difficult-to-read and slightly reluctant expression, as well as her comfortable elegance. It suggests elusiveness, with an edge of daring and, ultimately, an unnerving authenticity. There is nothing too familiar about Lupino in this image, which instead suggests only a deepening mystery—a paradox that remains unresolved.

LEFT: *Lupino photographed along Poverty Row on Hollywood Boulevard in the mid-1940s.*

Chapter 1

A STAR STUDY

I worked against my success by refusing to do roles that I did not believe in.

Ida Lupino in Ida Lupino and Mary Ann Anderson, *Ida Lupino: Beyond the Camera*

Gender can blinker our perceptions. We can see female actors, but we can't see female directors. What do you do with someone who can't be seen? Ida Lupino began directing Hollywood films in the late 1940s, when the industry was in the heart of Hollywood's classic period, an era marked by the silencing of women directors.

Lupino did little to resist this oppression. Instead of promoting what she did or seeking to curate her legacy, she was reticent when compelled to discuss her work.[1] She was similarly guarded about her private life. Working against this inclination, though, was her status as a prominent actress, first in film and then in television. "Stars matter," as Richard Dyer has observed, but when stars become commodities, they can lose control of how they are perceived, not only by their audiences but also within the industry.[2] Constant rebranding likely played a role in causing Marilyn Monroe, Orson Welles, and even Marlon Brando to disappear into unstable personas. As Francis Coppola famously said, "As soon as you become that big, you get absorbed."[3] Lupino's answer was to rebrand herself strategically by revising her image when her work in the industry changed.

As an actress, Lupino was a known visual commodity, often playing a tough femme fatale with heart and intelligence, who couldn't escape self-destruction.[4] Film critic J. Hoberman evaluates her roles on both sides of the camera and considers Lupino "the most complex" of the many actresses who appeared in noir films: "Ms. Lupino could be as sultry and sassy as Lauren Bacall while

Director Lupino on the set of Not Wanted, *1948.*

projecting an aching vulnerability. As world-weary as Gloria Grahame, she never came across as fragile, particularly in her subsequent work as a director." Hoberman is especially taken with her role as a blind woman in Nicholas Ray's *On Dangerous Ground* (1951): "Delivered largely in close-up, her subtly tremulous performance is worthy of a D. W. Griffith silent star."[5]

Lupino's acting abilities often outstripped those of the people she starred with as well as the quality of the material she was given, as David Thomson has noted. He also pairs her with Gloria Grahame, who is perhaps best known for her noir role in *The Big Heat* (1953), observing that they "could have played wicked sisters—they looked alike, and they were both too odd for placid movies." Thomson extols Lupino's "astonishing emotional explosion" in *They Drive by Night* (1940), directed by Raoul Walsh, and her role in Jean Negulesco's *Road House* (1948): "We could be meeting a woman from [pulp author] Jim Thompson—burned, dangerous, impatient, and pitiless."[6]

When Lupino transitioned from acting to directing, first in film and then in television, she drew on her own lean, taut performances to elicit the best from her actors. As she moved behind the camera, she reinvented herself so that she could make the movies she wanted. Her striking physicality, ideal for Hollywood's classic period, had always been foregrounded, and her fame in front of the camera led to her wide range of skills being suppressed and often silenced. Yet as a director, she used her early success as an actress as leverage with the studios, the censors, and her crews to get what she needed on film. She carved out her own noir landscape and directorial and collaborative persona. Using her technical expertise and her experience as an actress as well as a producer and screenwriter, she turned to creating B movies, eventually producing and directing six independent films in five years. When she returned to acting, this time for television, she was older, and she altered her identity again. Then, as a television director, she added more pixels to her image.

There are multiple photos and multiple portrayals of Lupino, all crafted to present a carefully constructed public persona. We see the noir actress or the independent director, and we can sense the imprisonment she felt from her femme fatale image, her uneasiness with her dual role as actress and director, her fear and discomfort caused by being the only woman in a male-dominated industry. Her image was frequently rendered in printed contexts such as recipes, how-to columns, even paper dolls—all intended to feminize her. Placing Lupino in the kitchen was particularly effective, and recipes for English Boiled Chicken with Cream Sauce or Ida Lupino's Good Eggs Scramble allowed the women who read the *Chicago Daily Tribune*'s Weekly Illustrated Food Guide or the *Los Angeles Times*' Celebrity Cookbook column to believe that the life of the glamorous Hollywood figure wasn't so different from theirs. *The Celebrity Cookbook*, containing a collection of recipes from well-known figures ranging from Jimmy Durante to Jacqueline Kennedy to Yehudi Menuhin, includes Lupino's recipe for fruitcake.[7]

Gender bias was always present and frequently blatant. For example, Lupino wrote, acted, and directed for the television anthology series *Four Star Playhouse*, just like her coprincipals, David Niven, William Powell, and Charles Boyer, yet Christopher Anderson doesn't mention her in his history of Hollywood television.[8] Over the course of her long career, different elements dominated and different histories prevailed, and today Lupino's star image and her labor remain contradictory.

During the five-year stretch in which she made her six independent features, Lupino continued acting in films and began a transition to television. In 1951, she divorced Collier Young, her second husband (after actor Louis Hayward) and her partner in the Filmakers. She married Howard Duff that same year, with whom she had a daughter, Bridget, in 1952. Throughout these life and career events, her private persona was never on display, even in the television series *Mr. Adams and Eve*, in which she and Duff portray a Hollywood married couple. She dances around real life in the series, which symbolizes, satirizes, and then shatters the ideas of fame, the star image, and Hollywood itself. When she and Duff appeared on *I've Got a Secret* to advertise the first episode of their Friday night show—and to promote sponsor R. J. Reynolds, the manufacturer of Winston cigarettes—viewers hoped for a glimpse of the real Ida. With an unscripted show like *I've Got a Secret*, almost anything could happen. Lupino kept her professional distance, however, slipping only once when host Garry Moore botched the title of the new show. She threw a quick glance at her husband, who corrected Moore. The audience might have missed it, but Lupino wasn't happy.[9]

Lupino had a long career, and although different personal stories prevailed during different periods, her consistent goal was to work. In the 1950s, to avoid running afoul of the postwar film industry's masculine hierarchy, whose support she needed to make her films, she downplayed and domesticated her vast intellect and her creative power, ultimately minimizing her authorship and her legacy. She wanted to avoid certain types of publicity, so she fashioned a self-representation that was complex while adhering to the industry's expectations. Throughout her years in Hollywood, whether she was in front of or behind the camera, Lupino was represented as overtly feminine. The publicity supporting Lupino's role as a director focused on maintaining her femininity to dilute the masculinity of her job. As a result, she didn't match the criteria that many postwar film critics had fashioned for successful male directors, particularly those they regarded as auteurs, so they tended to ignore her. Feminist scholars also had trouble: Lupino was a woman in a man's field, but she didn't fit into their feminist framework.

An assessment of her prolific directing work between 1949 and 1968, in film as well as in television, offers a new perspective on her career that allows us to understand her true place in media history.[10] As a director, she had a clearly defined style that blended the genres of film noir and film gris—bequests of the Poverty Row studios that began making low-budget films in the 1920s—with the neorealism of documentaries. She was a groundbreaking filmmaker, not only because she was a woman working in an industry completely dominated by men but also because she chose to make compelling films about subjects that were considered off-limits. The uncertain, unsettling endings of these narratives are marked by an ambiguity that fits with the ambiguities of her persona. Ultimately, though, Lupino's most important role was as a gifted, canny professional whose directorial accomplishments set the scene for the generations of women directors who would follow.

Self-Reflexivity as Commodity

When Lupino began her career behind the camera, few women had worked as directors. Wheeler Winston Dixon identifies four women who directed silent films in Los Angeles in the 1920s and 1930s—Lois Weber, Ida May Park, Ruth

Stonehouse, and Cleo Madison—as well as Dorothy Arzner, who was the first woman to direct classic Hollywood features. Dixon notes that when Arzner stopped making features in 1943, "women had effectively been dismissed from the director's chair" in Hollywood.[11] In the late 1940s, when Lupino moved into that chair, she was the only woman directing in Hollywood. It was inevitable that she would be compared with Arzner and that feminist critics would take the lead. Between 1960 and 1990, increasing numbers of women entered academia, driving a growing interest in women's studies. Arzner was accepted by feminist critics, becoming the poster child for theorists writing in the 1980s and early 1990s, but Lupino was not. By most accounts, Lupino was problematic. Unlike Arzner, she didn't fit into the theoretical box that feminist critics had devised to evaluate women's contributions to film.

Comparisons of the two filmmakers were always gender centered, even though their work was very different. For example, Ronnie Scheib characterized Arzner's "feminine eye" as "a rather lascivious one of looking at women's bodies."[12] Lupino, on the other hand, was not voyeuristic. Her narratives were not focused on or around sex; she was interested instead in social problems and how they affected her drawn-from-life characters. Her camera was more like Lois Weber's than Arzner's in its adherence to suspense. Lupino rarely used static or wide shots, keeping her camera moving, while using expressionistic lighting to demonstrate emotional imbalance, claustrophobia, and entrapment. As an actress turned director, Weber displayed a female ambivalence. While she seemed to believe in marriage offscreen, onscreen she was an independent, modern woman.

Lupino publicly rejected a feminist identity throughout her career, and early feminist critics allowed these statements to color their assessments of her work. They complained about the "anti-feminist content" of Lupino's filmmaking, pointing to "the gap" that they saw between her career and "the values she promulgated."[13] Such stark criticism persisted, provoked by Lupino's offhand comments about marriage and men. Many critics assessed Lupino's acting work as gritty but complained that her directing efforts presented far more ordinary narratives. Film critic Molly Haskell, a respected feminist voice, approved of Lupino's tough, gutsy acting roles while disparaging her directing, and Patricia White, writing in *Village Voice* in 1991, discussed the virtues of Lupino the actress but expressed ambivalence about Lupino's conventional treatment of the women in her screenplays.[14]

In fact, Lupino's written characters are the antithesis of the tough femme fatale characters that she so often inhabited as an actress in the 1940s. These characters were male fantasies, crafted primarily by men who had no concept of the loneliness of lower-class desperation or the frightening vulnerability of women in postwar America. Defining women onscreen as mother figures, eternal muses, or Mother Nature was symptomatic of a patriarchal cinema that relied on limiting and stereotypical portrayals. Lupino's instinct was to tell a truer story about the lived reality of the post–World War II women who worked menial jobs and had a bleak future, who were traumatized by rape or displaced by unmarried pregnancy, who felt trapped and thus were mentally or emotionally unstable. The focus of many early critics on Lupino's avoidance of feminist issues blinded them to the subtext of the actual stories that she told. Haskell called her films "conventional, even sexist," a comment that suggests Haskell had not seen *Outrage*, Lupino's film about the trauma of rape and its repercussions in a small American town.[15]

These critiques, together with a polarity in feminist film studies, have plagued Lupino's legacy for decades. In the 1970s and 1980s, cinema-centric feminist scholars such as Laura Mulvey and filmmakers like Cynthia Scott and Sally Potter began to document different aspects of women's lives, including oppression, sexuality, trade unionism, education, and advertising. The 1990s ushered in a new point of view in critical studies that offered a fresh historical context within which to reread the past. Critical consensus resulted in a reevaluation—and a recuperation—of Lupino's work. Her rigorous work ethic and the quality of her output supported this, particularly in regard to her phenomenal work in television.

Claire Johnston, Mary Desjardins, William Donati, Pam Cook, Christine Geraghty, Richard Koszarski, Martin Scorsese, Debra Weiner, Winston Wheeler Dixon, Michel Mourlet, and others lauded Lupino's rare abilities as a writer and director. Annette Kuhn and Carrie Rickey saw the enduring quality of Lupino's films early on and understood that the director had been undervalued and misunderstood.[16] The contributors to Kuhn's 1995 anthology, *Queen of the 'B's*—Ellen Seiter, Mary Celeste Kearney, Ronnie Scheib, Pam Cook, and Diane Waldman—discuss Lupino's themes and style in conjunction with her writing and directing. Carol Clover, indirectly, and Cook situate Lupino within the low-budget, B-movie exploitation pantheon, finding her films similar to Roger Corman's oeuvre in their subversive criticism of the repressed social construct of the 1950s.[17] Amelie Hastie's close reading of *The Bigamist* and Lucy Stewart's exploration of Lupino's authorship each contribute to the dimensionality of research on Lupino.[18] Rickey dismisses the claims that Lupino's films are anti-feminist in one cogent phrase: "That's an epithet, not a description of Lupino's considerable directorial skills."[19]

Now, over one hundred years after her birth in 1918, Lupino has become a model for women writer-directors, who are once again forging their way into the studios. They are making their mark particularly in episodic television, the very medium that critics saw as a dead end for Lupino—a role without agency for aged-out talent.[20] To know Lupino, we have to understand that her career was essentially an unstable process marked by continual rebranding across time and media and in both film and television.

Rebranding: A Star Reconsidered

In her examination of what she calls "recycled stardom," film scholar Mary Desjardins has divided celebrity into three distinct phases: fame, decline, and return.[21] These phases reflect changes in American culture, particularly the decline of the Hollywood star system. As the studio system waned, its stars capitalized on the cultural shifts and slipped into early television. This was a crossover stardom that repromoted these "new," yet returned, television stars. It worked because of the existing interrelationships that tied together the industry, the stars, and the fans.

The nostalgia for aging stars was particularly visible in televised anthology series, in which former female film stars were actively involved in writing and producing—and in Lupino's case, directing—their own television series. These women, who wanted control of their work and their image, included Lucille Ball, Loretta Young, Maureen O'Hara, Ann Sothern, Barbara Hutton, and Gloria Swanson, to name just a few. Ball was the first to make this move, with *I Love Lucy*, but she couldn't do what Lupino did. She didn't have Lupino's fundamental power. The same was true for Gracie Allen (*The George Burns and Gracie Allen Show*) and Harriet Nelson (*The Adventures of Ozzie and Harriet*). They were limited by their television roles, in which they portrayed overtly domesticated women who were in alignment with America's postwar culture. Lupino, in contrast, was already acknowledged for her acting, producing, writing, and directing in the film industry. She was the only woman who could bring all those skills to early television. Arzner—who couldn't do what Lupino did either—had retired, and Lupino thus became the only woman in the Directors Guild of America until 1971, when the brilliant Elaine May was added, producing a new total of two women.

Lupino was unique in a variety of ways. Her work had a strong noir and action profile, a drive toward social realism that resonated with Italian neorealism, a clear understanding of both the dramatic and comedic versions of stardom, and a desire to expose and parody the underside of fame. Lupino wrote or cowrote all her screenplays, and she was tech savvy, which some men found intimidating. She also had a deep understanding of performance and casting from her continuing work as an actress. As Coppola has noted, "More actors have become directors than any other group, because they know performance."[22] In fact, it may be because she was a well-reviewed and well-remembered actress that her unique narratives, which comment provocatively on her historical moment, have been neglected. When she moved from in front of the camera to behind it, such a shift was seen to be outside the boundaries of a star's role. Lupino, however, had always been courageous. She was skilled and prepared, and she made the transition easily.

Neither her writing nor her directing was foregrounded in Lupino's work for the television industry. She simply wanted to work. Sol Saks, the showrunner for *Mr. Adams and Eve*, pointed out that "TV was where the jobs were. You went for the jobs."[23] Lupino was an aging star, whose image could be too easily defined by scandal sheets, gossip columns, movie magazines, or an appearance on *This Is Your Life*, where the host tried to catch the star off guard so that spectators could catch a glimpse of the celebrity's reality. Female viewers identified with the aging stars, who demonstrated their resiliency as they remade themselves through the emerging medium of television. Articles and promotion pieces often emphasized Lupino's clothing, makeup, and looks—a tactic that the Hollywood publicity machine had used with Arzner before her. In her biography, *Directed by Dorothy Arzner*, Judith Mayne compares Arzner's feminine and masculine roles to poses or performative masks.[24] Arzner's mask was manly, although Hollywood was determined to deny her butch persona. Lupino's mask, however, was motherly to promote her refeminized renewal. The role of everyone's mother was a workable disguise for Lupino, because it discreetly minimized her actual power.

She moved into the new medium of television in 1954, as an actress on the anthology series *Four Star Playhouse*. The series was produced by Four Star Productions, which listed Lupino as its fourth member, together with Dick Powell, Charles Boyer, and David Niven. As she started writing and directing for other television series, she quietly took control of her image. She purposely kept it underdefined, and as a result, she ultimately became an obscured figure. She remained fiercely independent, but her freelance life sometimes led to financial insecurity. Steady work and raising a family were her two priorities, a choice that was influenced by the stories told by her father, whose childhood had been scarred by hunger and trauma. To keep working, she adjusted her persona to fit the circumstances. A recurring theme in interviews and remarks from this time is Lupino's public denial of her agency. She did not want to be seen as a groundbreaker, and she minimized her technical skills. Being a director was simply another aspect of her role as a multifaceted celebrity. Scholars Mary Celeste Kearney and James M. Moran have suggested that Lupino's "public image and private aspirations were at war."[25]

Lupino enhanced her brand as she moved into television by combining her immense skill set with her established status as an actress. Female stars functioned effectively as spectacle in the press, on television, and on film. Christine Geraghty suggests that the private space of the female star, including personal and private relationships and domestic concerns, fits easily into the discourse of celebrity.[26] Lupino must have intuited this, because she used that public-private binary to establish a career in the television industry. In some ways, she was mirroring the industry's—and America's—focus on women at home. It was in the television industry that Lupino began shaping her own brand as an auteur, using her star status plus her skills as a bona fide writer and director to land jobs. Lupino had a distinctive way of working out her gender roles, sidestepping the masculine patriarchy and avoiding any identity that would code her as either feminine or masculine. This allowed her to establish projects on her terms. Her version of feminism was highly personal, a response to the circumstances that surrounded her.

As her career progressed, Lupino developed an auteur approach that was collaborative yet also antithetical to the strict gender conventions of 1950s and 1960s America. It was in this unsettled cultural period, when the idea of home disguised uneasy undercurrents, that Lupino insisted on her independence. This was a difficult time for any woman to challenge conventions, much less emerge as a successful actress, writer, producer, and director in a young industry. Francine Parker rightly saw Lupino as a Renaissance woman, provocative and powerful. "As the living antithesis of single-mindedness, the word for Lupino is daring":

> daring to sacrifice security to realize a vision, rather than playing it safe . . . daring to be inventive in concept and different in technique; daring to do "A" movies on "Z" budgets long before it was fashionable; risking unknown faces, gambling on untried subjects; daring to shoot big, while shooting fast; daring to direct at a time terrifyingly tough for women, daring to be daring. She has been playwright, screenwriter, author, dancer, singer, artist, designer, musician, song-writer, composer . . . as well as actress, television and motion picture producer-director, and all-around film maker.[27]

Chapter 2

CERTAIN WOMEN OF POST-WORLD WAR II

You see my films are about people who get lost, who really don't have a home anymore.

Ida Lupino in Ginger Varney, "Ida Lupino, Director"

After World War II, American society embraced a new model of suburban living, one that emphasized the nuclear family and glorified the housewife, considered a woman's proper role. To work successfully as a director in the film industry, Lupino had to offer some deference to the men who dominated it. They included Joseph Breen, director of the Production Code Administration (PCA), which was tasked with enforcing the Motion Picture Production Code of 1930. Lupino was forced to compromise to make her films, as consistently indicated in archival documents in the Margaret Herrick Library at the Academy of Motion Picture Arts and Sciences.[1] Despite the constraints that the PCA imposed on her, Lupino used her skills and savvy to produce a number of spare, modernist, female-centric narratives that contradicted the studios' hard-and-fast rule linking masculinity with physical strength and femininity with sexual purity. Her first directed film, *Not Wanted* (1949), for example, examines the contested rights of an unwed mother and her illegitimate child. Lupino did not comply with all the alterations and cuts that the PCA decreed, but no one at the agency seemed to notice, because Lupino adroitly managed their reading of the film.

Change was occurring throughout the arts in postwar America. It was encouraged by the burgeoning economy, which provided relief for the expanding white middle class and led to the growth of a progressive political majority. Change was also taking place in society more broadly, and tensions arose as increasing numbers of white middle-class women began working outside the home—a move contrary to the powerful patriarchal ideology. As Lupino began her directing career in the late 1940s, however, societal expectations still emphasized the ideal nuclear family, the new model of suburban living, and the glorified place of the housewife in society. Capitalism and consumption flourished, aided by Hollywood's total dominance of the film industry. Hollywood films offered relief from wartime deprivation and promoted a hunger for postwar products such as nylon stockings, records, refrigerators, and things that cleaned, including vacuums, washing machines, and soap. White middle-class women responded eagerly to the gospel of modern homemaking.[2] Even Lupino may have felt the same pressure as other women to live the suburban fantasy of a comfortable middle-class lifestyle.[3]

The Broken Postwar Promise, Conformity, and Momism

The postwar period was marked by an exodus to the suburbs. The white middle class moved into low-slung modern houses, populating a new type of cityscape that was sprawling and sophisticated. Suburban life was characterized by post–World War II innovations: fast food, planned communities, freeway travel, affordable cars, and television.[4] Mind-numbing conformity was ascendant, producing a loss of self that was cunningly obscured by notions of individualism. Trauma and collective memory shaped the consciousness of the generation that came of age in the 1950s. These Americans understood the sublimation of individuality as an expression of the service that was due one's country. The resulting loss of individuality and creativity was famously embodied in William Whyte's organization man.[5]

Although television became a critical component in this trend toward conformity as it shaped the expenditure of leisure time, the first live television broadcasts were often highly original and creative. Classic Hollywood fare seemed old-fashioned next to the new comedy sketches of Sid Caesar, Imogene Coca, and Ernie Kovacs. At the same time, the film industry was adjusting not only to the rise of television but also to a surge of independent filmmaking that was empowered by structural changes in the studio system. Studios had lost the vertically integrated power that had allowed them to control both production and exhibition. Hollywood needed "a different type of niche film product" that was distinct from the "A-class prestige" films that had defined moviemaking before the war.[6] Lupino seized this opportunity and began producing and writing, then directing, low-budget B movies that highlighted the very malaise and conformity that cultural critics like Whyte were denouncing. Within the era's cultural landscape, Lupino carved out a space as a creative and forward-thinking artist who persistently sought ways to bypass closed systems in order to work.

The 1950s were marked by a trend toward social conformity that was helped along by a continuing bureaucratization of U.S. institutions. Max Weber, writing in the early twentieth century, warned of the shortcomings inherent in bureaucratic systems—loss of ingenuity, initiative, personal independence, and freedom—which became more prevalent after World War II.[7] Whyte pointed out the harm of bureaucratic thinking by comparing the plodding organization man to the curious scientist: "Management has tried to adjust the scientist to The Organization rather than The Organization to the scientist. It can do this with the mediocre and still have a harmonious group. It cannot do it with the brilliant; only freedom will make them harmonious."[8]

One physical aspect of 1950s conformity was the new low-slung rectangles that filled America's suburbs. Efficient but roomy, they had planted outdoor spaces that were well suited to growing families. These were functional modern houses for modern living. This innovative approach developed in California in response to the state's booming population. Architects Luis Barragán and Max Cetto modernized housing from Mexico City to the Brentwood neighborhood of Los Angeles, and Joseph Eichler, Richard Neutra, Gregory Ain, and Vienna-born Rudolf Schindler built houses in the San Francisco area, Santa Monica, and a number of Los Angeles neighborhoods. These expressions of modernity relied on mass production.

When combined with good design, mass production could provide a "foundation for good living," as Keith Eggener has noted. This optimistic, instrumentalist thinking was "a holdover from the Bauhaus" and other utopian theories. Key to modern design was the "new and elaborate use of glass," which produced a feeling of community in the suburbs by "merging public and private spaces."[9] Sliding glass doors removed the boundary between inside and out, and in a similar way, television screens brought the public into the private space of the home. Television was, in the words of Thomas Hutchinson, a "window on the world."[10]

Although television, in its early days, may have seemed peripheral to Hollywood, the film and television industries quickly became interdependent rivals, tied together by the many performers, writers, producers, and directors who crossed from one medium to the other with frequency. Neutra's design for the entry to the Walt Disney Studios in Burbank was a modernist statement for the postwar entertainment industry. Moving into television was a progressive and freeing choice for actors and filmmakers, and Lupino effectively exploited the imbrication of the two industries. As one of the few directors working in early television, Lupino recognized the value of the emerging medium.

As Kathleen McHugh has noted, America in the 1950s saw the "dumbing down of the feminine while at the same time the stultifying environment of domesticity," domesticity that McHugh suggests conjured warmth and love, but with endless, repetitive housework, home was saran-wrapped inside psychological entrapment and claustrophobia.[11] This was the era of *momism*, a term coined by a sardonic Philip Wylie in *Generation of Vipers*, in which he ruminates on the post–World War II notion of motherhood: "Mom is an American creation. . . . Mom is everywhere and everything and damned near everybody, and from her depends all the rest of the U.S. We must understand mom before we lose touch with understanding itself."[12]

As a wife, a mother, and an employed cultural worker, Lupino had to negotiate a number of domestic expectations and concerns. She believed in marriage as an institution, even though ultimately her own life reflected unhappily on that institution, and she was primarily the sole financial support for Howard Duff and daughter Bridget at a time when few women worked outside the home. Motherhood was a crucial component of Lupino's life, even though she had a thriving career. In fact, motherhood both hindered and helped her career. Lupino turned down offers to direct out of town or out of the country, which would have furthered her career, yet the emphasis on her "mother" persona helped her secure a vast amount of television work. On set and off, Lupino asked her cast and crew to call her "Mom" or "Mother," while she downplayed her sexuality. Silent color footage shot by Gypsy Rose Lee on the set of *The Trouble with Angels* (1966) captures Lupino directing Hayley Mills and Rosalind Russell; the footage shows Lupino's director chair, prominently stenciled with "Mother" instead of her name.[13]

Lupino lived in stark contrast to the expectations of a conformist society. The disparity between established norms of behavior for women and Lupino's work was apparent. At the time, a white woman's "correct" choice was not work outside the home, but work *inside* the home for husband and family, which constituted a trap for many women, including Lupino. These tensions are reflected in her representations of home and domesticity. In her independent films, home is an unhappy, claustrophobic place, not at all a refuge, and it is filled with secrets, trauma, and fear. These portrayals bring to mind Chon A. Noriega's conception of home as "the uncertainty of a question rather than the security of a point of origin or a refuge."[14]

One response to the frustrations that women experienced after the war was a new wave of feminism. Lupino was not interested in aligning herself with its proponents, understanding that a film could explore feminist issues and be entertaining. A filmmaker did not have to moralize to make a point. Yet the critical response to *Hard, Fast and Beautiful* (1951)—a film that Lupino wrote and directed—was to label the director an anti-feminist. Lupino portrayed a mother who drives her daughter, played by Sally Forrest, to tennis stardom. The mother hopes that fame will give her daughter a better life than her own—one independent of men. The burned-out daughter ultimately chooses marriage over her career, leading reviewers to misjudge Lupino's ending. Rather than happily ever after, the conclusion is ambiguous because the story is equally the portrayal of an unhappy mother who is driven to extremes for the sake of her daughter. This is the strength of Lupino's work: unsettling endings that reflected the anxieties of postwar America. A comparison with *The Hard Way* (1943), which features Lupino as the ambitious Helen Chernen, indicates how far Lupino's conclusions moved the needle away from convention. Chernen is a housewife who leaves her empty marriage—a common and usually unacknowledged problem for white women in the 1950s—and becomes a financial success by managing her sister's career. But the ending of the film is a judgment on her ambition. Neither marriage nor independence could save a fierce woman in the male workplace.

Because of the raw power of Lupino's subject matter, the ambiguity was also necessary in the era of PCA censorship: it allowed her films to be made. Nevertheless, within that space were plenty of opportunities to explore the immense disappointment of the postwar American dream. This was the moment of the man in the gray flannel suit, when consumerism exploded and conformity crushed individualism. By portraying and writing about female characters who resisted the return of prewar expectations about a woman's role, Lupino was at the forefront of feminism—something that feminist critics writing in the 1970s and 1980s failed to see. Only Ronnie Scheib took a firm stand against them, pointing out that they were "more concerned with statement-making than with filmmaking."[15]

Not Wanted, Lupino's film about unmarried pregnancy, was made in 1949, four years before abortion was first mentioned in a film, in Otto Preminger's *The Moon Is Blue* (1953). This shift was the result of three trends: producers pushing the boundaries of acceptable representations of female sexuality, increasingly contested gender norms, and competition with television. Preminger made the film after the PCA had declared the script was unacceptable, and he distributed it after the PCA refused to approve it. It was the first American film released without the PCA seal of approval.[16] Creating *Not Wanted* was a precursor to Lupino's modernistic neo-realism and perhaps helped pave the way for Preminger's film on the same subject.

Lupino's Global Cohort

Lupino was subject to the same gendered expectations that other women encountered following the World War II, but her extraordinary and sometimes unexpected skill level was catching the attention of an industry dominated by men. Her remarkable double transition was possible only because of the range of her interconnected skills and experiences. Her overarching acting identity was of the strong, bad object—as in Raoul Walsh's *The Man I Love* (1947) and Jean Negulesco's *Road House* (1948). Lupino's striking physicality was always foregrounded, yet her roles were diverse. She was the "good girl" in Walsh's *High Sierra* (1941), and in 1945, *Pillow to Post*, directed by Vincent Sherman, she showed that she could excel in comedy.[17] Nevertheless, it was her work as a femme fatale that made Lupino famous—and she was powerful in those early film noir roles.

By the mid-1940s, she found herself exhausted by the stereotype, and when she refused roles assigned to her by her studio, Warner Bros., she was put on suspension. When she was on the sidelines, she observed and learned from other professionals while they practiced their craft, as she explained in an interview for *LA Weekly*: "I never was one who woke up in the morning saying, 'God, it's so great to be an actress!' I was always looking for ways to be less bored on the set, so I hung around the director and the cameraman, asking them questions and watching what they did."[18] Although she did not publicly divulge what fueled her drive to direct at the time, she may have been motivated by anger, boredom, or perhaps a disgust with the femme fatale characters that she had portrayed. She wanted to leave the stereotypes and create images that used the force of the feminine to create challenging narratives.

Lupino, the only female director working in Hollywood at the time, was part of an international wave of actresses who became professional directors after the war. They included Mary Ellen Bute, Maya Deren, and Shirley Clarke, American women who worked outside of the Hollywood studio system, creating avant-garde and experimental films. Another extraordinary woman was Kinuyo Tanaka, who may have been influenced by Lupino's rise to legitimate director. Kinuyo was filmmaker Kenji Mizoguchi's muse, and he tried to prevent her from directing. Tanaka ignored him, directing *Love Letters* (1953) and six more films over the next ten years—an output comparable to Lupino's. Tanaka's themes, like Lupino's, were subtle, layered, and rooted in humanism. Norwegian stage actress Edith Carlmar directed ten films between 1949 and 1959, all produced by Carlmar Film A/S. Her debut was a film noir titled *Death Is a Caress*. Bodil Ipsen, a silent screen actress from Denmark, directed ten features during the 1940s and early 1950s, including two noirs, *Melody of*

Park Nam-ok carrying her baby on her back to the set where she directed The Widow, *ca. 1955.*

Murder (1944) and the Cannes prizewinner *Red Meadows* (1945).[19] The latter, a war drama codirected with Lau Lauritzen Jr., depicts a POW's flashback just before he is executed.

Park Nam-ok is believed to be the first female Korean film director. She was a new mother in 1954 when she directed *The Widow*, and she carried her baby on her back to the set each day.[20] Motherhood was and is an important issue in the careers of many women in the film industry, including female directors. The image of Park with her baby, shown above, encapsulates her dedication to her duty as a mother. Taken in 1955, the photo makes it look like this was the future for women working in the industry who had infants and young children. Park's movie, which concerns a woman's struggle between duty and desire as she raises her daughter alone after a war, offers another take on the female directing experience, this one in postwar Korea.

Lupino maintained a wide network throughout the 1940s, 1950s, and

1960s. These connections were also an important factor in her double transition, and they are key to understanding how she created her distinctive films. Lupino often stated that she knew everyone in the industry who had worked between 1935 and 1978.[21] For example, Lupino collaborated with Michael Curtiz, born in 1886, and Steve McQueen, born in 1930. Although the difference is only forty-four years, it represents an enormous cultural shift. Curtiz began his career during the silent screen era and flourished during Hollywood's Golden Age; he is best known for the all-time classic *Casablanca* (1942). Conversely, McQueen was an icon of the 1960s and 1970s, one of the reigning kings of cool, youthful to the end.

Among Lupino's many connections were other talented women, notable novelists and screenwriters who were working in the industry. Daphne du Maurier's award-winning novel *Rebecca* was adapted for a 1940 film, directed by Alfred Hitchcock and starring Joan Fontaine and Laurence Olivier. Joan Fontaine later married Lupino's second husband, Collier Young, and she costarred with Lupino in Lupino's final independent film, *The Bigamist* (1953). Vera Caspary is best known for her detective novel *Laura* (1943), which was quickly adapted for a film by Otto Preminger in 1944 starring Gene Tierney and Dana Andrews. Dorothy B. Hughes authored fourteen noir books, mostly forgotten. Her 1947 book, *In a Lonely Place*, was adapted for a 1950 film directed by Nicholas Ray, which starred Humphrey Bogart; Frank Lovejoy, from Lupino's *The Hitch-Hiker*; and Gloria Grahame, wife of Nicholas Ray. Bogart had worked with Ida Lupino twice, a few years earlier on *They Drive by Night* (1940), directed by Raoul Walsh—Lupino taking billing over Bogart—and *High Sierra* (1941), also directed by Walsh, where Lupino again had top billing over Bogart. Grahame worked with Lupino in 1954, performing in *Private Hell 36*, which was directed by Don Siegel and produced by Lupino and the Filmakers. Science fiction author Leigh Brackett was also a screenwriter, best known for her work on the adaptations of Raymond Chandler's *The Big Sleep* (1946) and *The Long Goodbye* (1973) and the script for the Howard Hawks classic *Rio Bravo* (1959).

Other important connections were to male filmmakers, including Nicholas Ray, Robert Aldrich, Samuel Fuller, Joseph Losey, and Don Siegel. In fact, a consideration of Nicholas Ray is crucial to any study of Lupino. For his biography of Ray, Bernard Eisenschitz had complete access to the director and to RKO files, allowing him to establish a detailed chronology of Ray's life from 1911 through the 1970s. Lupino's name appears frequently in this document, evidence of their interactions and collaborations. Lupino and Ray worked together, for example, in *On Dangerous Ground* (1951), written by A. I. Bezzerides and starring Lupino and Robert Ryan. Ray's *They Live by Night* (1948)

Lupino with director Nicholas Ray and cast of On Dangerous Ground*: (clockwise, around the table) writer A. I. Bezzerides, Ray, Lupino, Ward Bond, and Robert Ryan.*

was shot by George E. Diskant, who was the cinematographer for *Beware, My Lovely* (1952), which starred Lupino and was produced by the Filmakers. Diskant was also the cinematographer for *On Dangerous Ground* and for Lupino's *The Bigamist*. In addition, Lupino and Diskant worked together on episodes for the television series *Four Star Playhouse*, *The Rifleman*, and *Mr. Adams and Eve*.[22]

Lupino's work for *On Dangerous Ground* may have included an unplanned, uncredited role. Ray is rumored to have had a nervous breakdown at the end of the shoot, and some say Lupino directed several scenes when Ray became ill.[23] When Eisenschitz asked Lupino if she had completed the direction of *On Dangerous Ground*, she was careful with her answer. She remembered the ending as a collaboration with Robert Ryan, her costar.

> In a way Bob Ryan and I did; we did it our way . . . the end was nothing like the way we had it in the script. It ended with me standing in the doorway and crying. I said to Bob, "I don't like it." He said, "Neither do I." And we decided we'd end the picture the way you see it now.

> When he comes back at night, she feels her way downstairs, and Bob is standing there. We told our cameraman [Diskant] that Bob's hand would reach out and touch hers. She smiles and says, "Oh, you're back." He says, "Yes, I never wanted to leave you." And as the camera comes into those two faces tight, then we have the camera go down to our two hands clenched together, and it says, The End.[24]

Ray ultimately had no objection to the last scene.

Parallels can be found in the work of Lupino and Ray. In their directed films, they foregrounded youth, with the adults often blurred, and they did extensive location scouting. Ray's preference for ambiguity is seen in Lupino's approaches as shown only from the teenagers' points of view. All Lupino's directed films end ambiguously, bleak in their knowledge of the social expectations for women during the postwar period. *Hard, Fast and Beautiful*, for example, is an indictment of the circumstances that ambitious women faced. In the final shot, a mother, played by Claire Trevor in a notable performance, is left alone on the Wimbledon tennis court after daughter Florence (Sally Forrest) drops her winning trophy, with contempt, into her mother's hands. Lupino knew the power of the camera's final statement, and the postwar period was astutely reflected in her desolate, ambiguous finales.

These interconnections reflect the budgetary and genre concerns that challenged independent filmmakers. Like a family of moviemakers, Lupino, Ray, Bezzerides, and Diskant worked together, crossing from film into television and back again. Lupino, as usual, was the only woman at the table.

This had started to change when Lupino spoke with Debra Weiner for an interview published in 1977. Lupino bemoaned the dearth of women directors, but she was able to note that it was "wonderful" that there were "more women going into the field."[25] Although several women were directing in the mid-1970s, most were working actresses, like Lupino, and by the 1980s, the system had again locked down.

Any discussion of Lupino's global cohort inevitably leads to the question of auteurship and why her work was so slow to receive the acclaim it always deserved. Lupino used her early success as an actress as leverage with the studios, the censors, and her crews to get what she needed on film, designing her own noir-hybrid landscape and her own collaborative style. She was an expert with lenses, according to cinematographer Archie Stout, who worked with Lupino on three films and worked often with John Ford. Nicholas Musuraca, a cinematographer who lent his talents to Val Lewton and Jacques Tourneur as well as to Lupino (for *The Hitch-Hiker*), marveled at her direction of actors. Smart and patient, and perhaps intimidating because of her renown as a Hollywood actress, she obtained subtle performances from her casts. Her expertise as a film director made her transition to television an easy one.[26] Often she produced and directed while also shepherding other writers. In 1956, for example, Lupino cowrote, directed, and produced her television directorial debut, "No. 5 Checked Out," a half-hour teleplay that aired on *Screen Directors Playhouse*. It starred William Talman, with whom Lupino had worked on *The Hitch-Hiker* (1953).[27]

Male directors in Lupino's cohort were lauded for work that was equal to hers in genre, style, and expertise. One example is Robert Aldrich's "The Bad Streak" (1954), which was produced for the second season of *Four Star Playhouse*.[28] Two of Aldrich's films were chosen for inclusion in *Cahiers du Cinéma*'s top-ten list for 1955: *The Big Knife*, which starred Lupino and Jack Palance, and *Kiss Me Deadly*.[29] *Kiss Me Deadly* and Aldrich's *Vera Cruz* (1954) are considered two of the most influential films of the 1950s.[30] Jean-Luc Godard called Sam Fuller, another in Lupino's cohort, an auteur and paid homage to him by casting Fuller in his *Pierrot le fou* (1965).[31] Lupino and Fuller are both considered modernists: their films are "characterized by urban landscapes, subjective narration, nonlinear plots, hard-boiled poetry, and misogynistic eroticism."[32] Lupino cowrote and starred in *Private Hell 36* (1954), a noir crime film directed by Don Siegel, another highly regarded filmmaker.[33]

None of these male directors was ever labeled as anything but tough, brilliant, and relentless. Lupino possessed each of these qualities, yet as the sole woman in this group, her producing, writing, and directing credits were consistently overlooked. These comparisons to her contemporaries—especially Ray, Godard's auteur exemplar—help clarify what Lupino could have accomplished had she been directing in a different era.

Reviewers and even critics have often asked, "What male directors influenced Ida Lupino?" Freelance journalist Debra Weiner asked Lupino this question in an interview in 1977, when Lupino's directing career was still largely undocumented:

> Q: You acted with many fine directors. Did any of them influence your directing?
>
> A: Not in style. I had to find my own style, my own way of doing things. I wasn't going to try to copy anybody. But certain directors, like Wellman, Charles Vidor, Walsh, or Michael Curtiz, couldn't help but rub off. And Robert Aldrich, God knows it was a delight to work for him in *The Big Knife* (1955). He's not only a fine technician, but he certainly knows the actor. He digs down into your role and pulls things out you weren't aware were there.[34]

Promotional poster for Private Hell 36 *(1954), produced by the Filmakers and directed by Don Siegel.*

A better question is, Who are the directors whom Lupino influenced? Among those who have acknowledged the importance of her work are Clint Eastwood and Richard Boone. Both directors acknowledged her skill and were surprised by her ability to garner excellent performances while at the same time knowing her way around lenses and setups, camera angles, and blocking. Boone was impressed with his performances when Lupino directed, and Eastwood was influenced by Lupino's economy and her spare working method. Actress and director Lee Grant understood the problems Lupino faced as a woman that male directors did not, observing, "Once I started directing, I realized how tough it must have been for her and what courage she must have had."[35]

Chapter 3

SIX MOVIES, FIVE YEARS

There was an absolute and ironclad caste system in the film capital in the 1940s and 1950s that had as its primary purpose to exclude females.

Ida Lupino in Manohla Dargis, "Revisiting a Film from Ida Lupino, Hollywood Star Turned Director"

Between 1949 and 1953, Lupino's company, the Filmakers, produced six of her directed features: *Not Wanted* (1949), *Never Fear* (1949), *Outrage* (1950), *Hard, Fast and Beautiful* (1951), *The Hitch-Hiker* (1953), and *The Bigamist* (1953). Lupino brought her signature style to each one, using elements of film noir and film gris, plus neorealism, which gave these films a documentary tone. These were B movies, produced quickly on limited budgets.

When the studio system was broken up and restrictions were lifted on the studios' distribution networks, the major studios faced competition from not only the growing television industry but also independent companies. The studios began to turn out films that featured the same narratives brought to the screen by Poverty Row production houses, which had been making low-budget B movies since the 1920s. Many of these were pop-up companies, which were not necessarily tied to a studio or even to an address. Several were on or near North Gower Street in Hollywood, which became known as Poverty Row. B movies, which were especially popular with young audiences, could be made in two weeks, and many were made for around $20,000 rather than the typical studio budget of $400,000.[1] To save money, the companies used cheap sets or exteriors; the more long-standing companies maintained permanent lots, where they reused the same sets. The films featured quickly written dialogue, emphasized light and shadow for suspense, and employed ultracreative camera movement to deliver thrills.[2]

Poverty Row was a creative outlet for artists who wanted to express themselves in an original way and had the skills to make movies on a very low budget.[3] It was also a training ground, and many talented people got their start by working on B films. Some went on to work for larger independent film companies or for the major studios, including actors Buster Crabbe, James Cagney, Humphrey Bogart, and Ava Gardner and directors Carl Foreman, Edward Dmytryk, Robert Wise, Fred Zinnemann, Anthony Mann, Joseph H. Lewis, and Edgar G. Ulmer. Ulmer's *Detour* (1945) and Lewis's *Minstrel Man* (1944), the latter nominated for two Academy Awards, were made for Producers Releasing Corporation (PRC), a Poverty Row company that was "arguably the cheapest studio in Hollywood."[4] In 1947, the company was acquired by Eagle-Lion Films, which distributed Lupino's *Not Wanted* and *Never Fear*.

Most low-budget B movies were genre films following narrative formulas that were familiar and enjoyable for audiences. As Ronnie Scheib so wisely points out, "Without a sense of genre you are missing a lot of what is most alive in the movies."[5] Westerns, mysteries, comedies, and horror pictures were staples of this segment of the industry. Some were crime thrillers (*Gun Crazy* [1950]), and others were offbeat yet serious (*Damaged Lives* [1933]). B films were titled to sell (for example, *Strange Illusion* [1945] and *Hollow Triumph* [1948], the latter of which boasts the cinematography of John Alton).[6] A few, like *Jane Eyre* (1934), have stood the test of time. B films tend to have a strong narrative drive with no-nonsense visuals, in which moments of horror or crime are played out in opaque shadows, changing the characters' lives forever. In a great Poverty Row movie, what you can't see is precisely what provides tension and cathartic release. For instance, in *Cat People* (1942), produced for RKO by Val Lewton and directed by Jacques Tourneur, the camera follows a discarded piece of paper as a gust of wind picks it up, while the audience hears the wild cry of a cat offscreen, intensifying the feeling of dread. Using sound and shadow, Tourneur, Lewton, and cinematographer Nicholas Musuraca, the director of photography for Lupino's *The Hitch-Hiker*, created horror on a budget.

One of the most successful of the B studios was Republic Pictures, which made thousands of movies, including genre films and serials. Film historian Imogen Sara Smith lauded Republic's output in a 2019 article, stating, "There is no equivalent today to Republic's economy line of well-crafted B-movies. . . . They didn't offer big stars, budgets, or concepts, but they had a streamlined classicism and concentrated focus on action and narrative. . . . They represented an era when movies were movies."[7] Among Republic's releases was *The Quiet Man* (1952), with John Wayne, which was shot by Winton C. Hoch and Archie Stout; Stout was the cinematographer for three of Lupino's films: *Outrage*, *Never Fear*, and *Hard, Fast and Beautiful*.

The actors, screenwriters, directors, and producers who began their careers on Poverty Row took their training seriously, and many moved on to independent companies with bigger budgets and to the mushrooming network television industry. Lupino's career was emblematic of the path that talented individuals could take from Poverty Row to the indies, itself a classic B-movie story.[8] As an actress in B films, she had learned how to shoot quickly and masterfully on location—and on a shoestring budget—by observing her directors. She shaped these skills to produce a highly personal brand of filmmaking. As a director, she was inspired by the brutal candidness of Roberto Rossellini's neorealistic filmmaking, creating movies that brought to life women's disappointment in the post–World War II American dream.[9] Her ambiguous, wistful endings reflect her frustration with the constraints that affected her work. Working within such strictures is a challenge that is often reserved specifically for women, who, according to the French writer Hélène Cixous, "must steal in or fly by."[10] It required not only Lupino's talent but also her courage to become an independent filmmaker, particularly one who produced intimate treatments of socially complex themes in which empathy is extended to characters who are exploited and damned. Director Martin Scorsese is among those who recognized Lupino's importance as a trailblazer: "She was a true pioneer; the six films she directed between 1949 and 1953 are remarkable chamber pieces that deal with challenging subjects in a clear, almost documentary fashion, and are a singular achievement in American cinema."[11]

Each of Lupino's six independent films offers a commentary on America after World War II, when societal expectations made few allowances for personal circumstances. Two focus on oppressed women with grim futures: the protagonist of *Not Wanted* works at various dead-end jobs before falling for the wrong guy; in *The Bigamist*, Lupino plays a waitress in a dreary Hollywood restaurant who marries an already married man. The main character in *Never Fear* is confronted with a different type of dread: a dancer with a bright future contracts polio—an overwhelming fear during the late 1940s and 1950s—and struggles to find independence while recovering from the disease. Another of the films, *Hard, Fast and Beautiful*, exposes white-collar crime in women's professional sports while exploring the dark side of domesticity using a fraught mother-daughter relationship as underpinning in which ambition destroys both women. *Outrage* addresses the taboo subject of rape. *The Hitch-Hiker* is a terror-filled crime thriller detailing a serial killer's murder spree that was even more frightening because it was actually current news. Lupino did not hesitate to focus on themes that were highly controversial in the late 1940s and early 1950s.

The creation of the Filmakers gave Lupino not only creative control to make the films she wanted but also the opportunity to discover and introduce new

Lupino with Sally Forrest. Various fan magazines and reviewers noted their striking resemblance.

talent. In 1949, when she and Young created the manifesto for their company, one of their goals was to find and cast unknowns, as she explained to Hedda Hopper in 1949: "We're working on the theory that the ticket-buying public is more interested in what's in a picture than who's in it. So we're surrounding ourselves with fresh talent. We want ability, not names." Lupino added, "With the exception of Mark Hellinger, nobody ever bought a story for me. Now I want to do that for others."[12] Discovering young talent was exciting for Lupino, but it also fulfilled an important practical need: to control her small budgets.

One of these unknowns was Sally Forrest, whom Lupino cast in *Not Wanted*. Forrest was reviewed so well for this first role, as an unwed pregnant teen, that Lupino cast her again in *Never Fear* and *Hard, Fast and Beautiful*. Reviewers and critics speculated that Forrest was Lupino's alter ego.[13] Essentially, Forrest looked like Lupino, and with women, it was always looks first.

The fact that Lupino worked with Forrest on three of her independent films undoubtedly encouraged these conjectures. Forrest had ability as well as freshness. She was athletic, which was essential for her roles as a dancer in *Never Fear* and a tennis star in *Hard, Fast and Beautiful*. She could remain relatively authentic while working within the tight schedules that Lupino set. Lupino became so close to Forrest that she was a bridesmaid when the young actress married agent Milo Frank in 1951.

Only in *The Hitch-Hiker* did Lupino break away from her focus on women.

The Hitch-Hiker is a dark cult classic in which violent crime and postwar male dislocation are explored hand in hand. After World War II, white middle-class women had new appliances, romance novels, and lifestyle magazines, but whatever independence they had found during the war was greatly constrained. Heroic vets returned to homes that promised security, but for some of these traumatized men, they found what seemed like intolerable situations and wanted only to escape. This dark dynamic plays out in *The Hitch-Hiker* through a cinematographic design that was as close to expressionism as Lupino could afford—dramatic contrast and impenetrable shadows required complex, expensive lighting systems. In this and her other five independent films, Lupino exploited the film noir and film gris genres to express the alienated and highly ambiguous postwar cultural moment. As critic Christoph Huber notes, Lupino's independent films are "prison pictures" in which people are "trapped by their own weaknesses and fears."[14] Indeed, Lupino found a way to shoot the vast, open road as a claustrophobic nightmare.

Lupino's Genre Hybrids

Lupino was a master of hybridization. Each of her independent films mixes genres, incorporating aspects of film gris and neorealism, as well as film noir. She drew story material from contemporary news accounts and used these elements of docudrama to intensify her exploration of the social problems of the period: teen pregnancy, polio, momism, rape, serial murder, bigamy. Suspense is an important element, reflecting her interest in ambiguity, irony, and horror. She acknowledged her affinity for horror and the grotesque in an interview in 1974: "I would not be good at *Doctor Zhivago*, *The Longest Day*, the tremendous plains of war. I don't believe that is my channel . . . suspense pictures, yes. Robert Aldrich things, yes. *What Ever Happened to Baby Jane?* Yes. That I would say is my slot. Suspense."[15] Through her expert depiction of uncertainty and menace, along with her skillful blending of genres, Lupino produced films that realistically reflected American anxiety in the postwar years.

The noir mode emerged in American cinema just after World War II, and the term *film noir*, first applied by French film critics to early Hollywood crime films, came to characterize the hundreds of American movies that were released back-to-back after the war.[16] Noir has been discussed and analyzed religiously by film historians and critics, and what the term signifies is debated. James Naremore, who has written extensively about this genre, argues that it "belongs to the history of ideas as much as to the history of cinema. It has always been easier to recognize a film noir than to define the term."[17] Paul Schrader similarly considers it to be less a genre than a mood or a tone that gives a film a dark, psychological atmosphere. Schrader notes that it is easier to say what noir is not rather than what it is. Foster Hirsch and Andrew Spicer, however, argue that noir is a genre. Raymond Borde and Etienne Chaumeton see noir as a cycle of films reflecting alienation. And Raymond Durgnat believes it is less a defined genre than a visual style with similar, recurring motifs.[18] Schrader comments that although the noir genre attracted postwar moviegoers, critics "disliked" it because a film's visual style was favored over its theme. "Critics," he states, "liked to write about themes."[19] By the 1950s, film noir was giving rise to the neorealist social problem picture, and it is at this point that Lupino began her first transition and moved into the director's chair.

In Lupino's case, the noir mode became part of her work in a variety of ways. Lauded as a quintessential femme fatale, she developed a strong affinity for noir's stylistic elements as an actress. Lupino was also drawn to the psychological thriller, which was influenced by German expressionism and was often set in an uncertain and shadowy urban landscape. The techniques of film noir ably presented the expressionist themes of alienation and moral ambiguity, both pressing social concerns during the 1940s and 1950s. Lupino infused her films with the noir mode especially through lighting and repeated visual motifs, as well as character psychology and narrative ambiguity. Her films incorporate dreamlike states, violent confusion, disequilibrium, flashbacks, and character voice-over—all elements of noir. Naremore calls the genre a "collective style operating within and against the Hollywood system."[20] In *The Bigamist*, Lupino deployed noir in just this way to desentimentalize the melodramatic ideas that the censors imposed on her work. Naremore notes that several of Lupino's films can be classified as noir, and he points out that she was the "only important woman director" of the 1940s—a rare tribute at the time.[21]

Lupino also used noir to suggest the sense of jeopardy that infused postwar domesticity. As servicemen returned, many found that neither home nor society offered any relief from the deep-seated anxieties that were related to their wartime experiences. The currents of existential anxiety that are reflected in Lupino's protagonists may have had a connection to her personal life: Lupino intimated that her marriage to actor Louis Hayward was spoiled by the trauma he carried home from World War II.[22] Postwar psychological stress sets the tone of *The Hitch-Hiker*, in particular. Gritty location was another hallmark of noir, and Los Angeles offered the quintessential noir environment. Mike Davis explains that after the success of the screen adaptations of James M. Cain's and Raymond Chandler's noir novels, "film noir began to exploit Los Angeles settings in new ways. Geographically, it shifted increasingly from the Cainian bungalows . . . to the epic dereliction of downtown's Bunker Hill, which symbolized the rot in the heart of the expanding metropolis."[23] The first shot of *Not Wanted*, filmed at Bunker Hill, is an immediate expression of confusion and madness, a clue to the interior lives of the film's characters.

Some commentators have characterized Lupino's films as "melo-noir," and Lupino's films do contain melodramatic touches.[24] Melodrama can heighten the emotional impact of a film, as Belgian filmmaker Luc Dardenne noted in a 2012 interview: "You dare to do things that seem larger than life, which aren't at all realistic. And then we arrive at a way to make them believable, to make them live in the spectator's heart."[25] Shonni Enelow, however, points out that "the essential content of melodrama is not the communication of suffering, but its incommunicability—identify with me completely, says melodrama, even though I know you can't. What melodrama speaks is the wish to identify with another's suffering."[26]

As Lupino emphasized the struggle of the marginalized and foregrounded female agency, she made subjective statements of objective facts by pushing against the excesses of domestic melodrama. In addition, she often produced a subtler narrative by allowing the dream state of noir to coexist with the hyperbole of melodrama. It is, in fact, this restraint that drives *The Bigamist*, a film that is vastly different in tone from any of her previous efforts. Grisham and Grossman identify the mixture of noir and melodrama in Lupino's work as "home noir." They describe the "double-bind" that ensnares characters "who escape their antagonistic homes, often driven by American myths of the new freedom of the road, only to be forced back into the 'real world' of home—or suffer the realities of the road."[27] "Home noir" is particularly prevalent in *Hard, Fast and Beautiful*, in which dreams bump up against the issues of character and identity that were prevalent in the 1950s.

Lupino's directed films are best described as neorealistic social problem narratives that are interwoven with documentary elements. Her determination to produce this type of hybrid film may have been directly influenced by Italian neorealist Roberto Rossellini, whom Lupino met in 1946 at a party in Los Angeles. Rossellini reportedly complained that "in Hollywood movies, the star is going crazy, or drinks too much, or he wants to kill his wife," asking, "When are you going to make pictures about ordinary people, in ordinary situations?"[28] Lupino had seen his *Roma Città Aperta* (*Rome, Open City*), which had been released in 1945. Rossellini's harrowing depiction of the Nazi occupation of Rome resonated with Lupino, who had empathy for "lost, bewildered people."[29] Her compassion for the marginalized was evident in her first film, *Not Wanted*, and that became the model for her subsequent narratives.[30] Even the psychopathic killer in *The Hitch-Hiker* is given an empathetic monologue that exposes a neglected, traumatic childhood.

Lupino was drawn to the noir mode, but she was also interested in film gris. Directors working in this genre portrayed socially realistic landscapes, naturally photographed, that were drab and depressed. Their narratives emphasized capitalist inequality, class division, and materialism. Crime is a social critique rather than defining the critical flaw of a single character. These are grim tales stewed in guilt and paranoia. Thom Andersen discusses film gris in his 1985 essay "Red Hollywood," characterizing a group of films made in that genre, between 1947 and 1951, by a set of directors including Jules Dassin, Cy Endfield, John Huston, Joseph Losey, Abraham Polonsky, Nicholas Ray, and Robert Rossen—all left-wing dissidents.[31] More pessimistic than film noir, film gris blurs the boundaries between crime and enterprise—corrupt cops, for example, are portrayed as the product of a corrupt legal system—and links crime to disadvantage. The movies are characterized by subtle performances, an absence of femme fatales and hence better development of female characters, a blurring of good and evil, and bleak or gray settings.[32] Notable examples are Rossen's *Body and Soul* (1947), Losey's *The Prowler* (1951), and Huston's *The Asphalt Jungle* (1951), films that are "characterized by a combination of crime and social critique."[33] Other examples are *Force of Evil* (1948), *They Live by Night* (1948), and *Road House* (1948), the last starring Lupino. Lupino understood this rarely used (and still understudied) genre, and she knew it worked well for her socially realistic stories.[34]

In *The Bigamist*, for example, Lupino made ideal use of film gris elements: the line between good and evil is blurred, female characters have backstories that are clearly understood, and the setting for the characters is emotionally, physically, and economically bleak. The social ills investigated by Lupino and other film gris directors often came from the news, adding a touch of docudrama. This is reflected in several of Lupino's films: *The Hitch-Hiker* considers the consequences of childhood mistreatment; *Outrage* recounts a story of rape without consequence; *Hard, Fast and Beautiful* portrays corporate exploitation of the individual; *Never Fear* explores an unfounded fear of those with diseases; *Not Wanted* depicts the community in opposition to the individual and examines the perils for women whose lives were constricted by meaningless domestic labor after World War II. Each of these narratives includes a large measure of compassion for the antagonists—the audience understands, for example, that the serial killer in *The Hitch-Hiker* and the title character in *The Bigamist* each had a past that had distorted his morality and therefore his ability to conform to society's mores.

To make movies about such controversial subjects, Lupino had to move the dial on the production code, seeking a nuanced equilibrium between the demands of the Production Code Administration (PCA) and her filmmaking goals. *Not Wanted*, discussed in depth in chapter 4, and *Outrage* were contested heavily by the PCA, but Lupino effectively subverted the censors' demands through her genre hybridization, adding docudramatic elements to the script—especially for *Outrage*—to tone down the melodrama as requested by the PCA. As stated, melodrama is a heightened, exaggerated genre, whereas docudramatic elements are realistic and therefore proffer subtlety. This hybrid allowed Lupino to sustain her vision and secure funding.[35] A subdued—even recessive—behavioral study, *Outrage* "captures the banality of evil in an ordinary small town."[36] Through this delicate balancing act, Lupino was able to get precisely what she wanted onscreen and still satisfy the censors. Even though her films dared to enter provocative territory, she never experienced the hell that other filmmakers did as they tried to have their work approved. Her success was the product of her experience and skill, which gave her the insight needed to rework her stories visually and economically, like a minimalist painter, and was also partially due to her status as a famous actress from the classic Hollywood period.

When Lupino began her transition to directing, she was under contract to Warner Bros. The hierarchical organization of the Hollywood studio system shaped the content and meaning of films, and the lack of risk-taking and the tension between art and business often led to a flawed product. Assembly line uniformity and motion picture originality were at odds. Lupino was frustrated with the limitations placed on her work by the studio. She refused roles that she didn't like, resulting in her suspension:

> For about 18 months back in the mid 40s I could not get a job in pictures as an actress. Along with Ann Sheridan and Humphrey Bogart and John Garfield (we were all under contract at Warners) I was on suspension. It seems we were always on suspension, because we wouldn't do some of the shows we were asked to do. When you turned down something you were suspended, and you stayed suspended.[37]

After Lupino's relationship with Warner Bros. ended and the Filmakers was established, she was able to turn away from slick studio products and concentrate on her own written and directed narratives. Tiring of the femme fatale stereotype, she moved away from factorylike industry standardization and formulaic content, developing a distinctive Lupinian brand of B films. She knew how to fracture the linear narrative convincingly, using shifting points of view and flashbacks that moved her stories into film noir and film gris hybrids, which created more suspense and lowered her budgets.[38] As she undertook her conversion to director, Hollywood was changing, responding to a burgeoning television market and an industry-wide movement toward independent filmmaking that had started in the 1940s and would peak in the 1960s. Lupino was at the center of a Hollywood in flux.

Lupino and the Critics

Although she was at the heart of the independent film movement, Lupino was overlooked by contemporary critics, perhaps because those who controlled and those who wrote about cinema from the late 1940s through the 1950s were almost exclusively male. The most influential publisher of the new criticism was arguably *Cahiers du Cinéma*, whose interest was the new cinema of the French New Wave. This new cinema called for new writing that analyzed rather than reviewed film, and one of the ideas promoted within the pages of *Cahiers du Cinéma* was that of "la politique des auteurs." Film critic Andrew Sarris is credited with translating the French phrase to "auteur theory" and doing much to popularize it.[39] The badge of auteur was given to directors whose style was so distinctive that their authorship could be immediately recognized; among these favored directors were Nicholas Ray, Alfred Hitchcock, Joseph Losey, and Samuel Fuller.[40]

Sarris dismisses Lupino as a director with a single disparaging comment that compares her acting, which he admires as intense and influential, unfavorably with her directing, which he does not: "Ida Lupino's directed films express much of the feeling if little of the skill which she has projected so admirably as an actress."[41] Sarris, like others, erroneously compares characters that Lupino portrayed with those that she wrote. The noir roles that Lupino had played with such power were created by men and were subjected to the male gaze; the women's roles that she wrote or cowrote were based on actual women in the 1950s and were intended to illuminate postwar women's concerns for both the men and the women in the audience. In her films, the man's passivity—his inability to act—is more pronounced when the woman's passivity is shown through her characterization as a dazed wanderer.

French critic Michel Mourlet shines a light on Lupino's sheer skill in a 1960 article in *Cahiers du Cinéma*, "In Defense of Violence": "The film-maker who strikes deepest into violence and demonstrates it better than anyone is clearly Losey . . . [who] merits comparison with some of those astonishing reflexes one sees in actors in the work of Ida Lupino or [Kenji] Mizoguchi." Mourlet argues that all art is involved with violence, but only cinema can reproduce it; because violence stems from man's actions, "the camera captures it naturally."[42] He makes these points about a specific type of violence, one that is filled to the bursting point with tension, and it is that potential for eruption that Mourlet sees in Lupino's work. He notes that this intensity also characterizes the work of Raoul Walsh.[43] Lupino worked with Walsh as an actress four times: in *Artists and Models* (1937), *They Drive by Night* (1940), *High Sierra* (1941), and *The Man I Love* (1947).[44] Although Lupino stated unequivocally that she would never copy any director, she freely admitted Walsh's influence: "Uncle [Walsh] *always* knew *exactly* what he wanted and because he did I could give him the goods."[45] Genre films were not particularly popular at the time (perhaps because they were too pulpy), but Lupino and Walsh admired them, particularly those with characters who were vulnerable and lost.

In his discussion of auteurs, French director and critic Jacques Rivette left out Lupino while extolling four others in her cohort: Nicholas Ray, Richard Brooks, Anthony Mann, and Robert Aldrich.[46] Ray was the favored noir hero, without question. François Truffaut noted the "moral solitude" of Ray's characters, and Rivette wrote of the "demon of violence" central to each of Ray's films, but they associated these themes only with Ray.[47] Neither mentioned Lupino, although Ray and Lupino were similar stylists who made films with parallel themes. Angela Martin has noted Rivette's assertion that of the "virtues" shared by the four men, "violence is the primary one," whereas Mourlet contradicts this assertion. Martin links this violence to a "gender-bound enthusiasm" displayed by Rivette and his fellow critics. She concludes that among the women filmmakers of that time, only Lupino and Arzner might be considered as auteurs because they produced "a body of work within a single production context."[48] Ultimately, Martin notes that the New Wave's demand for personal self-expression was vastly different from "the later feminist call for the personal to be political rather than ego-centric."[49]

Lupino was kept out of the auteur pantheon for a combination of reasons. When she began directing, the film industry was no longer interested in Poverty Row films. Even so, Lupino's status as a woman filmmaker was undoubtedly a factor. Like Lupino, Nicholas Ray and Akira Kurosawa wrote popular films that showcased marginalized characters without personal power (*Rebel without a Cause* [1955] and *Yojimbo* [1961], respectively); unlike Lupino, both men are historicized as world-famous auteurs. The narrow perspective of feminist inquiry in the 1950s and early 1960s also played a role. Edgar Ulmer survived his B-movie legacy, but he did not have to contend with the negative assessments of the feminist critics who misunderstood Lupino, like Barbara Quart, who asserts, "The anti-feminist content of her work becomes more explicit, and the gap between what Lupino herself did and the values she promulgated more dramatic."[50] Annette Kuhn, in particular, has suggested that it is this "gap" that made Lupino illegible for so many years.[51] However, one scholar who has written often about Lupino, Richard Koszarski, has observed that her directed films "display the obsessions and consistencies of a true auteur. . . . In *The Bigamist* and *The Hitch-Hiker*, Lupino was able to reduce the male to the same sort of dangerous, irrational force that women represented in most male-directed examples of Hollywood *film noir*."[52] He deflects the criticism leveled by some of the early feminists while making a compelling case for Lupino's auteurship.

More recently, Lupino's accomplishments have been getting increased attention. A&E released two documentaries on Lupino in 1998, and MoMA's retrospective on women in film in 2000 concentrated on Lupino. In 2018, a film series at UCLA's Billy Wilder Theater showcased Lupino as actress and director.[53] These efforts signal a recovery of Lupino as director, as have essays in critical film studies and cinema anthologies.[54] Amelie Hastie's monograph on *The Bigamist* elevates Lupino's legacy. According to Hastie, when Lupino moved behind the camera, she traded her "position of visibility" in front of the camera for "one behind the scenes" and became invisible to film critics. Had she remained visible, Hastie argues, her stylistic filmmaking would have defined her as an auteur.[55] Therese Grisham and Julie Grossman have also offered textual analyses, descriptions of some of Lupino's best television work as actress and as director, and some infrequently discussed archival content.[56]

Lupino was a nimble strategist who overcame her gendered otherness, rejecting the assumptions, often published in *Cahiers du Cinéma*, that promoted a males-only conception of auteurism. She merits exemplary status—that is, as an author—if only for her volume of work, which outstripped that of many of her directing peers in both film and television. As a working film and television director as well as a mother supporting her family, Lupino led a life that was in stark contrast to the midcentury cliché of the compliant woman. A cultural critic of her time, Lupino worked against the repressions of the period, which eventually led to more freedom, particularly for independent filmmakers. Moreover, for the generation of women filmmakers who emerged in the late 1960s and throughout the 1970s, she was the only example of a woman who had directed independent features within the Hollywood system.[57]

Part II

CASE STUDIES: THREE INDEPENDENT FILMS

Lupino and Dina Merrill, bridesmaids at Sally Forrest's wedding to William Morris talent agent Milo Frank, August 5, 1951.

SNAPSHOTS

In 1950, Lupino was chosen by the all-male Screen Directors Guild to present the prestigious and coveted Academy Award for best director. Paul Douglas, president of the Screen Directors Guild and host for the awards ceremony, introduced Lupino with a quip that would be condemned today as flagrantly misogynistic:

> As you may have guessed, it's been our aim here tonight to choose our presenters for their fitness for the honor, and we also felt that if they were good to look at, that didn't hurt a bit. And to present the award for the best achievement in direction, the committee has chosen the best-looking director in town. Stanley Lupino's daughter must have been born wise in the ways of show business. . . . She has lately added writing, directing, and producing to her busy and distinguished career as an actress. Ladies and gentlemen, Miss Ida Lupino![1]

Lupino glides onto the stage amid loud applause and moves up to the microphone elegantly, her brief notes to the audience perfectly memorized. She speaks softly but clearly: "If a genie ever gave me a wish, I think I'd know how I would like to spend it. I'd want my name to be on a list like this."[2] Lupino announces the winner's name, "Joseph L. Mankiewicz, for *A Letter to Three Wives*," and Mankiewicz strides to the stage. He continues where Douglas left off: "Thank you brother Lupino. Ms. Lupino's name, incidentally, on the membership list of the Screen Directors Guild is Irving Lupino. That way we can keep the same informal tone to our meetings, and there's the building costs to be considered."[3] There was as much laughter as applause, but Mankiewicz was stating clearly that the guild was a closed boys' club. Lupino laughed along with the audience, perhaps enraging some early feminists, and then Mankiewicz grabbed her around the waist as they walked offstage together. That's entertainment![4]

In this photograph, Lupino is with actress Dina Merrill at Sally Forrest's wedding. Lupino's gaze suggests that she is aware of being watched and photographed; Merrill, in contrast, seems more accessible, smiling and squinting a bit in the sun, without self-awareness. Shots like these, with Lupino dressed in white tulle, tend to feminize her, but in this photo, she remains slightly inaccessible, even provocative. It is as if there is something pressing on her mind.[5]

Chapter 4
NOT WANTED

I did not set out to be a director. I was only supposed to coproduce Not Wanted.

Ida Lupino in Debra Weiner, "Interview with Ida Lupino"

A look at three of Lupino's six independent films—*Not Wanted*, *Never Fear*, and *The Hitch-Hiker*—provides an overview of her directorial work while emphasizing what makes each film unique in terms of its history and presentation. *Not Wanted* (1949) is not often discussed, but it was Lupino's first directed feature. Apart from its treatment of a forbidden subject—pregnancy outside of marriage—it reveals much about her skill and visual style as a director, her narrative inclinations, her lighting design and use of sound, and her work with actors, some of whom she discovered. It also shows how Lupino finessed the demands of the Production Code Administration (PCA).

Not Wanted marked Lupino's transition to film directing. Although moving behind the camera was a natural next step for the actress, writer, and producer, she noted in a self-authored article that appeared in the *Los Angeles Times*, "I never planned to become a director. The fates and a combination of luck—good and bad—were responsible."[1] The Filmakers had hired Elmer Clifton, an experienced Poverty Row director, but when Clifton had a heart attack three days into the shoot, Lupino took over. She knew the material and had cast the main roles, and it seemed the most economical way to proceed. It was her first directed film, although her role is not credited, as she noted in an interview published in 1977: "Since we were using my version of the script, I had to take over. My name was not on the directorial credits, however, and rightly so."[2]

Not Wanted is about a teenage girl who becomes pregnant out of wedlock and—because the film was made in 1949—is forced to give away her baby. Sally Forrest plays the teenager, Sally Kelton, and Leo Penn, another of

Lupino's discoveries, plays the destitute musician, Steve Ryan, who fathers her child. The emotional center of the film is the trauma, disorientation, and grief that Sally undergoes when her child is taken from her. The original script, titled "Bad Company," was written by screenwriters Paul Jarrico and Malvin Wald for Enterprise Productions. After being rejected as "utterly impossible under the Code" by the PCA, "Bad Company" moved to United States Pictures, a production company headed by Milton Sperling.[3] Sperling submitted a one-page treatment to the PCA on December 6, 1948. The PCA censors rejected the project, listing four primary objections:

1. The youngsters involved should be raised above the high school level.
2. The parents should not be depicted as inept nincompoops; this to avoid throwing the sympathy with the sin as well as the sinner.
3. He should be sure that in the preparation of his screen story, the sin is shown to be *wrong*. We told him that this was the *most important* item of all.
4. He would have to watch very carefully the *details* of the illicit relationships.[4]

The PCA relayed its concerns to Sperling personally, wanting to stay off the record to avoid setting a precedent for movies about "unwed motherhood."[5]

By February 1949, the project had moved to Emerald Productions, where Lupino was on the roster as a producer.[6] Working with Jarrico and coproducer Anson Bond, Lupino took charge. She changed the name to *Not Wanted* and rewrote the script with the help of Wald, Jarrico, and perhaps Collier Young. Then she negotiated with the PCA to reinstate the project. Lupino took a risk by showing up in person at the office of Eric Johnston, head of the Motion Picture Association of America (MPAA), but she was aware of her clout as a famous Hollywood star and the power of her presence. Although her looks subjected her to gender discrimination, they also gave her agency, which she used to get what she needed. Lupino knew how to flatter and cooperate, and this allowed her to work around the obstacles she encountered. She walked the censors through the objected-to "adult only" scenes and secured their approval. She agreed, for example, to make the seduction scene—where Sally becomes pregnant—"beautiful." The censors insisted that the unwed mom not be glamorized.[7] Lupino consented, and the project was green-lighted.

George Fisher, a radio personality and gossip columnist, spoke favorably of Lupino and her gumption in a KNX radio broadcast on February 6, 1949:

> Ida Lupino, the pretty movie queen—who made what Hollywood considered a come-back after two years of screen silence—in "Roadhouse," in which her figure dazzled movie-goers, her singing stunned them, and her acting brought back memories of her great performance in "They Drive by Night," which drove her to the top in Hollywood, is the filmtown's newest lady producer.[8]

Fisher noted that Lupino "amazed reporters by stating that the movie censors aren't big, ugly beasts, after all, but nice, broadminded, human beings!" and added that, as far as he knew, it was the first time "anyone had anything nice to say about the movie censors."[9]

Lupino used the studio's publicity machine to calm the fears of the censors, as an account published in the *San Diego Tribune-Sun* reveals:

> Ida is currently doing much of the writing on the "NOT WANTED" Script and has conferred with the Nuns at St. Anne's Home for unwed mothers. Naturally with such a subject, she has heard also from the industry censors at the [PCA director Joseph] Breen Office. I expected a blast at the scene *snippers*. But no soap.
>
> "I found them amazingly helpful," she said. "We went over the script with them and they pointed out what it must do. . . . They showed us that the story must be aimed at three classes:
>
> "TEEN-AGE GIRLS, since the majority of unwed mothers are between the ages of 11 and 18. Their emotions are immature, and their biggest fear is pain. Therefore, we must show as much of Labor as we can.
>
> "OLDER GIRLS, whose emotions are more developed. They must be shown the painfulness of having to give up their child, as most unwed mothers must, for economic reasons.
>
> "PARENTS, we must show that because they have brought a daughter into the world, they must share the responsibility for her, no matter what happens."[10]

According to Fisher, Lupino wanted to make *Not Wanted* not only for commercial reasons but also because she believed the movie could scare teenagers into being more careful during their early sexual encounters. Fisher related that Lupino "plans to show scenes in the labor room—never before done on the screen. It's grim—but the censors decided maybe it's about time." He added, "Ida is signing people like crazy and an unknown will play the lead. The picture will get underway in a couple of weeks with the hearty approval of the so-called ogres of the censor board!"[11]

As Lupino was in the midst of trying to secure the censors' okay, reporter Virginia McPherson published an article suggesting that Lupino detested the PCA.[12] Lupino sent a telegram to Breen to express her anger with McPherson, who had, Lupino said, misrepresented her comments. In the letter, Lupino stated unequivocally that she had only

> gratitude and appreciation for the constructive help of the production code administrators in trying to make my production *Not Wanted* a picture both of truth and good taste. . . . Such irresponsible reporting is unforgiveable. Any protest you may wish to make will find me in hearty support. . . . Because I am so deeply grateful for the aid of your office in treating a delicate subject, we shall leave nothing undone to give the reading and listening public the correct impression. Kindest regards, Ida Lupino.[13]

Through all these efforts, Lupino successfully negotiated for a more feminist vision of *Not Wanted.* Film historian Diane Waldman observes that "the ending presents a much less preachy Drew and a much less penitent Sally and is certainly less explicit than the script which received PCA approval about the rehabilitation of the unwed mother through marriage and reconciliation with the family."[14]

The reviews for *Not Wanted* were mixed, although they were generally good in regard to the technical aspects of the film. A review in *Variety* stated:

> *Not Wanted* has a chance at excellent returns in those situations that will take advantage of its exploitation possibilities. . . . [T]he makers have not sensationalized its unwed mothers theme, but present it openly enough to . . . help ticket sales. . . . [F]or a production debut, [the] picture offers usually good values for the budget and economy practiced doesn't detract from the excellent sight polish given by Harry Freulich's top flight lensing. . . . Elmer Clifton's direction helps the pathos and bathos of the Paul Jarrico–Ida Lupino script together rather well. . . . Sally Forrest clicks strongly as the girl who errs for love and goes through the shame and agonies of unwed motherhood. Outstanding is Keefe Brasselle.[15]

Lupino received no credit for the film, even though it seems likely that the reviewers knew she had stepped in to direct it. The *Hollywood Reporter* was more enthusiastic:

> *Not Wanted* is a strong entry into the independent market, whose highly exploitable story of an unmarried mother is done with taste, dignity and compassion. For the production team of Ida Lupino and Anson Bond, the enterprise is an auspicious start. While they have the courage to people their cast with talented unknowns, they also show the sagacity to compose their technical crew of men with unquestioned experience and ability. They give *Not Wanted* a decided advantage over the usual low budget effort. . . . The script for *Not Wanted* is an example of restrained, intelligent writing. It is somewhat slow in getting into the story, but happily there is the direction of Elmer Clifton to compensate for this lack of pace as he explores the characters of the people involved.[16]

Notably, the *Hollywood Reporter* gives only slight credit to Lupino with Anson Bond in its review, even though Lupino cowrote, coproduced, and directed the film, as well as having saved it from being corrupted by the censors. In London, however, Lupino's film brought rave reviews that called it a "Human Story" and stated, "Men Will Hate This Film."[17] Sixty-seven years later, the film reviewer for the *New Yorker* wrote:

> Ida Lupino's first film as a director . . . from 1949, is a startling blend of compassion and invention. . . . Lupino displays a documentary avidity for the details of work and play. She conveys Sally's unworldly, impractical passion with tender, intimate closeups and an intense, effects-driven subjectivity. . . . An incongruous yet majestic chase scene, highlighting a photogenic array of Los Angeles locations, projects the intimate melodrama onto the world stage.[18]

The main character in *Not Wanted*, like many of Lupino's heroines, has the kind of job that nobody wants, with low pay and long hours. She is a lower-income, hard-luck girl. A production photo for the film shows a small, frightened Sally standing between two much older-looking men: Keefe Brasselle, in the role of Drew Baxter, on the left, and Leo Penn, as Steve Ryan, on the right. Sally wears a simple, hand-me-down dress, while the men are in suits and ties, suggesting they are members of the professional class with jobs. They loom over Sally, while she looks unmoored. She holds a small suitcase, suggesting that she is homeless, a wanderer with few belongings. Brasselle looks angrily at Penn, while Penn looks off seemingly at no one. His stance implies that he is morally weak and without empathy. He is the antagonist, the slightly older, more worldly bad boy who impregnates Sally and then takes off.

This production photo may have been taken before the final PCA draft of the script. Penn's character, Steve Ryan, was originally an irresponsible, wealthy white guy, but the PCA censors insisted that he be semidestitute. Lupino, compromising, made him impoverished and living at the margin of society, even though her original character was more realistic. Since she could no longer make the sociopolitical statement that she had intended, she negotiated to give the character a creative dimension—that of a jazz pianist. Lupino also had to suggest that Sally was a sinner, but she successfully created a sympathetic character, diminishing any judgment the audience might feel toward her.[19] Waldman draws attention to the skill and persistence that Lupino employed to push such a film past the censors. She notes the "very careful path that had to be negotiated in order for a film such as *Not Wanted* with its theme of unmarried motherhood, to get past the PCA at this time" and adds that "this was true also of *Outrage* (1950) [and] other productions with which Lupino was associated."[20] For *Not Wanted*, Lupino convinced the PCA that juvenile delinquency and unmarried teen motherhood were becoming national problems and that her docudrama could bring the discussion forward and serve as both a warning and an antidote.[21]

Not Wanted opens with what would become a Lupino signature: a message that had the dual purpose of engaging the spectator and satisfying the PCA. The first thing the audience saw was a card with this statement: "This is a story told one hundred thousand times each year. We wish to express our deep appreciation to the many hospitals and institutions of mercy the country over, without whose gracious help this picture could never have been made." The message suggests that the audience will be familiar with the story's central problem—that it may have happened to one of them. It alludes not only to the film's theme, unmarried pregnancy, but also to the larger issue of juvenile delinquency. This was a central parental fear in the late 1940s and early 1950s and an ongoing point of control at the PCA.

As the credits begin to roll, Sally is at the center of the screen, moving toward us from a distance, walking slowly up Bunker Hill in downtown Los Angeles. Lupino knew that decay is cinematic, and in the late 1940s, Los Angeles's downtown was highly visual and visceral. The credit sequence, which runs one minute and twenty-seven seconds, was shot in a single take by a locked-off camera, but it conveys movement and strength. At the end of the sequence, Sally arrives onscreen in a close-up. She is clearly troubled, but she is introduced to us with Lupino's usual restraint. We hear the first human sound, a baby's cry, and we watch as Sally lifts an infant from a carriage. The baby's mother cries out in panic, summoning a police officer, and Sally is taken to jail.

This documentary-style opening is freighted with uneasy anticipation. In the background is a cityscape, and Lupino's camera suggests that it could be in any city—it could be in your city. Along the street are two storefronts, a laundry and a grocery. These impart subtle messages. A sign for soda in the grocery window and the presence of the laundry emphasize the domestic nature of motherhood. Juxtaposed with the advertisement for soda is one for wine; wine and spirits were staples in many households in the 1950s. Lupino's frame is always active, and the images are often more important than the text. "I'm terribly against dialogue," she said in her interview with Francine Parker.[22]

The next scene shows Sally in a jail cell, where she asks herself, in a voice-over, "How did I get here? How did I get here?" With this, Lupino draws us into Sally's point of view, and we bond with the character. Lupino, who has suppressed information about Sally's past until this point, dissolves the shot and flashes back to how Sally became a criminal. Lupino employs careful dissolves combined with a spare use of flashbacks and voice-over—elements of noir—to push the story forward. Edgar Ulmer was another director who made use of voice-over and flashbacks for budgetary reasons; flashbacks gradually reveal the film's exposition, and voice-over always refers to the subtext—it is never on the nose. In *Not Wanted*, Lupino uses voice-over in much the same way: not to dramatize the exposition, but to provide insight into Sally's unstable mental condition. Later in the movie, the audience is given information that Sally does not have, a device that creates an atmosphere of Lupinian suspense, anxious and disturbing for the viewer.

The structure of *Not Wanted* is aptly represented by David Bordwell's description of the suspense thrillers of the late 1940s: "The framework of the suspense story is the continual struggle of the frightened protagonist to fight back and save himself in spite of his pervading anxiety, and in this respect, he is heroic. The action of the story does not consist in mere activity, but in the hero's change of mood in response to changing circumstances."[23] Lupino's flair for suspense led Alfred Hitchcock to call her "the female Hitch"—a fitting compliment from the widely acknowledged master of the genre.[24]

Sally comes from a troubled household. Her angry, stressed, unacknowledged, and repressed mother, played by Dorothy Adams, is tired of doing thankless housework. Her father, played by Wheaton Chambers, is a passive man. Bereft of attention from his wife, he focuses all his affection on his daughter. Their home, like so many of Lupino's domestic spaces, is a trap. Sally's bickering mother and weak father are blurred and inexpressive; they have already surrendered to the trying aftermath of World War II. Sally cannot wait to get away from her parents, which motivates her to stay out all night and eventually to leave altogether.

The object of Sally's affection—indeed, her fascination—is Steve. He is an intense, brilliant musician, a classical pianist who plays boogie-woogie at a local club and practices in the bar of the restaurant where Sally is a waitress.

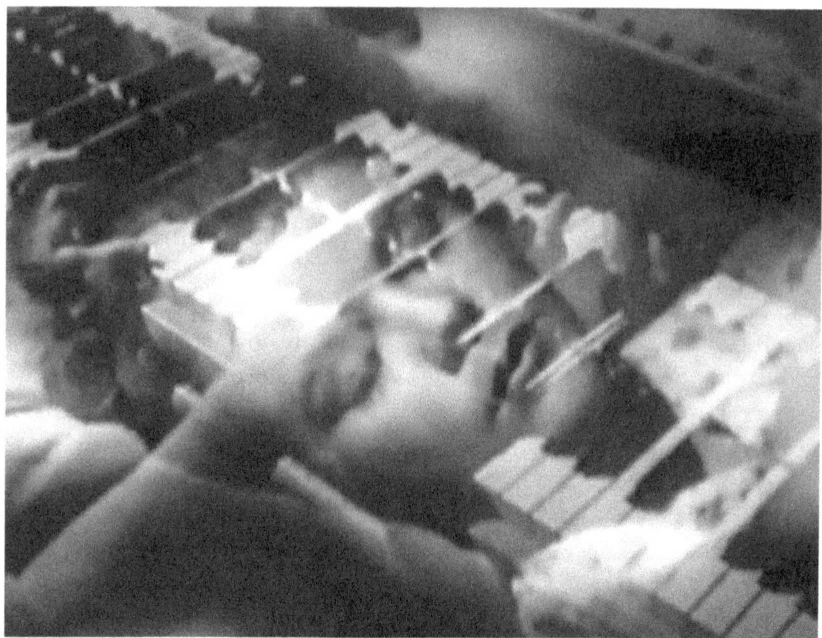

Sally dreaming of Steve (Leo Penn) in a Lupinian dissolve suggesting she is in love with his passion for music.

The artistic Steve does not want Sally. He wants acclaim for his music, and on his terms. He is also frustrated, broke, and going nowhere—except out of Sally's life. Steve's nocturnal existence is emphasized by Lupino's cinematographer, Henry Freulich, who used shadows, dark backgrounds, and low light in most of Steve's sequences.[25] Steve is shown outside during the day in only one scene, and the daylight seems too bright for his character. He looks out of place. Nosferatu-like, he sleeps during the day and begins to wake as night falls. Sally, on the other hand, is cheery and bright, innocent as she falls in love with the wrong guy. When she is working, she watches Steve practice through a porthole-style window in the restaurant's service door.[26] Even when Steve is practicing alone, Sally's face dissolves across the piano keys, signaling that she is always thinking of him.

Lupino was a master at using locations or combining shots to minimize dialogue and save time. She preferred an immediate, clear picture—a pure image—like all great directors. A shot of a dejected, pregnant, and out-of-work Sally with the window of a diner behind her reflects her loss of self personifying the confusion of postwar America. The camera's point of view reverses the words painted on the window—"Help Wanted Waitress"—suggesting an inversion of the phrase, "Waitress Wanted Help." Sally does need help: she is excluded; she is feeling *not* wanted.

A shot of Sally with a café window behind her. The camera's point of view reverses the words painted on the window, "Help Wanted Waitress."

The music by Leith Stevens plays an integral role in defining Steve's character. When we see Steve move from the jazz he plays to make money to the modern classical music he loves, Stevens's score conveys the passionate, artistic side of this failed musician. In this way, Lupino expressed sympathy even for the antagonist. Stevens had a unique talent for generating gripping suspense, with simple orchestrations conveying tension even during quiet moments. Music played a vital role in Lupino's films, and she often used jazz to enhance her version of hybridized noir. Stevens's scores for *Not Wanted* and *The Bigamist* are distinctive for the composer's use of jazz idioms. Lupino and Stevens continued to work together after Lupino moved to television.

In pursuit of Steve, Sally escapes her unhappy home and boards a bus that is traveling along Interstate 90. An exterior shot shows the bus rolling along a featureless highway. This image is a signature metaphor, used by Lupino to signify freedom, restlessness, or flight. On the bus, Sally meets Drew, a decent guy whose war injury has left him with a wooden leg—another of Lupino's acknowledgments of the human toll of World War II. Drew, played by Keefe Brasselle, a Lupino discovery, is as sunny as Steve is dark. He is introduced to the audience through a sweetly comic scene, in which Lupino put the two side by side on the bus. Drew is hidden under the jacket he is using as a blanket while he restlessly sleeps. As he turns this way and that, Sally becomes increasingly irritated. Drew's face finally emerges when he drowsily rests his head on Sally's shoulder, and he wakes when she gives a sharp shrug to dislodge him. The sequence—perhaps a shout-out to Lupino's comedic forebears—shows that Sally Forrest is surprisingly hilarious. This type of opening, of the lovers-to-be who initially don't like each other, is an enduring trope in romantic comedies from *The African Queen* to *Pillow Talk* to *Pride and Prejudice*.

Lupino's scene, however, upends the usual narrative. Although it has romantic moments, *Not Wanted* is not a comedy. How Lupino used this sequence is more important than any projected assumption that the film will have a doggedly plotted "happy" ending. Adding a new character—a costar—exactly twenty-five minutes into a ninety-one-minute film, and expertly folding him into the action while reversing the mood, is an expert twist on the comedic standard. Indeed, the writers set up the narrative's many shifts and unexpected reversals with great dexterity.

As Sally begins to forget Steve and care for Drew, Lupino presented a contrast between the dark interiors associated with Steve and the daylight-filled scenes in which Sally and Drew interact. This reminds us that we are watching ordinary people through the techniques of documentary filmmaking. These elements are incorporated throughout *Not Wanted*. Footage shot by the second unit infuses the film with docudrama, grounding it in everyday life. For example, Lupino shot the scenes at Drew's "gaseteria," an actual gas station and eatery. The footage captures the ambient noise and the sights of a busy enterprise: a Coke machine, trash cans, cars filling up with ethyl.

Sally becomes aware that she is pregnant with Steve's child during a scene with Drew at a carousel. Her realization is embedded in an agonizing sequence that begins after Sally and Drew ride together on the carousel. Drew proposes, and Sally experiences complete happiness for the first time. As they talk, however, she becomes disoriented. Her confusion and fear are portrayed through a series of cuts that alternate expressionistic shots of a wildly spinning carousel and Sally's face. The sequence culminates as Sally's vision blurs, she passes out, and Drew takes her into his arms. The film then cuts to Sally's rooming house, where a doctor explains her sudden fainting spell: she is pregnant. Sally has not consummated her relationship with Drew, so the audience understands that it is Steve's baby that she is carrying. Unable to tell Drew that she is pregnant, Sally once again boards a bus, seeking escape in a new city. Increasingly unwell, she eventually collapses outside a neighborhood church and soon finds herself in a boarding hospital for unwed mothers.

The sequences depicting the hospital have an air of reality because Lupino shot them in the hospital corridors of St. Anne's, a maternity hospital in Los Angeles, with ambient light and little or no music.[27] Sally and a friend stop to peer through the windows of the hospital's nursery, and here Lupino inserted a shot of a room full of newborn babies, crying and sleeping. This material seems to have been taken in a hospital ward or inserted from documentary or archival footage. Scenes set in hospital offices and dormitories were shot at the studio, and their realism apparently satisfied the PCA. The continuity between the studio scenes and those shot at St. Anne's is excellent, a tribute to Lupino's editor, William Ziegler. Zeigler, one of Alfred Hitchcock's favorite editors, worked with Lupino on her next feature, *Never Fear*, and following that, *Hard, Fast and Beautiful*.[28] Indeed, Lupino credits Ziegler with her initial understanding of film editing.

The PCA would not allow Lupino to shoot a reenactment or acted version of actual labor and delivery, so she negotiated a compromise to shoot the birth completely from Sally's point of view in a kind of hallucinatory, expressionistic dream sequence. The doctor and nurses in white are seen in and out of focus, and the eerie soundtrack by Stevens, which may have been manipulated in postproduction to distort the sound of the piano, heightens our sense of disorientation.[29]

Lupino's artistic use of her subjective camera is exemplary, combining neorealistic and noir effects to produce a scene that captures Sally's semidrugged state and suggests her underlying anxiety. The audience understands that escape can be as much a trap as the darkness and drudgery of home. For another neorealistic touch, Lupino had wanted to show the diversity of teen pregnancy, but this was disallowed by the PCA. Nevertheless, Lupino slipped one Asian American woman into a hospital scene, placing her among the six other "unwed" mothers, who are white.[30] Lupino was forced to make this and other changes to her script to ensure that the film would be produced, "sacrificing some of the acute articulations of gender and class," as Waldman points out. As cowriter and director, however, Lupino was able to move the film in a direction that was "female centered."[31]

Sally's shame early in the film is supplanted by guilt after she chooses to give up her baby. Lupino wrote a monologue that Sally delivers to her newborn as she holds the baby in her arms. It would be a difficult scene for any actress, but with Lupino's precise direction, Sally's performance is exquisitely moving. If the PCA wanted this movie to be a warning to young girls, to their parents, and to society in general, Lupino did a frighteningly credible job. The intensity of the psychological shame and guilt around pregnancy without marriage is portrayed with absolute validity. This kind of stark honesty may have been one reason *Not Wanted* made almost ten times its cost. By most accounts, the budget was $154,000 and the film made a quick million, which led to Howard Hughes's interest in the Filmakers.[32]

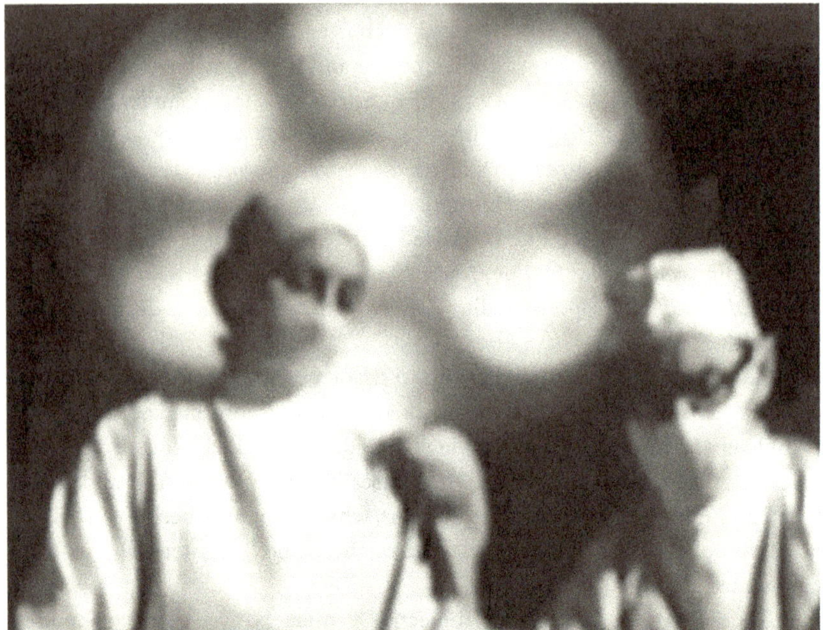

Part of an expressionistic sequence from Sally's point of view, purposely blurred by Lupino, as Sally is anesthetized at this point while being prepped to give birth.

The final scene of *Not Wanted* presents the essence of the film, which Parker describes as "the poverty of a woman's fantasy life." As Parker notes:

> The silent long last scene of the film is one of the most moving, beautifully shot scenes of any film: a chase by a crippled young man to save the woman he loves from suicide. No word is spoken, the last eight pages of dialogue having been thrown away on the day of shooting.[33]

The final image is intense: once Drew falls, Sally stops running; once Drew is vulnerable, Sally opens up; and once Drew forgives Sally, they can both be free. Lupino understood that audiences did not necessarily need happy endings; what they needed was truth.

Lupino's films acknowledge and lament the false promise of the postwar American dream. She was a master at capturing the sheer disappointment that corrupted the lives of adults and, in turn, their children. *Not Wanted* reflects the failure of the American promise for women who had to return to domestic labor and confront the physical and psychological damage that fathers and husbands brought back from a devastating war. Through her engagement with noir, Lupino evoked a "powerful sense of belatedness and the inability to escape the past" that resonated with women whose hopes for "more flexible gender roles, including expanded fields for female work and agency," turned out to be empty. This was especially true for those women who "bore the heavier burden of these failures," as Grisham and Grossman observe.[34]

Some feminist reviewers have criticized Lupino's films for endings that are too optimistic. In addition to the final reconciliation in *Not Wanted,* the marriage that finishes *Hard, Fast and Beautiful* is often cited to show that Lupino's films end unrealistically. A careful consideration of that narrative, however, reveals the opposite. The pushy mother, Millie Farley (played by Claire Trevor), winds up alone in an empty tennis stadium following her daughter's Wimbledon victory. The daughter, Florence Farley (Sally Forrest), walks away, leaving her mother holding the trophy, which is now reduced to a mere memento. The antihero is not the daughter, but the mother, who dominates, sacrifices for her daughter, and undergoes the most significant and dramatic change in the narrative.

To conclude that *Not Wanted* has a happy ending is to misunderstand the structure of Lupino's characters. Also ambiguous is the subtext of the film, which asks who it is that is not wanted: the child, the mother, or both. It could even have been Lupino herself, struggling to work within a studio system dominated by men. Some analyses of *The Bigamist* have described its conclusion as a representation of women's acquiescence to a male-dominated, and also passive, post–World War II ethos.[35] Here again, however, Lupino crafts an ending that is ambiguous. Neither Phyllis Martin (played by Lupino) nor Eve Graham (Joan Fontaine) stays with the bigamist, Harry Graham (Edmond O'Brien), whom Lupino shows as passive, weak, and psychically flawed. *New York Times* critic Howard Thompson identified the "real text" of *The Bigamist* as "an insidious point of no return for the lonely."[36]

Lupino's ambiguous endings are often bittersweet, but they are always fraught with uncertainty, indecision, and doubt. As her final scenes come to a close, Lupino's women, like *Not Wanted*'s Sally, are trapped in a delusion, and we realize that their exploitation is bound to be repeated. The men, like *The Bigamist*'s Harry Graham, are emasculated, unable to find resolution in their existential search to redeem their maleness. Of the early feminist critics, Claire Johnston was the only one who understood the significance of Lupinian ambiguity, stating that *Not Wanted* reveals "reverberations within the narrative" that have a relationship to the "sexist ideology" that existed in Hollywood.[37] By disrupting the usual cinematic representations of women and women's point of view, Lupino was quietly challenging Hollywood's long-standing attitude toward women. Annette Kuhn points out that in the field of early feminist film criticism, Johnston stood alone in her appreciation of Lupino's

The poster for Not Wanted, *warning, "The drama that is being lived each year by 100,000 American girls!"*

accomplishments.[38] Lupino's written and filmed narratives were not commentaries on her beliefs; rather, she used them to reveal the undercurrent of women's experiences and feelings in the 1950s.

Lupino chose provocative subjects—the trauma of rape, pregnancy out of wedlock, bigamy, the polio scare, corruption in female professional sports—that were considered daring at the time. Essentially, she extended the social problem film to a larger forum, building her narratives as national issues. This national framework, which was empowering as well as subversive, is reflected in one of the promotional posters for *Not Wanted*: "Unwed mother . . . her story—the nation's problem!"

A production photo of Sally Forrest's character fills in the ellipsis. In it, the character seems desperate, completely alone, and her pregnancy is just apparent.[39] *Not Wanted* is a social problem film, but it is wrapped inside an exploitation film. To produce *Not Wanted*, Lupino skirted the censors in various ways, resisting an ending in which a chastened heroine finds "Mr. Right." The film contains no discussion of Sally's immorality or repentance for her sexual activity. Lupino questioned the old moral code yet refused to define herself as a feminist as she offered this noir docudrama with an ambiguous conclusion. Wheeler Winston Dixon notes that *Not Wanted* was "enormously influential among those viewers who went out of their way to see it," and "it remains a remarkable directorial debut."[40] *Not Wanted*'s astonishing profit likely came from a large and captivated female audience that understood and resonated with Lupino's compassionate message.

Chapter 5

NEVER FEAR

If Hollywood is to remain on top of the film world, I know one thing for sure—there must be more experimentation with out-of-the-way film subjects.

Ida Lupino in Louise Heck-Rabi, *Women Filmmakers*

Never Fear (1949) is about a promising modern dancer, Carol Williams (played by Sally Forrest), who suddenly contracts polio myelitis and is told she will never dance again. Carol's fiancé is Guy Richards (Keefe Brasselle). He is pushed away by a depressed Carol, who wants no reminders of her past life. Carol is full of guilt for delaying Guy's career, a plot point that recalls Sally's guilt in *Not Wanted*. Carol is a victim, but only until she regains her courage and confidence at the end of the film.

Never Fear is Lupino's most overtly autobiographical film. In the late 1940s, before vaccines were available, polio disabled more than 35,000 people each year.[1] In 1952, when the outbreak reached its height, 57,879 cases were reported, 3,145 people died, and 21,269 people, mostly young, were left with mild to disabling paralysis.[2] Lupino had contracted polio in 1934, when she was a young adult, and it left her right hand slightly impaired.[3]

Ronnie Scheib credits Lupino with an "almost 'documentary' sense of locale" that created "a very special tension," and this is especially evident in *Never Fear*.[4] The film opens with a warning to the audience that the story is from real life, that it will have a bearing on their lives, and that it was filmed on location.[5] As she did for *Not Wanted*, Lupino widened her marketing campaign, creating concern for a larger, national problem. Much of the movie was filmed at the Kabat-Kaiser Institute, a rehabilitation facility for people who had contracted polio and other neurological disorders.[6] Lupino employed the setting to create a deftly directed docudrama that depicts the realities that were then experienced by polio patients and rehabilitating U.S. servicemen.[7] When Lupino shot *Never Fear*, it was at the institute's Santa Monica location on Ocean Avenue. One news account from 1952 described it as akin to a "luxurious beach resort," noting, "Every person in sight is either in a wheel chair, walking with crutches or body braces, or being pushed along on a gurney. Everyone appears happy and busy, going to or from a water therapy room, a physiotherapy section or exercise room."[8] Lupino incorporated all these activities into the film, shooting scenes in the pool and therapy rooms, as well as in the halls. Lupino also filmed one of the institute's popular recreational events, a wheelchair square dance, in which her characters participate alongside Kabat-Kaiser residents. In fact, throughout the movie, many of the people in the background are patients at the institute. The traumatized victims of war are represented by patient Len Randall, played by Hugh O'Brian (another of Lupino's discoveries) in his first major role. Len is permanently disabled and, like many of the actual patients, dependent on his wheelchair for mobility. *Never Fear* addresses the cruelty of polio, the debilitating fear that accompanied its spread, and the hope offered by therapies that helped victims who were diagnosed with polio. This message was an important one, as noted in an online history of the Kabat-Kaiser Institute:

> Given the center's proximity to Hollywood, it was often the site of cameo appearances by movie stars. But that relationship took a deeper step when the actress Ida Lupino directed (and co-wrote, and co-produced) a film there. Never Fear . . . , a story about a beautiful young dancer with a promising career who contracted polio and struggled to recover, had personal meaning for Lupino, who had contracted polio herself in 1934. Lupino made the film to combat the public fear of polio during the 1948–49 epidemic, and captured the power of the center's program using actual patients and, yes, a wheelchair dance.[9]

The authenticity of the setting helped Lupino work around the censors at the PCA. On August 10, coproducer Collier Young had sent a letter and two copies of the script for *Never Fear* to Geoffrey Shurlock, a PCA administrator. Young wrote that he and Lupino were contemplating starting production no later than September 15, 1949.[10] PCA director Joseph Breen replied eight days later, asking decorously for five routine items, including a brief synopsis. He signed the letter, "Cordially yours, Joseph I. Breen."[11] Just as she had learned the basic techniques of film directing by watching others behind the camera, Lupino had also learned how to check the right boxes on the forms required by Breen's office before a picture could be green-lighted. On the form titled "Analysis of Film Content," Lupino listed *Never Fear*'s settings as "*Balboa streets*—theater night club, dressing room, beach, doctor's office" and "*Los Angeles*: hospital room, highway; Kabat-Kaiser Institute (for polio) including elevator, corridors, rooms, gym, pool, auditorium, office, garden, therapy rooms, real estate offices, park, car, countryside, apartment," emphasizing the realistic tone of the film.[12] On another titled "Cast of Characters and Synopsis Form," Lupino summarized the plot in simple language: "This is a story of how a young dancer gets polio; of how her resulting feelings of self-pity lead to a break-up with her fiancé; and of her partial physical recovery and reconciliation with the fiancé."[13] For type of ending, Lupino had four choices: "Unhappy," "Moral," "Other," and the one she checked, "Happy."[14]

Because of her adroit management, Lupino was able to begin production of *Never Fear* on September 21, 1949, close to Young's targeted date. Lupino and Young sent a handwritten note to Sally Forrest to wish her luck, writing, "Here we go again" at the top. With a clever reference to the film, the note closes with "Never Fear!" The note is written on stationery from the Club Del Mar, which was adjacent to the clinic, suggesting that Lupino and Young were staying at the hotel on or just before the first day of shooting.[15] *Never Fear* was released on December 29, 1949, which meant the cast and crew worked through the winter holidays.

The University of California, Los Angeles, holds a script for *Never Fear* in its special collections that was autographed and donated by Hugh O'Brian.[16] Although this may be the final version, scripts rarely reflect what appears onscreen. Changes are often made during shooting, and this was particularly true for Lupino and others working with microbudgets in the independent film world. One difference between the script and the film occurs at the film's beginning. At some point during production, the card that introduces *Never Fear* was rewritten. The script reads:

> ON SILENT SCREEN BEFORE TITLES
>
> This is a true story. Like so many stories drawn from life, it happens every day—everywhere. That is why you may have known a girl like Carol.[17]

The card that appears on film is quite different:

> This is a true story. It was photographed where it happened. Our grateful thanks to the many who made this motion picture possible.

The final opening lines emphasize Lupino's on-location shooting, creating more realism and even some suspense. Then Lupino thanks those who were involved in the making of the movie, another nod to maintaining realism,

CLUB DEL MAR

1910 OCEAN FRONT · SANTA MONICA · CALIFORNIA

Sept. 20

Dearest Sally—

Here we go again! We know you're going to do a great job because we know *you* so well. Thanks for your hard work and your loyalty.

Never Fear!

Affectionately,
Ida and Collie

Note written on Club Del Mar stationery from Lupino and Collier Young to Sally Forrest, September 20, 1949, the day before shooting began.

keeping it current in the viewer's minds. The most surprising difference, though, concerns the title. O'Brian's script is titled *Never Fear*, but onscreen we see "The Filmakers present an Ida Lupino Production, The Young Lovers." Judging from Lupino and Young's note to Sally Forrest, the film was being called *Never Fear* immediately before shooting began, and posters produced subsequently by the studio promoted the release of *Never Fear*.[18]

Also notable is the somewhat unusual order of the credits. Sally Forrest, Keefe Brasselle, and Hugh O'Brian are at the top of the sequence, followed by the costars. Next come the screenwriters, Ida Lupino and Collier Young.

Following, however, are the music director, Leith Stevens; the director of photography, Archie Stout; and the head of production design, Van Nest Polglase. The credits then end, as usual, with frames for the producer and the director. It's possible the prominent positions of the music director and the production designer were Lupino's way of acknowledging Stevens for the tension and suspense he brought with his musical arrangement, and Polglase for sets that looked authentic but were affordable.

A number of scenes in Lupino's script did not make the final cut to screen. They may have been dropped for a variety of reasons, including budget concerns and scheduling difficulties. Shots that were deemed repetitive or unnecessary once on set were not filmed. Indeed, Lupino was always on a tight budget, and notes made to the script before shooting may have been consolidated or deleted once filming began.

Never Fear opens with a single shot that is decidedly modernist. Economical, minimalist, and active, Lupino's camera was always on the move.[19]

MUSIC up and WE DISSOLVE to:

EXT. BALBOA STREET—INSERT

We SEE a small bouquet of flowers through a glass window, and the CAMERA PANS UP to meet our POV

EXT. GUY RICHARDS—SAME

CAMERA continues, moving to pick up Guy in a SINGLE who looks longingly at the flowers, checks his trouser pockets for money, doesn't have any, begins to take off when

A DELIVERY BOY

With a gigantic flower delivery catches Guy's attention, as he moves fast out of the flower shop, momentarily cutting Guy from our view, flowers now filling the screen. Once the flower arrangement has passed, we SEE that Guy has cleverly plucked a small Gardenia arrangement from the bouquet making his own tiny spray, and pleased with his stolen gift, spins a U-turn around a lamppost, and the MUSIC reflects Guy's carefree life.

ON GUY—MOVING

He continues down the street with a Chaplinesque walk away from the momentarily still camera, strolling to the beat of the music.

Lupino gives us a lot of information in this single shot: Guy is a main character; he probably has a girlfriend; he has no money and is content to take a few gardenias (a recurring motif that represents his love for Carol) from an over-the-top floral arrangement; and he is optimistic and happy-go-lucky—the character's most positive aspect.

Lupino then makes her first cut.

EXT. ANOTHER STREET—BIT LATER

Guy walks past the entrance to Club 18, where his picture is posted prominently. He takes a quick look at himself, gives his picture a quick fingertip kiss, and continues inside.

INT. THEATRE STAGE—MOMENTS LATER

Guy walks into an open space of a large theatre, a full floor above the proscenium, where the CAMERA angles down and we SEE Sally Forrest's character, CAROL WILLIAMS, in a high, wide-angle shot, where she is rehearsing a dance segment. Guy looms large here from the balcony above, as --

BELOW ON STAGE—SAME

Carol is tiny, almost like a dancer in a music box, someone we can barely see from Guy's high vantage point.

A look at the script held at UCLA shows that the planned initial action in the opening shot was deleted.

EXT. BALBOA STREET—DAY—LONG SHOT

A YOUNG MAN carrying a paper bag under his arm, exits from a drug store with great speed zigzagging in and out of the passing pedestrians and briefly clad sunworshippers. He makes a sudden stop and, at the same time, nearly pushes off balance a rather portly gentleman who is in the act of bending down to purchase a paper from a news rack. The young man, Guy Richards, gives a vague smile of apology, spins around and makes for a small florist shop one door down. He peers in the window for a moment, then digs in his pocket, brings out a few coins, gives a little shrug of disappointment and is about to leave when one of the florist assistants exits from the shop carrying a huge floral centerpiece about five feet long. As he passes Guy, the flowers held aloft and heads for the florist van, Guy deftly whisks a couple of gardenias from the rear end of the bouquet and starts gaily down the street again. He comes abreast of the portly gent once more, who has been eyeing all this. Guy gives him the hush sign, and, before the man can open his mouth, beats it around the corner.

Lupino may have thought that this opening added nothing to the narrative or that it would take too long to shoot.

Lupino's preference for focusing on imagery is immediately evident. The first line of dialogue comes nearly two and a half minutes into the film, when Guy yells out to Carol, telling her to take a break. We then see the lovers together, happily musing about their future. They seem to be on the cusp of breakthrough fame. Despite the upbeat mood, Carol is unusually nervous about the upcoming performance, giving the scene an undercurrent of tension. Her uneasiness sets up the viewer to expect something more serious. This—imparting a sense of impending doom—is a Lupinian pattern, also used famously by Hitchcock.

Carol is Lupino's wandering girl-woman from *Not Wanted*, but here she is burdened with what Scheib calls "half-formed expectations" that increase the emotional stakes when her life is suddenly changed by a traumatic event.[20] Lupino came from a family of dancers, including her mother, Connie Emerald, and her sister, Rita Lupino, so she had a keen knowledge of the dance world and how vital the body is to a dancer's identity. Trauma is the essential component of another Lupinian pattern, which Scheib describes as "a brief opening positing a continuing 'normal' life, a sudden traumatic interruption of that flow, an overwhelming sense of alienation and disorientation, a brief respite at some sheltered communal refuge, a reversal of trauma by the active assumption of what was initially passively experienced, and a tentative start of a new life." She suggests that Carol's fear—that polio will keep her from fulfilling her dance ambitions and, ultimately, becoming a choreographer—reflects Lupino's feelings about her transition from actress to director.[21] Both of these professions, choreographer and director, were dominated by men in the late 1940s.

Lupino used Forrest's capabilities as a trained dancer and an athlete in all three of their collaborations: *Not Wanted*, *Never Fear*, and *Hard, Fast and Beautiful*, in which Forrest's character is a tennis player. Critics and writers have commented on the close physical resemblance between Lupino and Forrest. They were often mistaken for each other, and there has been some speculation, as well as innuendos, that by casting Forrest, Lupino was casting herself as the protagonist of these three films.[22] Forrest's agent and future husband, Milo Frank, who sent her to audition for *Not Wanted*, thought that her strong physical resemblance to Lupino may have gotten her the role: "I think she reminded

Ida of Ida."[23] It is more likely that Forrest met several criteria for Lupino: She was a young unknown whom Lupino could afford. She was athletic, necessary because each of the three narratives demanded that the protagonist foreground her athleticism, which Lupino equated with femininity and power. And equally important, the two worked well together. There was an ease on set that Lupino wanted to maintain, since tension could threaten her small budgets and tight schedules. An undated interview in which Forrest spoke with someone identified only as "D" offers a glance into the productive relationship between the two women:

> D: [How] did you find Ida Lupino[?] . . . [*Not Wanted]* must have been the very first thing she directed, one of the first things?
>
> Forrest: Yes, I think it was.
>
> D: Did you find her an effective director?
>
> Forrest: Marvelous! Because I had never even taken acting lessons, I had never tried to be an actress, and there I was, a star in, true, a small show, but I was the star of the show. I don't know how, but she just guided me. She was, if not the best, one of the best directors I've had. And wonderful for women, just fabulous. When I had the chance of working with her as an "actress" in another picture, it always astounded me; she was one of these people who knew where the lights were, if the light wasn't right, she knew it. There was nothing she didn't know.
>
> D: In her directing, how did she work with actors?
>
> Forrest: Very intimately. We became very close on the set. Never other than that, but she knew me. And I was really a child, you know.[24]

For Forrest, the most challenging and satisfying of the three films may have been *Never Fear*, where her role as Carol demanded a complete character transformation, from an ambitious gifted dancer to a struggling polio survivor. In fact, Sally Forrest had wanted to be a dancer since childhood, having drawn pictures of costumed dancers and prima ballerinas from an early age.[25]

Carol is an active, vital, creative woman. She is a trained dancer, much like Lupino's sister, Rita, and even Lupino herself, whose once-athletic body had been compromised by polio. When Carol contracts polio, she and Guy have just premiered their new nightclub act, an intricately choreographed fencing match with an overt sexuality. Lupino used a moving camera to photograph the dance, which was created by the expressive Billy Daniel. Close-ups and medium shots capture the dancers' work without intruding on the audience's point of view as the two main characters do mock battle under key lighting, with the audience in shadow. The new act is a triumph, but suspense builds as the audience begins to understand that the celebratory feeling can't last.

As the next scene starts, Lupino's "camera dollies in, and holds on Guy, working on a new routine at the piano, offhandedly throwing enthusiastic remarks over his shoulder." We can barely see Carol, who is huddled behind him, in front of the stage. As Guy breaks into an exuberant waltz, the film "cuts unexpectedly to Carol," who is struggling to stand. The camera focuses on the "dawning awareness of her illness, exploring the silent disaster, the invisible process of change within her."[26] The waltz ends abruptly when Guy notices Carol's collapse. Just as she did in *Not Wanted*, Lupino helped define the lead male character as a starving artist by giving him piano expertise. In *Never Fear*, Guy has choreography as well as piano skills. These artistic talents were unusual attributes for a male character in the postwar 1950s, and in *Never Fear*, they indicate Guy's inability to succeed financially in the new, male-dominated American society.

Guy takes Carol to a doctor, who makes an urgent telephone call to General Hospital in Los Angeles. The doctor gravely makes arrangements for Carol to be admitted, then pauses before he gives his diagnosis: "Suspected polio." Another person stricken by poliomyelitis! The camera follows as an ambulance delivers Carol to the front entrance of the Kabat-Kaiser Institute. The film quickly establishes the physical devastation of polio with a sequence that introduces O'Brian's character, Len, as he is cheering up a young boy who is, like Len, in a wheelchair.[27] Lupino's frames are often full of activity, allowing multiple ideas and images to be accessed by the audience at once. As Len wheels around to the elevator, images, camera angles, and bits of dialogue immediately signal that he is a positive force at the institute. Later in the film, Dr. Middleton (played by Lawrence Dobkin), the retired surgeon who heads the institute, tells Carol his own story of polio, which ended his surgical career. The disease left him without the full use of his right hand, which was Lupino's own physical remnant from her bout with polio. Here Lupino is represented by both the male surgeon and the female dancer.

A docudramatic montage of Carol's rehab in six shots elegantly conveys the challenge she faces as she begins to reeducate her muscles and the difficulty of persevering. Although Carol's body is on display throughout this sequence, it is "active in its struggle against inactivity of accepting a mutilated, dependent, intersubjective version of womanhood," as Scheib notes.[28] Lupino's camera then deftly cuts away to Guy, who is beginning a new life. He applies for a job in real estate and is hired by an obnoxious boss, who recalls cinematic representations of studio moguls like Jack Warner and Louis B. Mayer. Lupino always looked for space where she could inject a satirical comment about the business. This character, Mr. Brownlee, was played by Jerry Hausner, who was also known for playing Ricky Ricardo's agent in the iconic *I Love Lucy* series.[29] The camera then cuts back to Carol and Len, allowing us to get to know O'Brian's sagelike, Sirkian character—a selfless, asexual being. Godlike in his empathy, he has a complete understanding of others. O'Brian's wisdom is expressed by his positive nature and his connection to the children at the institute. Nonetheless, accompanying his buoyant demeanor is an undercurrent of tragedy. We suspect that, unlike Carol, Len will never leave his chair. He is a hopeless case who remains hopeful.

The documentary aspects of *Never Fear* are enriched by the attentiveness that Lupino gave to the background characters, including the actual Kabat-Kaiser patients who were there at the time. The patients constitute a community: they socialize together, and they take care of one another. We see Carol and Guy enjoying the institute picnic with the other patients, listening to an uplifting song about Guaymas, Mexico (a location that figures in the plot of *The Hitch-Hiker*), and we watch Carol and Len participate in the wheelchair square dance. Lupino foregrounded the real-life patients as much as possible in the docudrama scenes, showing polio's unjust attack on the innocent, which included many children, from infants to teenagers.

As in *Not Wanted*, when Sally discusses her fears with her roommate, there is a noteworthy camaraderie between the two women. Lupino subtly demonstrated how women help women as they explore their deep, specific fears of childbirth, motherhood, and entrapment. In a scene at the institute, Carol, who is worried about the destructive impact that polio has had on her relationship with Guy, asks her friend Josie (played by Lupino's sister, Rita Lupino) for advice. Josie, whose husband has been with her throughout her illness, says, "Nothing can come between us now that we're going through this together." The emotion of this exchange is heightened by director Lupino's intimate blocking. Carol stands above Josie. As she brushes Josie's hair, she holds her close and, like a wise and trusted sister, listens to her speak. Lupino shot the scene economically, with no cuts and with both actresses in a two-shot. Stevens's music is quietly soaring, supporting the shift in mood as Carol resolves to work harder to overcome her paralysis.[30] The next scene is a close-up of Carol's feet as she takes slow steps with the help of steel crutches. A voice-over repeats Josie's words: "Nothing can come between us now that we're going through this together." This signals the turning point in Lupino's script.

Lupino used exchanges between Carol and Guy to show Carol's fragility and to expose the mixed emotions that ongoing trauma can produce. Lupino and Young wrote a quiet scene in which Carol, frustrated and unhappy with her slow progress, refuses the engagement ring that Guy offers. The scene suggests the many relationships that were affected by veterans' post-traumatic stress disorder, and for Lupino, it may have had an autobiographical undercurrent that was related not only to the trauma her first husband had experienced after the war but also to her own bout with polio. Carol's moments with Len suggest a potential romantic connection, similar to the relationship that develops between the main character in *Outrage*, Ann Walton (played by Mala Powers), and the California preacher-redeemer, Bruce Ferguson (Tod Andrews).

When Carol is finally ready to leave the hospital, she has a last meeting with Dr. Middleton. In a telling piece of subtextual writing, he says, "Keep your hands off the rails, Carol," suggesting that she must stand on her own two feet, leave victimhood behind, and move forward by herself without rancor. As Carol walks out of the building with just a cane for support, she has a brief moment of independence. Then, in a reversal, Guy, unable to live without her, appears on the street, and the two lovers desperately embrace. This moment, in its Lupinian ambiguity, is similar to the ending of *Not Wanted*. Although it is the last scene, it does not feel final. Carol and Guy are secure in their love for each other, but their path forward is not clear.

The press for *Never Fear* was initially complicated by the title changes between *The Young Lovers* and *Never Fear*. A rare poster used for European distribution seems to title the film "I Want to Live," with these words in both French and Dutch. "Never Fear" appears, too, but in smaller type.

There was a concerted effort to take advantage of *Not Wanted*'s critical and financial success, and some posters tout the film as "The Dramatic Successor to *Not Wanted*." Others proclaim, "Another Box-Office SMASH" or "The Filmakers present an IDA LUPINO Production, *NEVER FEAR*."

The title change reveals what was important to Lupino, and perhaps to Young as well. Instead of a bland story about young lovers—which had been a slight criticism of *Not Wanted*—Lupino insisted on a more complex narrative that hinged on a character's battle with a virulent contemporary disease that everyone feared. The narrative promoted the point of view that was at the heart of the therapies offered at the Kabat-Kaiser Institute: beating the disease had more to do with a patient's willingness and determination than with the medical interventions themselves, early mind-body focus. This idea of psychological health emanating from faith and courage had its roots in a late-1950s notion of the redemptive benefits offered by a community of like-minded people. In *Not Wanted*, Sally finds friendship and acceptance within the group of unmarried pregnant women at the home for unwed mothers. In Lupino's *Outrage*, the main character, who has been raped, finds solace in a pastoral setting.[31]

Rare promotional poster for Never Fear *in French and Dutch.*

Like *Not Wanted*, whose message focused on the terror of teen pregnancy, *Never Fear*, which highlighted the consequences of polio, was an exploitation film. These films illuminated real social problems, which justified the exploitative aspects of the narrative. Exploitation films were historically sold using a variety of manipulative promotional materials designed for specific demographic profiles. The producers knew whom they needed to target in order to sell tickets. Even with their variations and differing implications, the posters for *Never Fear* were all titled and produced to sell, in true Poverty Row fashion. The studio's pressbook, issued for local theaters and media, exploited the team of Sally Forrest and Keefe Brasselle by suggesting that they were a couple in real life: "The sensational new stars from the team of 'Not Wanted'—together again—in a taut, tense, turbulent romance, 'NEVER FEAR.'"

The *Hollywood Reporter* noted their acting skills: "Sally Forrest and Keefe Brasselle are young actors with splendid dramatic resources."[32] Eagle-Lion Films promoted the movie's director—"Ida Lupino makes it two hits in a row . . . 'Not Wanted,' 'Never Fear'"—and offered radio spots that featured her: 'Get your FREE radio spot announcements! The disc allows for live playdate announcements after each spot. Several of these spots are narrated by Ida Lupino who directed 'Never Fear.' The platter contains one-minute, 30-second and 15-second spots. Send your request to Exploitation Manager, Eagle Lion Films."[33]

The marketing also talked up the film's tie-up stills—"Several 'Never Fear' stills are exceptionally well-suited for tie-up purposes: window displays, counter cards, and co-operative ads"—and listed the products and businesses that could benefit from being associated with the film: "soda fountains and drinking cups, dressing gowns, sportswear, bakeries, beachwear, jewelers, art supplies, drawing schools, bathing suits, beauty shops, pearls, children's clothing, photographers, women's fashions and cosmetics." But the studio was careful to limit its liability: "Use of these stills is authorized providing that no endorsement of any product read or implied, appears in accompanying copy." Other types of promotion depended on a human touch: "On the street! Street bally on 'Never Fear' can utilize several young couples who stroll along the main streets of town arm in arm and wearing placards reading: All the world loves a lover . . . that's why all *Blanktown* will love 'Never Fear' Thursday at the Rialto."[34] Promoters played up the love story, probably to mute the subject of the film.

Lupino knew the branding potency of a world-famous actress turned director, and promotion for *Never Fear* capitalized on her star power in various ways. One documentarylike promotional release featured an unglamorous, serious photo of Lupino that stressed her career as a director rather than an actress. The copy is titled "Why I Made 'Never Fear' by Ida Lupino."

> Where there is human courage, there is drama. When everyday people fight for life and love, you have the very essence of heroism. These are the real-life ingredients of "NEVER FEAR."
>
> Because I saw this story happen . . . because it thrilled me with its truth and hope . . . that's why I wanted to bring "NEVER FEAR" to the screen, photographed where it happened.

A candid, off-the-set publicity shot of Sally Forrest and Keefe Brasselle together.

Naturally, I was also encouraged by the enthusiastic support the American public gave to "NOT WANTED." It proved to me that most people do want something different out of Hollywood.

These are the reasons why I am proud of "NEVER FEAR." I sincerely hope this intimate story of the heart will have a lasting meaning for you.[35]

The addition of Lupino's signature, reproduced below the copy, suggested to readers that Lupino knew from personal experience the fear that polio induced and the courage needed to fight the disease.

Never Fear was not a financial success for the Filmakers. The title change from *The Young Lovers* was confusing, and the few reviews were lukewarm.[36] The *Christian Century* magazine gave *Never Fear* only a small mention: "Unpretentious, making documentary use of current rehabilitation progress. Commendable in its picture of triumph over despair."[37] The *Rotarian* magazine was slightly more enthusiastic: "Produced and directed by Ida Lupino. Drama. Disheartened and embittered when struck down by polio, girl dancer eventually learns that her usefulness is not necessarily at an end, triumphs over her misfortune. A simple, unassuming story that makes use of considerable documentary footage, is inspiring in its demonstration of what determination and subjection of selfish concern can do."[38] Probably more damaging was the theme itself. The December 13, 1950, issue of the *New York Times* called it polio's "second worst year ever, with [a] record 598 cases for the 48th consecutive week bringing the total to 31,989."[39] Audiences just did not want to be reminded they could wake up in the morning with polio.

Scheib sums up *Never Fear* as a film about "'being a woman'—or, more precisely, about the difficulty of accepting a dependent, truncated version of womanhood disturbingly close to its most traditional limited social definition," a statement that might also be applied to *Not Wanted*.[40] Yet even though the female protagonists in *Never Fear* and *Not Wanted* were portrayed by the same actress, and both films present the female protagonist's traumatic journey, Carol Williams is a vastly different woman from Sally Kelton. At the end of *Never Fear*, Carol is able to stand on her own, leaving the institute without the help of a protective man or a new lover. In *Never Fear*, Lupino explored not only the dangers of passivity but also the strength needed to overcome it. Similarly, the father of the main character in *Hard, Fast and Beautiful* enacts the harmful passive psychology that was prevalent in approaches to parenting during the repressive 1950s.

Nicholas Ray's characters—including, notably, the father (played by Jim Backus) in *Rebel without a Cause*—also battle passivity. Scheib draws a parallel between Lupino and Ray, arguing that their work challenged "the subjective heroic consciousness structures of traditional Hollywood film."[41] She points out that their films, as well as those of Samuel Fuller and Robert Aldrich, are products of a "postwar consciousness" that reflected the "disjunctive transition between trauma and a possibly even more traumatic return to normality."[42] Lupino had experienced her own return to normality after battling polio. And just before production began on *Never Fear*, she suffered an injury that immobilized her, requiring her to direct from a chair. This put her at the physical level of the wheelchair-bound Carol and most of the extras. Charles Silver considers these circumstances in a discussion of what sets *Never Fear* apart from Lupino's other films:

> *Never Fear* definitely brought out a distinctively feminine side to Lupino's direction. It's difficult to define precisely, but there is an unusually physical, tactile quality to the way the film's characters relate to one another. So although it would be hard to argue that the film has a conventionally feminist sensibility, it would also be hard to imagine it having been directed by a man. *Never Fear* must have had a special resonance for Lupino . . . since she had, like her heroine, experienced polio as an adolescent. The fact that she had to direct the film from a wheelchair (due to an injury) must have been a constant reminder of how close she came to a grim early fate.[43]

Lupino recovered and went on to create a body of work that "remains singular, a vital contribution to the evolution of women in cinema and of American independent film production in general."[44]

As Lupino's second film, *Never Fear* had to do solid business to confirm her legitimacy as a director. Although there were some good critical notices, it wasn't a topic that interested the moviegoers, and the film did not do well. Lupino kept directing, however, making the movies she wanted and keeping her budgets low. Her next two films, *Outrage* and *Hard, Fast and Beautiful*, received good reviews, particularly for Lupino's lead actresses, Mala Powers and Claire Trevor, respectively. *Outrage*, about rape, was the more difficult project to get past the PCA restrictions. Lupino liked only the first half of the film because she thought that she had allowed the second half to wander away from a focus on the exploitative nature of the topic. It was her penultimate film, *The Hitch-Hiker*, about a true-life serial killer, that gave her career a significant boost. Its gritty reality and cinematic suspense astounded the public and critics alike.

Chapter 6

THE HITCH-HIKER

[Billy] Cook granted me the release. . . . I found him to be cold, calculating, and I was afraid of him. I could not wait to get the hell out of San Quentin!

Ida Lupino in Ida Lupino and Mary Ann Anderson, *Ida Lupino: Beyond the Camera*

The Hitch-Hiker (1953), which Lupino cowrote and directed, represents a break from her other films in that there are no women in credited roles. This conspicuous absence, together with the minimal cast and pared-down script, signals a refinement in Lupino's approach to filmmaking. The plot is straightforward: a fictionalized, docudramatic version of the real-life story of Billy Cook, who had just gone on a murder spree, killing six people between 1950 and 1951. Two men, Gilbert Bowen (played by Frank Lovejoy) and Roy Collins (Edmond O'Brien), are in their car, headed to a fishing vacation, when they pick up a hitchhiker, Emmett Myers (William Talman, in a stunning film debut). A psychotic killer on the run, Myers forces Gil and Roy to head toward Santa Rosalia, Mexico, where he plans to take a boat across the Gulf of California to freedom. This is a compact narrative of a life-and-death struggle, whose economy not only reflects Lupino's directorial principles but also foreshadows the aesthetic of the live television dramas that were to come.

The opening frame of *The Hitch-Hiker* just skirts docudrama as it directly addresses the viewer, while telegraphing the dread that suffuses the film. Lupino's admonition to the audience—"This could have happened to you"—could not be more threatening. The two opening shots that follow, which provide background for the titles, are as spare and intense as the plot itself.

A promotional poster for The Hitch-Hiker.

#1) EXT. ASPHALT LANDSCAPE – DUSK

We SEE a man's torso, leather jacket, boots. He walks along a highway. Hitchhiking. We don't see his face. A car pulls up to a stop in front of us. Picks up the HITCHHIKER. Car pulls away and we SEE the license plate: "2650 400." MUSIC up.

DISSOLVE to: Darkness.

#2) EXT. OFF ROAD TERRAIN. LATE NIGHT.

Headlights at a distance dart across the dark frame. A CAR rolls to a sudden stop, the door opens, and we SEE the same boots we saw before. Then we HEAR a woman SCREAM. Followed by two GUNSHOTS. Silk evening purse falls open in the dirt at the man's feet. A HAND reaches down to pick up an object that's fallen from the purse. Boots walk away. CAMERA stays focused on the ground. Dissolve to a flashlight moving across the ground from left to right and up to the previously seen license plate, "2650 400." The camera follows the flashlight, panning along the side of the car to the open passenger door. INSIDE THE CAR, legs and then hands of a WOMAN dead in the passenger seat. Cut to law enforcement officer, then back to the flashlight, which moves to the driver's seat. A DEAD MAN is slumped over the wheel. Both victims remain faceless. FADE OUT![1]

Within two and a half minutes, Lupino's camera has jumped time, moving the story far forward and setting up the next sequence—which will show us the next victims—without dialogue. Lupino presented only the essentials, using a compact aesthetic that illustrates the grace and sophistication of her directing. We hear the scream and the gunshot, and "like the sudden illumination of a sulphur match," we glimpse the threat that waits just ahead.[2] Leith Stevens's music swells, and the suspense that pervades the film is established. Nicholas Musuraca's rule-bending lighting and intense black-and-white palette command our attention. Lupino's work is direct, non-judgmental, and ultimately revelatory. The narrative brings a frightening true story to life without melodrama or frills. Lupino knew her audience. These men and women, whose lives might be constrained by misfortune, prejudice, or fear, were fascinated by stories that had been ripped from the headlines. They wanted to know only whether Roy and Gil would survive. True crime stories, like B movies, were cathartic in their thrills.

With *The Hitch-Hiker*, arguably Lupino's best independent film, Lupino broke away from the emphasis on social realism that characterized her earlier films. This is a new noir landscape, but it still employs Lupino's docudramatic blend of styles. It is "Lupino noir," a term coined by Carrie Rickey to express Lupino's iconic cinematic idiom.[3]

Another breakaway is the storyline, which centers on three men. Except for the faceless victim in the opening and a young Mexican girl in a brief scene midway through the film, no women appear in *The Hitch-Hiker*. This is a striking change for Lupino, whose previous films were tightly focused on women and women's issues. (The absence of the feminine in this drama could be a projected mirror of Lupino's absence in film history.) Although Lupino uses this stark absence to darken the movie, women maintain a powerful spectral presence, supplying the subtext that explains the psychological makeup of the three men. We feel their spirit when Roy and Gil discuss their wives as they drive south. However, when Roy mentions hooking up with a prostitute from their past, we see the pain and guilt that would cause Gil through his internal reaction. As Gil begins to miss his wife and daughter and, ironically, the safety of domesticity, the women's importance becomes more tangible. In this film, Lupino touches not only on the postwar trauma of men but also on that of the women who, after experiencing new freedoms outside the home, were sent back into the home as domestic workers. She successfully reframes the wives left behind as a constant and conscious, if ghostly, presence.

Reviewers showered praise on Lupino for this low-budget, eight-reel, 6,369-foot chiller.[4] Reviewer Barry Parker lauded the film in 1981 as "a disturbing piece of film noir," cautioning that "people shouldn't be alone when they see it." He added, "It scares me even today.'"[5] In 1953, RKO deposited a 35 mm print with the Library of Congress for copyright purposes. The print was chosen for the Library of Congress National Film Registry, and it remains in the library's collection, but *The Hitch-Hiker* was not seen again until 2003.[6] Then in 2013, Kino Classics announced the release of Blu-ray and DVD editions of a new high-definition transfer from a 35 mm archival restoration by the Library of Congress. Orson Welles's *The Stranger* was released by Kino at the same time, another circumstance that denotes Welles and Lupino as peers.

Although contemporary reviews for *The Hitch-Hiker* were strong, at times they undercut Lupino's abilities as a director. Some reviewers seemed almost surprised by how gripping and tense the film was. *Boxoffice* noted the film's hard action, which apparently was unexpected from a female director:

> RKO has a genuine sleeper in this hard-hitting, suspenseful program melodrama. The taut screenplay is enacted almost entirely by three actors, [including] William Talman who gives a memorable portrayal of a vicious escaped convict and murderer. Produced by The Filmakers

> and splendidly directed by Ida Lupino, who also wrote the screenplay with Collier Young, the picture is vividly realistic from the tense start to the violent finish. There is never a suggestion of romantic interest—none is needed.[7]

Variety praised the film's direction but made no mention of Lupino—the coproducer, cowriter, and director.

> Grim melodrama on perils of aiding ride-thumbers; excellently done . . . thorough both in acting, writing, and direction conceptions. Talman's roadside murderer is a frightening elemental portrayal. O'Brien's character is expertly drawn to show the gradual breakdown of man under the strain of capture. Lovejoy's is the character with a strength that comes out under the ordeal. Production makes good use of rugged outdoor locations, which Nicholas Musuraca's camera shows to advantage, Leith Stevens' music score is apt to the melodrama.[8]

Reviewers usually focused on the surprising muscularity of the diminutive (that is, female) Lupino. One wrote as recently as 2014:

> *The Hitch-Hiker* is a taut, compelling, and at times brilliantly suggestive film noir thriller. The film showcases Lupino's *idiosyncratic strengths* as a director while offering an unusually direct and cogent critique of American masculinity's investment in and estrangement from a culture of fraternity and brotherhood.[9]

Ronnie Scheib recognized Lupino's undervalued technical brilliance, summing up the lack of understanding shown by masculinist reviewers, some of them women:

> The striking compositions[,] . . . the on-pulse kinetic editing[,] . . . and the full utilisation of contrasts between night and day, inside and outside (the constantly revitalised and restructured tension between the three men in their fixed car positions . . .)—these are elements very hard at work in all of Lupino's films, and very much responsible for the mysterious "feelings" critics are willing to ascribe to her films while denying to her the means of creating [them].[10]

The Hitch-Hiker is now noted by critics and scholars, as well as spectators and fans, as Lupino's best directorial accomplishment and her biggest critical and financial success. It was also her personal favorite—speaking to Francine Parker, Lupino noted that it was "her pride"—of the independent films she directed.[11]

The Hitch-Hiker was shot in the empty, high-desert setting of the Alabama Hills, near Lone Pine in California's Inyo County. The desolate spot often stood in for scripted locations in the deserts of the southwestern United States and northern Mexico, including, in Lupino's film, Baja California.[12] Lupino became a curiosity to the press, and a reporter and photographer from United Press International arrived on the desert set to "photograph Lupino in action."[13]

Lupino avoided suspense-film clichés in *The Hitch-Hiker*, using her camera and the spartan landscapes to produce a charged, and ultimately claustrophobic, atmosphere. The film has been favorably compared to Jacques Tourneur's *Out of the Past* (1947) and Edgar Ulmer's *Detour* (1945).[14] Lupino's understanding of metaphor and her unsettling technical minimalism produced spare images and stylistic components that recall Ulmer's noir B films and Tourneur's A-list canon. John D. Thomas, writing for the *Village Voice*, notes that "Lupino's fantastic use of high-contrast lighting presages Welles's work on *Touch of Evil*, and the way she pulls the bug-eyed killer's face out of the darkness makes him look like a demonic jack-o'-lantern."[15]

The script for *The Hitch-Hiker* was adapted from a story written by Daniel Mainwaring. Lupino, Young, and Robert L. Joseph are credited with the screenplay. Mainwaring also worked on the script, but his contribution was not credited.[16] Joseph wrote the first treatment, titled "They Spoke to God," and he ultimately received story credit. Mainwaring's book was based on a true crime story about William Edward Cook Jr., a twenty-two-year-old Missouri ex-con who killed six people, including three children, during a hitchhiking crime spree in the U.S. Southwest in late 1950. A short time later, in January 1951, Cook hitched a ride with two prospectors, James Burke and Forrest Damron, in California's Imperial Valley. Cook's prisoners for eight days, they were forced to drive him across the border, before being captured in Santa Rosalia by Mexican police.[17] When he was caught, Cook proclaimed, "I hate everybody's guts and everybody hates mine."[18] Cook was ultimately convicted in California for the murder of Robert Dewey, his last victim. The jury deliberated for only fifty minutes before delivering a guilty sentence, and Cook was sent to the gas chamber on December 12, 1952. His warden at San Quentin stated, "He was the most completely alone young man I have ever encountered."[19]

Time and *Newsweek* covered the "Billy Cook Story" in depth. Cook was described as a "desperado," in the mold of John Dillinger, and in some articles he was romanticized, with his looks compared to James Dean's. He was quoted as saying, "I'm gonna live by the gun and roam," the gun a .32 caliber snub-nosed pistol.[20] Psychologists weighed whether Cook's troubled childhood was

Cinematographer Nick Musuraca's use of uplighting to pull the villain, Emmett Myers (William Talman), out of the shadows.

a cause of his deviant behavior, a theory that Lupino and Young incorporated into their screenplay.[21] Cook's mother died young, and Cook and his seven siblings were abandoned soon after by their father, who left them in a deserted mine shaft. Cook had a deformed right eye, sometimes described as a lazy eye, which may have been why he was not adopted after the children were rescued. Unlike his six siblings, who were all adopted, Cook was shuttled in and out of government institutions and spent his adolescence in reform schools. He wound up in the Missouri State Penitentiary. At some point along this familiar route, Cook had "Hard Luck" tattooed onto his fingers.[22] This triggered Lupino's empathy, and those words were incorporated into several titles as Lupino and Young worked on a screenplay that would do justice to Cook's tragic story.

Payroll cards in the RKO Collection at UCLA list several preliminary titles for *The Hitch-Hiker*: "They Spoke to God," "The Persuasion," "The Difference," "The William Cook Story," and "The Cook Story." Joseph, who was given a "story by" credit, authored what appears to have been the first treatment in the story file and an early 98-page screenplay titled "They Spoke to God: The Cook Story," dated April 10, 1951; it was synopsized by Richard Bluel. Lupino and Young wrote a 104-page screenplay titled "The Difference," dated October 1, 1952, and synopsized by Lewis Clay. Another document in the collection, headed "Dialogue Comparison," was likely prepared to indicate who should receive credit for the script. Two versions of a scene (which was entirely cut from the final draft), one from Joseph's "screenplay" and the other from Lupino and Young's "final script," are typed out side by side. The dialogue is extremely similar. Joseph used the men's actual names, but Lupino named the two characters who picked up the hitchhiker Gil and Roy. She also made the two protagonists war veterans, dramatically altering their character and connecting them subtextually to a postwar America. Unfortunately, these documents offer only clues about how authorship evolved; the collection does not tell a complete story.[23]

Fragments in the RKO files show that there were eight reels of film, timed at a tight seventy minutes and forty-six seconds; a "revised final script" of 103 pages; and a "second revised final script" of 104 pages. Since a 70-page script will generally yield a seventy-minute film, either the actual final draft is not extant or Lupino cut about 30 pages from her script on set. Most likely is that Lupino economized resourcefully on the original shot lists as she filmed. Lupino was on a tight, twenty-six-day schedule. Initial photography began on June 23, 1952, and finished on July 19. The daily call sheets show that work usually began at 9:00 a.m., with a few earlier calls at 6:00 a.m. for unscripted wild footage. All days were expressly "rain or shine."[24]

Collection documents reveal that the budget for *The Hitch-Hiker* was Lupino's largest. Bill Talman's fee for the film was $11,333.33. Other talent was paid by the day, and according to daily requisition forms, Lupino was over budget only one day of the twenty-six days scheduled for the shoot. Her expenditures for July 16, 1952, for a street scene with extras, exceeded her budget by $38.36. Expenses included two Plymouth sedans for a total of $100.00. The "Transportation Lunch Sheet" designates breaks at Portuguese Point, located on the Palos Verdes Peninsula. The archives show that Lupino's documentary touches included shots of trucks, cars, police motorcycles, and fishing boats. Adherence to the schedule and the budget meant that this was a tough shoot, with no room for error. Lupino found creative solutions while making a critically sound movie. Lupino was a lyricist, vitally interested in the scoring of her films, and she sometimes composed cues. The RKO collection contains a title page for a cue titled, in Lupino's handwriting, "One Eye Sleeper."[25] There is a substantial amount of sheet music in the collection, showing that the music for *The Hitch-Hiker* was scored for full orchestra, including piano and guitar. The score for the film reflects Lupino's taste for jazz and noir-inspired music. It is spare and quiet, like Lupino's visual directing, and it relies on subtle underscoring that does not overwhelm the images onscreen.

Lupino consistently said that she liked to "do pictures about poor bewildered people, because that's what we are."[26] She wanted her audience to side with characters who are trapped by their circumstances, regardless of the moral ambiguity of their decisions. She sympathized with dangerous figures who acted outside of behavioral norms. This embrace of the marginalized is at the forefront in *The Hitch-Hiker*, which, of her six films, employs the least subtext. Lupino was not the only filmmaker interested in Cook's story. An interagency memo to PCA director Joseph Breen, dated January 23, 1951, notes an inquiry made by Lindsley Parsons from Monogram Productions.

> Mr. Lindsley Parson [*sic*] (Monogram—Normancy 2–9181), called up to ascertain whether it would be possible to make a picture on the life of William Cook, the notorious murderer, at present in the papers.
>
> Parson says he has a friend who is the assistant to the Governor of Lower California, who has written him and told him he would help him in every way possible.
>
> Parsons is awaiting an answer by telephone.[27]

At the bottom of the letter, in bold handwriting, Breen wrote, "Not good! We couldn't go for this," and signed with his initials.[28]

A week and a half later, on February 2, Hedda Hopper's column in the *Los Angeles Times* revealed that Lupino was planning to do a picture "based on the harrowing experiences" of the two men captured by Cook.[29] This prompted Parsons to contact the PCA again, resulting in another interagency memo, this one with the subheading "Killer William Cook and the Two Hunters Kidnaped by Him and Held Prisoner for Eight Days in Baja California." The memo states that a film on this subject was "impossible under the Code." Neither Parsons nor Lupino would be allowed to make a film about an incarcerated killer. One of Breen's employees called Lupino's office and "read to them Clause 13 of 'Special Regulations re Crime' of the Code," which described the limitations on how crime and criminals could be portrayed.[30] Subsequently, on February 6, the *Hollywood Reporter* and *Daily Variety* announced that Lupino would be making the movie, giving Lupino and Young some vital free publicity. The same PCA memo reproduced the salient points in each story:

> "Filmakers has acquired film rights to the story of the experiences of Forrest Damron and James Burke, two El Centro engineers who were abducted and held captive for eight days in Baja California by escaped killer William Edward Cook. Filmakers has tentatively titled the story 'I Spoke to God' and is beginning production preparations immediately. Ida Lupino will direct." REPORTER.

> "Filmakers, indie unit releasing though RKO, yesterday bought chase yarn based on desperado William Cook's abduction of Forrest Damron and James Burke, El Centro engineers. Two men were held captive for eight days in Baja California, by the escaped convict. Picture is tentatively titled 'I Spoke to God.' Collier Young will produce, Ida Lupino will direct, Malvin Wald will write screenplay."—VARIETY.[31]

The censors at the PCA discussed the matter again and determined that "while no story could be produced with Cook (a notorious killer), as the main character . . . it might be possible to tell the story of the two prospectors." This was relayed to Parsons, who told staff member "H. H. Z." that Lupino "had gotten the jump on him by contacting the prospectors."[32]

On March 31, 1952, James V. Bennett, director of the Federal Bureau of Prisons, weighed in, contacting Joseph Breen to complain about Lupino, who had tried to secure a deal with Cook while he was imprisoned at Alcatraz:

> Miss Lupino's organization made an effort to obtain his signature to a release for the purpose of screening a picture dealing with his sadistic career. This we declined to allow in accordance with our usual policies.[33]

After Cook was transferred to a state facility in California, wrote Bennett, Lupino tried again:

> But when Cook was turned over to the California authorities, Miss Lupino, through his attorney Mr. John Connelly of Oklahoma City, apparently obtained his signature to such a release. This underhanded trick, I think, is a sad commentary not only on the attorney but on Miss Lupino's organization, and I believe that the release is invalid. As soon as pending appeal proceedings are completed, we intend to present this matter to the Grievance Committee of the Oklahoma Bar Association and take other appropriate steps so far as Mr. Connelly is concerned, because we believe that he had no more right to smuggle this document to Cook and get his signature than he would have to smuggle a gun into the institution.[34]

Naturally, Lupino and Young fought back, sending a three-page letter to Bennett from their office at RKO Studios on April 10, which said in part:

> Dear Mr. Bennett:
> We have delayed an answer to your letter of April 1st until we could check and recheck all points of procedure in connection with the

> preparation of a screen story dealing with the true experiences of Forrest Damron and James Burke while in the captivity of William Edward Cook. This we have now done with considerable thoroughness and will now set down the facts.[35]

Lupino and Young proceeded to explain that although they did obtain a release from Cook while he was standing trial in El Centro, no one approached Cook directly, as they knew that would not be possible. They did contact Cook's attorney, John Connelly of Oklahoma City, they said, and told him that they wanted to make a film and would need a valid and legal release from Cook. Connelly was amenable to the idea and subsequently accepted $3,000 from the Filmakers for life rights to Cook's story. The contract was signed by Connelly and Cook himself. Lupino and Young reiterated that the Filmakers had previously obtained similar releases in exchange for cash payments from Damron and Burke. They also visited California's governor, Edmund G. "Pat" Brown, who did not want to be involved but suggested that Lupino and Young might be able to pursue a signature once Cook had passed into California jurisdiction. Lupino and Young also spoke with the district attorney of Imperial County, Don Bitler, and U.S. marshal James J. Boyle, who said that the best approach to Cook would be at the precise moment he passed into custody of the state of California. To persuade Bennett, Lupino and Young cited their track record:

> Frankly, our intention at this point is to make a picture in which Cook does figure as one of the characters. In keeping with our past production record, we propose to make this picture with taste and distinction. There could be nothing further from our minds as citizens and producers than turning out a film of bloodshed and violence. I do modestly think we have made somewhat of a name for ourselves in the presentation of social problems which have been well received by critics and public alike. For this reason alone it would be folly for us to put our names on a cheap or sensational picture. . . .
>
> We are now in the fortunate position of being able to send you the script which we propose to shoot, calling especial attention to the fact that there is no bloodletting whatsoever and that the entire action of the piece is confined to the last eight days and nights of Cook's freedom before his final capture in Mexico. As you will see, the entire script is written from the viewpoint of the peaceful minds of two perfectly average men. We first became interested in this subject due to the compelling nature of the moral and religious experiences of their captivity. In writing this screenplay we found that Cook simply became

> the symbol of evil—the enemy of society. As you will see, we at no time apologize for Cook's conduct, nor do we attempt at any point to glorify his criminal activity. The obvious reasons for portraying living people on the screen is that we specialize in the documentary film and have found that when dealing in facts we can produce pictures of greater import and impact.[36]

They concluded the letter by restating that they were in no way trying to elude departmental policy. Lupino implied that they would welcome any suggestions Bennett might make vis-à-vis objectionable aspects of the Cook character or anything that might reflect badly on Bennett's official activities. They then pointed out that because they had expended a lot of money, there was some urgency. Finally, Lupino offered to make a trip to Washington, D.C., to meet Bennett in person.[37] A postscript notes that the script would arrive separately. At this time, the title was "The Difference (The Billy Cook Story)."

It wasn't until April 11 that Bennett responded, and then not to Lupino and Young, but to Geoffrey Shurlock. Bennett stated flatly that he did not believe the filmmakers had spoken with Governor Brown, District Attorney Bitler, or Marshal Boyle, essentially calling them liars.[38] By May 21, Lupino and Young had sent their final script to the PCA, and Breen was communicating with RKO publicist William Feeder, who was representing Lupino and Young.[39]

In May, Feeder reported to Lupino and Young that Breen had written to him that "The Difference (The Cook Story)" was essentially acceptable under the provisions of the PCA, and it could go forward if ten changes were made.[40] Most of these changes were to details, but some were to facts of Cook's story that were essential to Lupino's docudramatic style. For one, the PCA suggested that "the Narrator refer to the 'second and third' victims rather than the 'third and fourth.'"[41] To comply, Lupino cut her own voice-over narration; she may have thought it was unnecessary and would only add to the budget. Much like Guy de Maupassant, who wrote little dialogue, Lupino preferred to tell her story with her powerful images, relying on the audience's intelligence to interpret them. Another request was more intrusive: "The reference to the paralyzed right eyelid and the tattoo on the back of the left hand seem to identify this killer with Cook. We ask that these items be changed or eliminated."[42] Lupino tried to prevail on this note, but she was forced to compromise. The PCA allowed her to choose either the deformed eye or the tattoo. Lupino chose the eye, and she made excellent use of it throughout the narrative.

Other objections had to do with religious piety (here, a lack of it), the depiction of firearms, and identifying a location by name:

> We respectfully direct to your attention the fact that Gilbert gives a recitation of his entire schedule on Sunday, without making the slightest reference whatsoever to God or Church. We feel that for public relations purposes you would want us to point this out.
>
> The flaunting of weapons by gangsters, or other criminals, will not be allowed. . . . Having this provision in mind, we trust that you will handle this item in your story with restraint and discrimination.
>
> We ask that the town of Santa Rosalia be given some other name; again, having in mind the necessity to disconnect your story, as much as possible, from the original Cook story.[43]

Lupino emerged triumphant on the last point, using the name "Santa Rosalia" and even showing its location on a map.

Finally, the letter stipulated that ultimate judgment would be based on the finished picture. This was a deadly threat: after all the cost, effort, and time that went into a film, the PCA could deny its distribution, basically killing the picture. Lupino won most of her battles with the censors, however, and she ultimately won the war.[44] The back-and-forth negotiations show how dogged Lupino and Young were and, in fact, how determined any filmmaker had to be not only to secure rights to a news story but also to have the movie greenlighted. The arduous three-way tussle between the Filmakers, the Bureau of Prisons, and the PCA generated news as well as publicity, giving a boost to the Filmaker's promotional campaign for the film. Lupino worked carefully, applying pressure without anger and never taking anything for granted, because she understood the tenuousness of the PCA's approval process. When she had to, she drew on her cachet as a respected actress to get what she needed, all in service to her films.

The Hitch-Hiker is far more than a simple story of good versus evil. While she terrified her audience, Lupino addressed some of her favorite themes in a narrative that is uniquely dependent on an all-American technology: the automobile. Cars were everywhere in the 1950s, especially in the movies. They were employed to signify twentieth-century modernization, and their ubiquity had an indelible influence on American culture. The automobiles manufactured in this era were powerful machines, capable of high speeds. They promised escape from the domestic space, which felt confining to men and women alike in postwar America. Not everyone could own a car, however, and it was relatively common to pick up hitchhikers, so Lupino's dire warning at the opening of *The Hitch-Hiker* would have resonated with her audiences. As they watched a psychotic man commandeer two automobiles and murder two people, viewers would have realized that the events portrayed in the film could happen to anyone who picked up a hitchhiker. Ultimately, the narrative emphasizes the danger rather than the freedom of owning a shiny American car.

Lupino and Young's two travelers are war vets, a departure from the contemporary news stories that identified them as prospectors. They are married—Gil has a child—and we sense the relief these men feel as they seek freedom from another weekend of claustrophobic, domestic obligation. Gil's relief is not as unequivocal as Roy's, however, and he pretends to be asleep when Roy proposes visiting a Mexicali brothel. Gil opens one eye to the camera, but Roy, who is driving, doesn't see this. It is a subtle but telling moment hinting at a moral dissimilarity between the two bonded males that creates a complex relationship. Lupino's rewrite of the Cook story allowed her to explore one of her major themes: the failure of the American dream and the disillusionment of veterans who struggled to reenter American society, particularly the confines of domesticity. The home was now a place of free-floating anxiety, particularly for heterosexual men who had experienced the trauma of war. These issues were immediately understood by movie audiences at that time. In Lupino's hands, the narrative became unexpected, volatile, and moving.

When we meet Roy and Gil, they are ordinary guys. Myers, however, intuits that Gil is the more intelligent of the two men, and he focuses on Roy as the easier to influence. When he takes these men hostage, he takes control of their lives. He has the upper hand: he has the gun, and he understands the weakness and vulnerability of the two domesticated males. Film scholar David Greven points out that Myers is an "unclassifiable presence that threatens to explode the male status quo. He violates the codes of male bonding and exposes masculinity as a form of gender drag."[45] The impact on Roy and Gil is greater than a loss of freedom—it is the ultimate emasculation.

Through Myers, Lupino reflected on and exposed masculine postwar anxieties about retraumatization and death.[46] As soon as he pulls a gun on Roy and Gil, Lupino's camera begins to define their predicament. In Lupino's hands, the automobile becomes a steel trap, emphasizing the fragility of the fantasies of freedom that Roy and Gil had expressed in their opening dialogue. Such dreams constitute an "unreal happiness, a suspension of existence, an irresponsibility," which Jean Baudrillard equated with the mobility and speed offered by the automobile.[47] Lupino also isolated Roy and Gil in the vast space of the high desert, an empty terrain with plenty of secrets. The landscape offers an oppressive sameness that promises death, which can come quickly to those without water.[48]

Perhaps envious of Roy and Gil's friendship and their "normal," middle-class status, Myers calls the two buddies "suckers, up to their necks in IOUs," and "hypocrites" because they had changed the destination of their trip without telling anyone. Myers points out that if they hadn't lied to their wives, they wouldn't be his prisoners.[49] When Roy scoffs at trigger-happy Myers for missing a shot taken at a scurrying rabbit, Myers retaliates tenfold with a sadistic game of humiliation that forces the two friends into an even more frightening situation. Myers compels Gil to shoot at an empty beer can that Roy must hold close to his face. Gil is an accomplished marksman, terrified but steady.

He safely shoots the can out of Roy's hand, but the experience begins to psychologically destabilize Roy. Gil, for his part, realizes that Myers is even more unhinged and menacing than he had thought. The sequence significantly increases the narrative stakes, and the suspense is heightened by the underscore. When the cue was composed, it was titled "Sadistic Target Practice."[50] Even Myers's deformed eye is an advantage. Because this eye never completely closes, Gil and Roy cannot tell whether Myers is awake or asleep. With a gun, a damaged eye, and a life filled with desperation, Myers has all the motivation he needs to maintain control over these men. Interestingly, the importance of Myers's disability is foreshadowed early in the film, when Gil opens one eye as he pretends to sleep to avoid Roy's suggestion for an escapade in Mexicali.

Once strong and mentally solid, Gil and Roy—and their friendship—are steadily weakened by the humiliation and terror they endure. And as Myers brutally reopens their war wounds lest his own wounds be exposed, Lupino's shot list probes undercurrents of alienation, denial, and psychological claustrophobia. Location shooting was a vital and constant stylistic component of Lupino's essentials-only filmmaking. There were budgetary reasons for location decisions, but she also knew that the location could enhance the film's realism and improve the actors' performances. Lupino also used her settings—whether a noirish Los Angeles cityscape, the pastoral countryside, or the merciless desert—as a reminder to her audience that they could be inhabiting these spaces after they left the theater and returned to reality. *The Hitch-Hiker* was released in 1953, three years before passage of the Federal-Aid Highway Act of 1956, which provided for the modern interstate highway system linking U.S. cities. Billy Cook's crime spree was aided by the badly maintained roads, many unpaved, and the indirect and isolated routes that travelers had to take. In the western part of the United States, these roads often traversed vast and frightening expanses of nothingness.

The shots from above the desolate dirt roads are full of portent, suggesting an unsettling end for the characters. Lupino's camera is situated low, shooting up into the crevices of the looming, ancient rock formations that border the road. The tight framing increases the suffocating effect of the barren badlands.

Myers, always in control, setting up Gil to murder Roy.

Sadistic target practice on Roy.

This is a place of dread, of silent spaces that become frightening sites of near death. An abandoned well suggests a gruesome end for Gil and Roy, and Myers, seeking revenge for his own childhood abandonment, enjoys watching the two friends imagine the horror of their death. Lupino tied everything together with her trademark cinematic economy.

When Gil and Roy, angry and demeaned, try to escape by running across an abandoned airstrip—recalling too-recent memories of war—Myers pursues them in their own car. The two headlights are like two eyes—recalling Lupino's opening shot—as the car gains on the two men. Roy trips and falls, and Gil runs back to help. Myers stops just short of murdering the two men, who crouch on the tarmac. They are trapped, illuminated in the glare of the headlights. Myers gloats and points out that if Gil had not helped Roy, he might have gotten away. It is another moment of economy, in which the two headlights remind us that Myers doesn't have two normal eyes. It is the reason he was seen as defective and thus unwanted—a recurring Lupino theme.

Roy, whom Myers had pegged in the beginning as the weaker and less intelligent of the two men, now begins to unravel. Lupino's camera shows us, without judgment, the collapse of the masculine myth as Roy succumbs to Myers's psychological torture. We watch Roy's fear mount as Myers forces him to exchange clothing, making Roy the target of the police who are searching for them. That killer and victim have become interchangeable is the final travesty.[51] Lupino presented Myers's masculinity as uncertain. Instead of the classic psychotic male who terrorizes women, as portrayed by Robert Mitchum in Jacques Tourneur's *Out of the Past* and Charles Laughton's *Night of the Hunter*, Lupino's murderer is an intelligent opportunist who enjoys terrorizing the two men. Lupino's feminist focus on male-male relationships gives the film a rare volatility. The reactions among the men are unexpected, and Myers's monologue has an unsettling intimacy. He reveals uncanny insightfulness as he probes Roy's moral weakness, and in a moment of compassion and psychological strength, he tells his own story with some vulnerability. Again, we see Lupino treating a despicable character with sympathy.

This Lupino film presents the viewer with a spectatorial truth about postwar impaired masculinity that is relayed not only by Lupino's story and camera work but also by Musuraca's cinematography. The desert location gave Musuraca a challenging palette of high, bright light during the day and deep blacks at night. His use of sharply contrasting tones produces a sense of space within the tightly framed shots. Wide, high shots emphasize the feelings of confusion and hostility that the desert landscape evokes, while slightly overexposed shots suggest the unrelenting heat. Light and imagery merge as the shots move in and out of darkness—a recurring note in noir narratives.[52] Shadow is expressive and mysterious, adding truth and suspense to the image. The harder shadows produce a dramatic tableau, one in which the light serves as its own set decoration. In daylight shots, the harsh light projected against the walls of rock with a high-key light keeps the blacks intact. The nightscape is a shroud of merciless darkness, illuminated only by flashlights, headlights, and a crackling campfire. The darkness binds the three men together, with each man's face painted in half-light and shadow. These scenes aptly demonstrate how Lupino used elements of "Lupino noir" to express and expose the shifting relationship of hierarchical male power.

The exterior shots of open desert offer some relief from the claustrophobic interior of the Plymouth in which the men are trapped for hours. Movement is restricted inside the car, exacerbating the brutally edgy silent sequences. Lupino directed Myers to wield his .32 as if it were an appendage, keeping it trained solidly in front of the camera or pointed right at the audience, escalating the quiet terror. Within the confined space, the movement of the car is conveyed by light moving across the men's faces, creating rhythmic tension. Musuraca often lit the characters from below, so that they moved toward darkness rather than light, destabilizing the viewer. In fact, Musuraca drew a line around everything he wanted his audience to see, balancing foreground, midground, and background.

Lupino and Musuraca used rear screen projection to suggest movement for some of the shots inside the car, but the device is barely noticeable. Lupino's use of this technique is vastly different from Hitchcock's. In *Marnie*, for example, Hitchcock used obvious rear screen projection to emphasize Marnie's fantasy life: she rides her mythical horse, a child's libidinal, but plastic, image. Lupino, in contrast, used the device to keep the audience's perception of movement as real as possible, enhancing the feeling that they are watching a life-and-death situation. The interior of the small sedan becomes a surreal landscape.

Critic Vivian Sobchack sees rear screen projection as a neglected aesthetic element of film noir, one that serves its theme of existential entrapment and "eternal return" in a world with no exit. She argues that the device is as important for defining space in film noir as flashbacks are to the genre's representation of time.[53] Back projection literalized noir's worldview, making the metaphoric terms so often used in critical readings of noir (particularly of a psychoanalytic kind) quite literal. Rear projection adds a phantasmatic, dreamlike element to the screen image. As a stand-in for filming in a moving vehicle, it also constitutes a conspicuous blind spot for noir characters—and viewers—by forestalling or foreclosing any sense of the characters' existential freedom. This claustration becomes intelligible to viewers sensually as well as cognitively. The unsettling feeling of watching rear screen projection further complicates

Lupino's documentary style. The contrast between the confinement of the interior shots and the agoraphobia-inducing shots of the desert's expanse are jarring, and the vague but persistent promise of escape is unsettling. Lupino also skillfully incorporated objective correlatives, such as the vultures hovering over the shimmering desert, waiting for something, anything, to die. It all adds up to a nerve-racking experience for the viewer.

The tension produced by the direction and cinematography is supported by the script, which contains little dialogue, and starkly lit close-ups often take the place of a verbal exchange. Lupino and Young knew when to release information and who should release it. The first beat of dialogue between Gil and Roy—when they consider reliving their bachelor days by visiting a prostitute—reveals who is the weaker of the two.[54] Gil wants to go to San Felipe, but Roy wants to go to the mountains. Roy complains there is nothing to do in San Felipe but fish. Gil is direct: "That was the idea, wasn't it?" Roy will lie to his wife, but although Gil may be tempted, he overrules Roy. Myers understands what the audience already knows, choosing Roy as the man to manipulate as the film reaches its climax. All three characters are animated by their backstories, which are established through the specificity of the writing and carefully integrated into the action. They also represent three levels of consciousness: O'Brien's character, Roy, is a lost child; he is Lupino's bewildered character. Lovejoy's Gil, a draftsman, is clear and theoretical. Talman's killer is depraved—and powerful. Lupino was not positing a simple Manichean relationship between the characters; she was reflecting life itself.

The Hitch-Hiker is what Scorsese would term a "quiet film," in which Lupino allowed the camera and the lighting to tell her story.[55] She recorded only what was necessary, without any stylization that might suggest commentary. Lupino compelled the viewer to engage, decipher, and fill in details. This becomes a literal exercise in the scenes in which the characters speak Spanish. The Spanish dialogue is not translated, and this unusual absence of subtitles increases the documentary feel. Rather than directing actors who were native Spanish speakers to communicate in English with Spanish accents—something they would never do in real life—Lupino chose to increase the authenticity of the narrative. In these scenes, in which the three men interact with Mexicans, Lupino shifted the power to Gil. Because he speaks Spanish and Myers does not, Myers momentarily becomes the vulnerable character, as he admits, "I don't know what they're saying." When Myers needs to buy rations or gas for the car, he keeps the gun on Gil and threatens him not to say anything in "Mexican" that could tip off the police or be a coded call for help. Gil carefully gauges any opening he might have, which intensifies these sequences for the audience. Lupino's script cross-cuts between the practical conversation of traveling and the psychotic exchanges between the killer and his captives. The language confusion is real, with the mismatch fueling the building sense of dread. The foreign setting intensifies the audience's sense of dislocation.

Lupino seemed to have a particular interest in expressing madness as response to frustration. Apart from Myers, several of her characters exhibit some degree of insanity: Sally Kelton in *Not Wanted*, Harry Graham in *The Bigamist*, and Shelley Peters in an episode of the television series *Breaking Point* titled "Heart of Marble, Body of Stone" (1963), directed by Lupino, in which the main character (played by Gena Rowlands) is an actress undergoing a breakdown. Some of Lupino's most-lauded film roles were of unhinged women, including in *The Light That Failed* (1939) and *Ladies in Retirement* (1941). These characters, both acted and filmed, may have reflected the psychological burdens of Lupino's unique, solitary position in the film industry, and putting their stories on the screen may have allowed Lupino to work out her own existential issues. Many directors do this; why not Lupino?

There is a dearth of scholarship on *The Hitch-Hiker*, perhaps because of the film's slim subtext. Besides various pages in Grisham and Grossman discussing Lupino's penultimate film with others of Lupino's movies, only one in-depth online article, "Ida Lupino's American Psycho: *The Hitch-Hiker* (1953)," can be found, in *Bright Lights Film Journal;* in it, David Greven discusses a familiar film noir villain, the American Psycho, an unsubtle reference to Alfred Hitchcock's later film, simply titled *Psycho*.[56] Another published piece, an essay by Lauren Rabinovitz in Annette Kuhn's anthology *Queen of the 'B's*, focuses almost exclusively on Lupino's "vision of hell," which she defines as "masculinity fragmented into neurotic components of maladjustment."[57] Lupino and Young were interested in the real story of William Cook, but their objective was to write a story that was *truer*, almost suprareal, akin to a literary fable by Don DeLillo. By maintaining intimacy as well as tension, Lupino produced a relentless action piece about the moral ambiguity of two men whose lives depend on their friendship and trust. Although *The Hitch-Hiker* is constructed from the elements of a noir thriller, the elements are reconfigured to present a meditation on postwar trauma and disappointment that is more complex than what Lupino had presented in any of her other independent films, *Not Wanted*, *Never Fear*, *Outrage*, *Hard, Fast and Beautiful*, or *The Bigamist*.

As a director, Lupino was always concerned with portraying real life and how the viewer would respond to the narrative, and her screenplays are remarkably objective. She did not make judgments about her characters. She never employed the histrionic aspects of melodrama, and she rejected the hyperbolic mode. When, for example, Myers reflects on his grim past, he does so by citing the facts, without any claim of victimization. Lupino's subject matter was always uncompromising—the trauma of rape, the dread of an unplanned pregnancy, the psychological confusion around bigamy, the isolation of polio, the anger and frustration of being forced into a professional sports career, and, in *The Hitch-Hiker*, entrapment. These were unusual, gritty, low-budget, real-world narratives, explored by the period's only woman working in the studio system.

Lupino's direction can be compared to Sam Fuller's, for her economy of method; to Alfred Hitchcock's, for her skill with suspense; and to Nicholas Ray's, for her focus on youth. Like these three men, Don Siegel was another director championed by Jean-Luc Godard and other *Cahiers du Cinéma* writers, and he and Lupino overlapped and linked in creative ways. Siegel's style, however, cut fast and free, while Lupino was more aware. Siegel's speed often detracts from the moral center of the film. In contrast, when Lupino's characters agonize, the audience shares that anguish. Lupino was concerned primarily with her characters; Siegel cared more about action. Lupino was praised for her ability to fluently link scenes, for her painterly dissolves, and for her use of a mobile, yet bulky and outdated 35 mm Mitchell camera.[58] Low-budget camera work could be static, often because cameras were heavy, and time for setups were limited.[59] Lupino always preferred to move her camera, but she could adapt as the situation required, as when filming the automobile interiors for *The Hitch-Hiker*.

The three case studies of *Not Wanted*, *Never Fear*, and *The Hitch-Hiker* demonstrate that Lupino's point of view was evenhanded: she treated males and females alike as flawed. With *The Hitch-Hiker*, Lupino was initially reticent to write a film that did not feature a woman. Nonetheless, Roy's and Gil's absent wives are a ghostly presence felt throughout. Even Myers is curious about and jealous of the postwar nuclear family. All three men are flawed and fully realized (albeit to varying degrees), just as Lupino's female protagonists are three-dimensional characters, all too human.

Lupino's women, though, are not victims. Sally Kelton (*Not Wanted*) overcomes her guilt and shame. Eve Graham (*The Bigamist*) is a brilliant businesswoman, barren but upbeat. Millie Farley (*Hard, Fast and Beautiful*) is an amoral mother who thinks she is providing the best life for her daughter. And in *Outrage*, the personal strength that Ann Walton (Mala Powers) exhibits after she is raped is compromised by the next relationship she forms, but Lupino never suggests that she is a victim. These are all strong women who reflect social problems of their times, and they must be appreciated within that context. Lupino was commenting on, rather than denying, the reality women faced after the war. Lupino's point of view was subversive. Her endings are necessarily ambiguous, and these films are perhaps difficult to watch. The men in Lupino's cohort of filmmakers, as a whole, are far less egalitarian with their female characters, advancing sexist notions of women as victims, sexual objects, or doting, mindless mothers. Lupino created complex women sadly trapped by the smallness of their lives. They are bewildered people, imprisoned in their own stories. Shelley Cobb argues that Lupino's women "struggle against the social and legal limits of the post-war era," with her characters foregrounding "the social exclusion and censure of women . . . and the ambivalent ways they attempt to escape those traps." She maintains that Lupino's "social critique . . . remains resolutely anti-utopian in [its] gender politics."[60]

Francine Parker notes that Lupino's independent films summarized the spirit of the 1950s: "There is an upbeat toughness of spirit in all of Lupino's films. The world of darkness is constantly, fearlessly fought and miracles are wrought. Never is there the least cynicism. Sardonic humor and wit, perhaps, but never single-minded cynicism. The sharp director with her pure and thoroughly brilliant economy of expression has wrapped up the Fifties for us."[61] Noir is a genre that especially lends itself to spare filmmaking, and Lupino was a master of essentials-only cinema. Director Barbet Schroeder has stated that "all movies are documentaries in the sense they record real people doing real things," and this is what Lupino did with such mastery, from the warning at the beginning of each of her movies through their ambiguous finales.[62] Today the subgenre might be called "dirty realism."

Lupino's segue into television directing was a natural next step, made easy by her ability to shoot fast and smart, together with her particular multigenre brand of expression and her ease with actors. She expanded into new genres, adding westerns, satire, and comedy to the thrillers and suspense that she saw as her "slot."[63] Her skills were ready-made for early television action dramas. As Rhona Berenstein notes, the "liveness" of television created a new form of "direct access" to performance that was "unmediated."[64]

As a prolific and creatively powerful filmmaker with a distinct voice, Lupino was on a par with her male counterparts. But her vision was also unique. In an ironic twist, given her career playing femme fatales, she inverted the voyeuristic gaze onto the male. The actors who portrayed ultramasculine characters trusted Lupino's techniques and her creative eye, asking her to rewrite and direct scripts, drawing on her cinematic wisdom and her female point of view. When Lupino was directing features in Hollywood, she was the only woman who was. This was not because her films were distinctly feminine or melodramatic—they weren't. Lupino focused on the miseries of women in the 1950s, portraying them as trapped, as underdogs in society, as misunderstood, as emotionally if not physically abused. Lupino empathized with the unsettled, the traumatized, and especially the dangerously disturbed, as Scheib has noted: "Lupino's films denaturalize passivity; it is unwanted, restless, anxious, important. Her characters are sleep-walkers, their subjectivity condemned to incompleteness, their faces swept by emotions that happen to them but never belong to them. . . . Between their subjectivity and the world there is nothing."[65] Lupino's written characters were linked to her own experiences, and her directed characters were murky and subtle—and original.

Part III

TELEVISION

SNAPSHOTS

Lupino was athletic, which perhaps was a genetic carryover from her acrobatic ancestors. As an actress, she was known for her ability to ride horses and to fight and carry a gun believably, and she drew on this athleticism as a director. A photo, probably taken on the set of *The Rifleman* in 1961, shows her coaching a stunt double for a lethal fistfight.[1]

Lupino directed other westerns, including *Have Gun—Will Travel*, starring Richard Boone. Clint Eastwood visited the set while Lupino was filming one of the eight episodes she directed, and he watched Lupino riding alongside Boone to find a specific shot. In a backhanded compliment, Eastwood said, "I believed that if an actress could become a director, it kind of made me think I could be a director."[2]

Because the roles of director and writer were both considered male occupations, stories about Lupino in the print media often mentioned her with a feminine touch: "The present Mrs. Howard Duff is known to actors and actresses as one of the most sensitive—and the toughest—directors in the business."[3] This description links Lupino to her husband and then to her career, alluding to her femininity first and her masculinity second. A photograph taken at Lupino's wedding to Duff depicts her as a domesticated and, more important, dutiful wife. There is no hint of the smart, skilled, powerful, writer-director. Ironically, Lupino's movies explored the dark sides of domesticity: entrapment, loneliness, and madness.

LEFT: *Lupino, in the white blouse, choreographing a fight sequence with a stuntwoman.*

Chapter 7

LUPINO AND EARLY TELEVISION

Darling, I love westerns, the sweep, the color, the very elementals—the violence. Darling, they're wonderful.

Ida Lupino in Cecil Smith, "Dainty Ida Takes Up Whip as Director of Westerns"

For professional women in the 1950s and 1960s, finding a balance between career and home could be a difficult challenge. For Ida Lupino, the television industry offered the perfect solution. She could work on a variety of shows and in a variety of genres, and the compressed production schedules allowed her to spend time with her third husband, Howard Duff, and their daughter, Bridget, while remaining creatively relevant. By altering her career to focus on television rather than film, Lupino was able to both maintain her author's touch and care for her family. Lupino, who had acted, produced, written, and directed film, was one of the only women at that time who had the skills to make this change. She moved seamlessly into early television, first as a star and then as a director. This choice placed Lupino in rare company. Only one other industry professional made the same double transition from starring in and directing films to starring in and directing television: Orson Welles.[1]

Lupino was a transgressive figure in the film industry, with her early exploitation films and her elusive identity, and she continued to be a transgressive figure in the television industry, disrupting the gender binaries of the 1950s both on- and offscreen. Born into the business, she had the experience and intelligence to stake her own territory, and she knew how not to follow the rules. Lupino refused to be coded as either feminine or masculine, although she played the game when she had to. She was willing to allow herself the nurturing characterization of *mother*, which she created to accomplish her goals as a director. As a result of her astonishing skill set and her uniquely varied successes in the film industry, she was "the most active woman working behind the cameras in the formative years of TV."[2] In fact, until 1989, Lupino held the record for having directed more episodes than any other woman working in television.[3]

The More Modern Medium

Tectonic changes were taking place in the entertainment industry in the early to mid-1950s. Television was an early disrupter. Americans' exposure to television rose rapidly as sets became more affordable and new broadcasting stations were established. Between 1946 and 1955, the percentage of American homes with television sets increased from .02 to 65 percent.[4] At the end of the decade, 85.9 percent of American households had at least one television set.[5] Television studios raced to keep up, and by the mid-1950s, network schedules were filled with comedies, westerns, soap operas, quiz shows, and dramas.

Television production became established in Hollywood in the early 1950s. Initially, actors in the studio star machine who wanted to supplement their work and income found opportunities in radio. Then, in 1954, television revenue passed radio revenue for the first time, and the new medium supplanted the old.[6] The studio contracts that restricted a star's autonomy were gradually eliminated, and stars became free agents who could seek work at television networks. They were untethered from the studio system.[7]

Television offered a different kind of workplace for film industry professionals. Although some programs were still broadcast live, most were filmed, which introduced an element of flexibility lacking in film production. The conventional wisdom in television's early days was that film stars should avoid the small screen because they would become overexposed and diminished in both media, but modern families enjoyed watching film stars in their living rooms—for free—and embraced this new, more intimate way to follow their favorite personalities. Blending film and television work became a common practice for actors.[8] In the mid-1950s, a Screen Actors Guild survey revealed that actors who made up to $7,500 a year—the "largest division" of its members—spent about half of their employment days acting for television.[9] A starring role in an anthology episode or a one-shot prestige performance could draw a big name because these appearances lessened concerns about the star's overexposure. For established stars, television appearances could be lucrative. Ginger Rogers earned $50,000 for a single appearance in a pilot for a proposed sitcom titled *The Ginger Rogers Show* (1961).[10]

A few stars never did cross over, including Cary Grant, Katharine Hepburn, Clark Gable, and Rita Hayworth. Others of equal prominence, however, such as Marilyn Monroe, William Holden, Gene Tierney, and Ingrid Bergman, sought the small screen for various reasons. They might have wanted wider exposure or had a specific need for publicity—perhaps for a new movie. Some feature stars began in television—including Paul Newman, Joanne Woodward, and Rod Steiger, who were graduates of the Actors Studio in New York and brilliant actors—but television studios preferred film stars because sponsors preferred them. The bigger the sponsor, the bigger the star.

Commercials for consumer products were the lifeblood of television production, and the companies that made them needed stars. Being associated with a star could link a company's products to a program's perceived altruistic or artistic value.[11] Sponsors could rely on star directors like Lupino, Nicholas Ray, Alfred Hitchcock, and Robert Aldrich to stimulate viewership because they attracted stars to series and series episodes. As Joseph Cotten, who segued smoothly into television, shrewdly observed, "No sponsor in his right mind wants to come right on and say, 'I'm the sponsor and here's what I'm selling.' . . . He needs a middle man to make the audience feel at home with him."[12] Television, which was gaining in both credibility and audience numbers, also offered free publicity for projects in other media. *The Ed Sullivan Show*, for example, was the place to advertise a record album, an upcoming film, or even a book.[13]

Programming tended to reflect the cultural expectations of the moment, including those for gender roles. Some early series did push these boundaries, if only a little. One was *Private Secretary* (CBS, 1953–1957), which featured actress Ann Sothern, who played Susie MacNamara, the secretary to a Manhattan talent agent. The character is a middle-class career woman living in an urban setting. Educated, and more charismatic than her boss, she organizes the office like a household while remaining submissive.[14] Another, *The Betty Hutton Show* (1959–1960, CBS) was helmed by Betty Hutton, who was just too wacky and explosive for early television.[15] Hutton apparently alienated the housewives who were watching, since *The Donna Reed Show* (ABC, 1958–1966), scheduled at the same time, won the ratings war for that time slot. Donna Reed portrayed the perfect housewife, and the show's sponsors maximized her farm-girl persona.[16]

Ida Lupino's *Mr. Adams and Eve* (CBS, 1957–1958) was not Lupino's first foray into television, but it was a departure from sitcoms like *Donna Reed* because Lupino played a version of herself, a movie star, and the show was satiric and self-reflexive rather than simply comedic. Lupino frequently denied a connection to typical Hollywood standards of glamour and femininity, and her character, Eve Adams, was not a typical Hollywood star.[17] This self-conscious depiction of the public and private lives of flamboyant film stars is striking even today. Unlike Lucy Ricardo (Lucille Ball) in *I Love Lucy* and Gracie Allen in *The George Burns and Gracie Allen Show*, Eve Adams escapes the domestic space, and her successes rather than her failures are emphasized in the show. She is allowed to fail as a housewife because she is too busy being creative and making movies. *Mr. Adams and Eve* was a family effort, with Eve's husband played by Howard Duff. Lupino and Duff formed Bridget Productions to make the show, which was based on an idea by Collier Young, Lupino's former husband and partner in the Filmakers.[18]

Television may have been seen as marginalizing for some of its stars, but as Therese Grisham and Julie Grossman point out, it was traditionally "less hierarchically organized" than the Hollywood film industry, so women began to find it slightly easier to find work that was not only in front of the camera.[19] As a director, Lupino sought out compelling stories that would attract a mass audience in the rapidly changing, chaotic, and contradictory media culture of the 1950s and 1960s. Through television, she could create modern narratives with multiple meanings. As television director Robert Butler has observed, Lupino worked against the usual practice by filming "not the words but the drama."[20]

Lupino's contributions to television were extraordinary, and the feminist history of American media cannot be told without recognizing the range of her accomplishments. Gwendolyn Audrey Foster has noted that feminist critics "too often" took Lupino's comments about women working in a man's world "at face value."[21] Many of the statements Lupino made seem to have been designed to irritate these critics. In a December 1965 news story, for example, she said in regard to her television directing, "Keeping a feminine approach is vital. Men hate bossy females. . . . Often I pretend to know less than I do. That way you get more cooperation."[22]

Lupino was not limited by her gender. In fact, most of her acting, writing, and directing work in television was male-centered, as evidenced by her work on programs such as *The Untouchables* (ABC, 1959–1963), *Have Gun—Will Travel* (CBS, 1957–1963), and *Bonanza* (NBC, 1959–1973). The stars were almost exclusively male, as were the crews, and the episodes presented male-centered texts. Lupino acknowledged this in a 1974 interview, when she was asked about the genres she enjoyed: "I was directing *Have Gun—Will Travel* with Richard Boone, *Hong Kong* with Bob Taylor, *The Fugitive* with David Janssen, *Manhunt*, *The Untouchables*. Who, me? I thought. Here I'd always done women's stories and now I couldn't get a woman's story to direct."[23] Amelie Hastie suggests this was because of Lupino's success with *The Hitch-Hiker*, her fifth directed film.[24] Although *The Hitch-Hiker* certainly increased Lupino's stature, directing for television was nevertheless a modern choice for Lupino, one that aligned with her determination to remain an intensely independent woman, as both industry professional and mother.

Value in the Mundane

Television was maligned by critics and often seen by entertainment professionals as a step down from studio film work, but for Lupino it was a step up. Her transition into the new, fast-moving medium was thoughtful, even cautious. "I was snobbish toward TV at first," she said, "but that changed fast. The pressure, the opportunities, the fantastic challenges—it's all fantastic, darling."[25] Her television career began with *Four Star Playhouse* (CBS, 1952–1956), first as an actor and then as a director. This was one of many televised anthology series that presented a different story with a different set of characters in each episode.[26] Some presented a variety of teleplays that ranged across genres; others were genre-specific, focusing on, for example, mystery and suspense. Regardless, each episode was essentially a short movie. Film and television scholar Christine Becker points out that the anthology series was "an essential component of television's early efforts to sell itself to audiences, critics, and sponsors as a culturally valuable and financially viable entertainment format."[27]

Anthology series offered film professionals a path into the television industry, and *Four Star Playhouse* provided a gateway not only for Lupino but also for directors Aldrich, Frank McDonald, and László Benedek, among others. Blake Edwards was a frequent writer as well as a director for the series.[28] The anthology series also changed the hierarchy that had been established by Hollywood filmmakers. Screenwriting became a privileged position, one that gave writers a great deal of creative control. The narratives presented in the anthology series focused on characterization, and writers created the characters.[29] The networks bought teleplays, and directors were hired as technicians, not auteurs. The director's mandate was to get the story on the air quickly, usually in three to four days. They were hired to realize, with consistency, what the writer had created. Directors like Lupino, who had experience and skill, chose the shots and camera angles, worked with the actors, often did some script rewriting, and closely collaborated with the cinematographer. These directors may have been for hire, working from episode to episode, but their contribution was essentially the same as it had been for film. Television studios and producers got an auteur for low pay.[30]

Lupino starred in nineteen episodes of *Four Star Playhouse*. The first was "House for Sale," which aired on December 31, 1953, during the second season. She also originated the story for two of the episodes in which she acted, "The Story of Emily Cameron" (March 29, 1956) and "The Stand-In" (July 19, 1956), both in the fourth season. The character that Lupino created for "The Story of Emily Cameron" is "a victimized wife and a shrewish manipulator" who is "both controller and controlled." The complex role represented a "tour de force of both scripting and acting" for Lupino.[31] Lupino's familiar themes of entrapment and escape are woven into this story of a passive-aggressive woman who is dramatically driven to excess.

Lupino's path into television directing was through another anthology series. Although it ran for only one season, *Screen Directors Playhouse* (NBC, 1955–1956) served as an elite showcase for film actors and, particularly, film directors, as the opening promised, "Screen Directors Playhouse: Bringing you each week an outstanding original screenplay chosen and directed by one of the country's foremost motion picture directors." John Ford, William Dieterle, Don Siegel, Fred Zinnemann, Frank Borzage, and Leo McCarey are a few of the directors who worked on the series. Each episode, running from twenty-two to twenty-seven minutes, was a movie in miniature, created with attention to lighting and set design, performance, framing, and editing. All were produced using the talents of highly skilled film industry veterans who worked fast to keep costs down. The episodes, which were filmed in different aspect ratios and with different film stock, were often elegant productions despite the limitations. Directors had to be seasoned to make a good product while incorporating the precisely timed commercial breaks, prescribed budgets, and limited shooting days that television production required. This was an ideal format for Lupino. Her directorial debut for television was a half-hour teleplay for *Screen Directors Playhouse*, "No. 5 Checked Out," which aired January 18, 1956.[32]

Lupino's transition to television gave her opportunities that had not been available in the film industry. She was able to work in a range of genres and genre hybrids and in series that had lucrative sponsorships, providing bigger budgets and more resources. Gender roles both onscreen and off were evolving as censorship was loosening. Moreover, Lupino's reputation as an in-demand television director afforded her a formidable position of authority, one usually reserved for men. Most of her work was for action, western, and thriller series, not the melodramas, musicals, comedies, or romances that might have been expected from a woman. Television offered not only the speed and variety that suited Lupino's style but also a climate that was "dense, rich, and complex rather than impoverished."[33]

Lupino in the opening credits for her Screen Directors Playhouse *episode, "No. 5 Checked Out."*

One of the best illustrations of the progressive nature of television, and a refutation to the argument that the medium was a marginalized mausoleum for industry professionals, is offered by the three anthology series hosted by Alfred Hitchcock: *Alfred Hitchcock Presents* (CBS and NBC, 1955–1962), *The Alfred Hitchcock Hour* (CBS and NBC, 1962–1965), and the reboot decades later, *Alfred Hitchcock Presents* (NBC and USA Network, 1985–1989). A look at the personnel lists for the series shows that Hitchcock put together a talented and varied group of writers, directors, and actors who made the transition from film to television or trained in television and then went on to film. All three of Hitchcock's series were, in some ways, a Roger Corman–like training ground.[34] Hitchcock was the apotheosis of suspense storytelling. He produced, directed, or wrote many of the shows, and he appeared in some of the episodes, creating his own promotion. These programs were an advertiser's dream.

Hitchcock, Aldrich, Ray, and Lupino were all working in television at about the same time, between 1956 and 1968. An appraisal of their work and working relationships illuminates the complexity of the new medium from the creator's perspective and underlines the exemplarity of Lupino's directorial methods. The three men are canonized in the critical literature, yet Lupino, whose work in television matched, and in some ways exceeded, theirs, has been generally overlooked by critics and theorists. Lupino was not ignored by Ray, Aldrich, or

Hitchcock, however. All four were part of a kind of guerrilla alliance of directors, writers, cameramen, editors, and musicians active in the entertainment industry through the 1960s, who moved between film and television as job opportunities arose. Lupino worked for Aldrich as an actress in *The Big Knife* (1955) and as a producer for his five episodes of *Four Star Playhouse*.[35] Ray and Lupino each directed an episode that appeared on *On Trial* (NBC and CBS, 1956–1959), a series hosted by Joseph Cotten.[36] Lupino also directed two half-hour episodes for *Alfred Hitchcock Presents*.[37]

The anthology format offered Lupino and her colleagues a more modern alternative to film. Episodes were produced quickly, which allowed Lupino to take enough work to support her family while having time to spend with them. Lupino could make choices that worked for her creatively rather than just monetarily. She turned down the lucrative lead role for an episode of *Alfred Hitchcock Presents*, "Sybilla" (December 6, 1960), for the chance to direct the same episode, even though directing paid far less than the acting. Instead of $5,000, Lupino was offered $1,250.[38] By this measure, her acting was worth four times more than her directing—or it may be that her gender allowed Hitchcock to offer her less for directing than what male directors were receiving. For *The Untouchables* and *Hong Kong*, Lupino directed some of the series' most violent hard-action episodes. Her episode of *The Twilight Zone* (CBS, 1959–1964), "The Masks" (March 20, 1964), is a twisted, grotesque morality tale. Richard Boone, the star of the long-running *Have Gun—Will Travel*, invited Lupino to direct an episode, and she was the first woman in television to direct a western. This episode, "The Man Who Lost" (April 25, 1959), was not "a stereotypical 'woman's story,'" but a script by Harry Julian Fink, who was famed for his graphic descriptions of physical violence. Kathleen Spencer writes that the episode presents "a dark character study of a man accused of killing a cattle rancher and 'attacking' his wife."[39] The "attack" is a rape, but the word *rape* was still not allowed on television in 1959.[40]

Lupino was known for her "skill at handling players of both sexes and her sensitivity to . . . the problems and needs of her cast," both products of her acting career.[41] The performance that she pulled from Boone, who was notoriously difficult, was so popular with reviewers that the star brought her back to direct seven more episodes in the next two seasons.[42] Boone told columnist Erskine Johnson in 1961, "Ida stimulates me as an actor because she knows acting." In a weekly show, he added, "you get into acting patterns. Ida gets you out of them."[43] Filming a television episode, particularly for an action drama, was demanding. The compressed schedule of three to four days did not allow multiple takes, and everyone on set had to be nimble and fast. A director who did not understand lenses, angles, and light would not be successful. Lupino's run with *Have Gun—Will Travel* is a testament to her mastery of her craft. Boone, who likely learned from and was inspired by Lupino, went on, after Lupino, to direct twenty-eight of the episodes himself.

Lupino quickly became one of an elite group of highly skilled film directors who worked, at least for a time, in television. Producers favored these directors—all male with the exception of Lupino—because of their expertise and efficiency. Like Lupino, they worked in a variety of genres and with a variety of stars.

Chapter 8

ACROSS MEDIA WITH RAY, ALDRICH, AND HITCHCOCK

"Television," I screamed. "Really, George [Diskant], you're out of your mind."

Ida Lupino, "Me, Mother Directress"

Ida Lupino, Nicholas Ray, Robert Aldrich, and Alfred Hitchcock were directors in common. All were considered modernists, and all made the transition from film to television, with Lupino being the only woman, and the only working actor, in the group. Discussing their work together serves to reiterate the skills and genre expertise that these great directors shared. Lupino was one among equals, yet her contributions to television are only recently being recovered and rediscovered, more than fifty years later.

Lupino and Ray

Ray's *Johnny Guitar* had just been released to good reviews when Jennings Lang, a Hollywood talent agent, producer, and writer, asked Ray to contribute to *General Electric Theater* (CBS, 1953–1962), an anthology series initially produced by Revue Productions. Ray directed an episode titled "High Green Wall" (October 3, 1954), broadcast during the third season. The episode was rebroadcast on August 17, 1959, as part of the final season of *The Joseph Cotten Show.*[1]

"High Green Wall" starred Cotten, an early favorite actor of Orson Welles, and Thomas Gomez, a Shakespearean stage actor and a top Hollywood supporting actor.[2] Cotten could portray psychotic characters with frightening reality, as he did in Hitchcock's *Shadow of a Doubt* (1943). Ray had worked with both stars on *Macao* (1952) on a three-day sequence for which the director was not credited. The source material was Evelyn Waugh's short story "The Man Who Liked Dickens," which had been given new dialogue by writer Charles R. Jackson (author of *The Lost Weekend*). Ray had one week for rehearsal and three or four days for filming. He began to rehearse, experimenting and hoping for something new from this exercise in a new medium.[3]

Ray shot "High Green Wall" in 35 mm, making the best of the studio's lighting limitations and the breakneck schedule, conditions that suited the intense theme of the episode. Most members of the cast and crew were new to television and thus new to its time constraints. The cameraman, Franz Planer (a trained portrait painter), was one of the few cinematographers that Ray worked with again.[4] Ray dispensed with the prologue that usually preceded episodes of *General Electric Theater*, opening with the protagonist, Paul Henty (Cotten), staggering through a Central American jungle. Clearly very ill, he collapses, and a tracking shot follows as two Indigenous people help Henty walk to the camp of Mr. McMaster (Gomez). This is the first of many shots that suggest a vast jungle inhabited by exotic people and terrifying, surreal possibilities.[5]

After the title sequence, the story resumes as Henty rouses after a four-day illness, having been cared for by McMaster, who has lived in the jungle all his life. His father was an American missionary and his mother a local Native; both are dead. Before McMaster's father died, he had read aloud to his son from the novels of Charles Dickens, and McMaster, who had never learned to read, longs to hear the stories again. McMaster relates that he had depended on a "guest," Barnabas, who had entertained McMaster until his recent death. Barnabas's task, reading Dickens out loud, now falls to Henty. Soon enough, Henty realizes that McMaster, who is armed, is not going to let him go. McMaster shows Barnabas's grave to Cotten in a not-so-understated threat: Henty should not contemplate escape.

Ray works efficiently within the confines of the small set, which he plays upon through "ruptures in tone, physical conflict, [and] dynamic exploitation of the setting."[6] As the teleplay advances, the passage of time is defined by Henty's reading and shots of a steadily diminishing pile of books. Like Lupino, Ray compresses sequences during shooting, eliminating conventional transitions. For example, as Henty reads, thunder interrupts and both men rush outside, the camera dollying out with them. When Henty declares that he will no longer read to McMaster, the story darkens further. After Henty's declaration, McMaster withholds food until Henty resumes reading—now from *A Tale of Two Cities*. Henty pointedly asks, in the character's words, to be released "from this prison of horror."[7] The dual forces of the rejection of civilization and the overwhelming power of nature are later repeated in Ray's *Wind across the*

Everglades (1958). Entrapment in mental and physical prisons is also a consistent Lupinian theme, expressed most overtly in *The Hitch-Hiker.*

One of the hallmarks of Lupino's and Ray's directing styles is the complexity of their camera movements, and these techniques are especially apparent in the filming done within the restricted space of the television studio. Ray did not bother to hide the cheap set for "High Green Wall" (which might be an homage to the B films so adored by the French New Wave critics), instead using special effects to suggest the wind, lightning, and torrential rain of a monsoon. Ray's episode has been noted for its "cruelty and despair," which foreshadows "the climate of madness" that marks others of Ray's works, such as *Bitter Victory* (1957) and *Bigger Than Life* (1956). Lupino was interested not only in the portrayal of madness, as shown in her episodes for *Breaking Point* (ABC, 1963–1964) and *Alfred Hitchcock Presents,* but also in the grotesque, as seen in "The Masks," her episode for *The Twilight Zone.*

Ray's camera, like Lupino's, is efficient and mobile. At the end of "High Green Wall," a pensive portrait of Henty holding an open novel is superimposed over a shot of busy Native people in their village. In a voice-over, we hear Henty intoning the opening passage from *A Tale of Two Cities.* The camera zooms in on Henty as the superimposed shot dissolves into a tree branch, swaying in the wind. As Henty recites, "It was the winter of despair," lightning strikes, the branch falls, and the screen fades to black, followed by the title card: "The End."[8] For Ray and Lupino, stressing the ambiguity of a story, particularly at its conclusion, was an act of rebellion against the neatly packaged endings typical of classic Hollywood films, endings that were devoid of resonance.

Lupino's episode of *On Trial,* "The Trial of Mary Surratt" (November 2, 1956, on NBC), demonstrates her skill with her camera.[9] As with most of the episodes in the series, the teleplay was based on actual trial records. Surratt was convicted of conspiring in the assassination of Abraham Lincoln and hanged in 1865. Her boardinghouse was used as a meeting place for a group of Confederate sympathizers who plotted to abduct Lincoln. Among these men were Mary Surratt's son John and John Wilkes Booth. The abduction plans were never realized, but after the Confederacy collapsed, a determined Booth devised his successful plan to assassinate the president.

In a 1977 interview, Lupino recalled the tight schedule that was required to film the episode: "It was shot in three days with three or four days to prepare. I sat up day and night doing all the research I could on the assassination of Lincoln. Television—there's nothing rougher, nothing rougher."[10] Lupino likely was interested in Surratt not only because she was the first woman to be executed by the U.S. government but also because, as a woman, she was an outsider.[11] Surratt claimed that she had no knowledge of the assassination plan, and the justice of her conviction is still debated. Lupino used this uncertainty to sharpen her examination of how Surratt's marginalized status may have affected her outcome.[12] Lupino's engagement with women's social problems and gender roles was foregrounded in her direction, as always, but this was not simply because she was a woman. More important was her experience as a postwar filmmaker who had moved from slick Hollywood products to B movies, with dark themes that had a vital undercurrent of repression and female claustrophobia.

"The Trial of Mary Surratt" is a twenty-seven-minute drama, including introduction and credits, and stars Virginia Gregg as Surratt.[13] A pivotal scene shows Surratt being unfairly interrogated by men in power: a senator and an attorney.[14] Lupino's framing of Surratt in medium close-up, in her dark, cramped jail cell, portrays her as a woman trapped by circumstances and powerless against her male accusers. When Senator Corbett (played by Ray Collins), asks Surratt, "How can I believe you?" she replies, "You can't. You're a man." Only her face is illuminated inside the bleak cell, as cinematographer George Diskant employs shadowy noir expressionism. Surratt looks off, frustrated and angry. "I fetched their meals, made their beds. Took messages for them. They didn't bother to tell me anything." She adds, her drawl pronounced, "What m-a-a-an tells a woman what he's plannin' till it's all done?" She turns on her interrogator, asking, "Does your wife know that you're here in the jail tonight? Did you ask her what she thought about your coming here?" The senator shakes his head. "No."[15] Lupino's Surratt is angry and impassioned: she meets the senator's passive-aggressive attitude with defiance and exposes women's invisibility in a male-defined, male-dominated world. "The Trial of Mary Surratt" is a reaction to postwar oppression of the feminine and the intolerable repression experienced by both sexes.

The distinction between justice and power is a common theme in Ray and Lupino's narratives. Both were wary of traps, imprisonment, and "adults" in power. Lupino used the drama and thriller genres to delineate issues of justice for and the victimization of women. In "The Trial of Mary Surratt," her focus was on the rush to judge Surratt guilty, a rush implemented by the men in power.

The success of the episode increased Lupino's stock in the television industry. After the Surratt episode wrapped, job offers increased, as she noted in her interview with Weiner: "And from then on it became like a snowball. They'd book me in advance because they had to have answers in advance and I couldn't direct movies again until 1966, with *The Trouble with Angels*."[16]

Lupino and Aldrich

When Lupino transitioned into television as an actress on *Four Star Playhouse*, she was careful to curate an elegant entrance. The four stars—Lupino, Dick Powell, Charles Boyer, and David Niven—were a troupe of compatible entertainers, much like Lupino's family of circus performers. She seemed to enjoy the speed and the variety of the medium, securing "story by" credit for two of the episodes in which she acted: "The Story of Emily Cameron" and "The Stand-In."

In 1955, a sophisticated new television series, *Screen Directors Playhouse*, debuted on NBC. Although it ran for only one season, the anthology series attracted journeymen and auteur directors alike, including Leo McCarey, Frank Borzage, John Ford, Fred Zinnemann—and Lupino. She directed a single episode, "No. 5 Checked Out" (January 18, 1956), which was written by Willard Wiener from a story by Lupino and featured Teresa Wright; William Talman, who had starred in Lupino's noir masterwork, *The Hitch-Hiker*, in 1953; and an aging but still frighteningly layered Peter Lorre. Lester H. White is listed as cameraman, but Paul Ivano, Nicholas Ray's cameraman on *They Live by Night* (1948), is credited as well.[17]

"No. 5 Checked Out" was shot at Hal Roach Studios in Culver City. Filming started on December 13, 1955, and wrapped just four days later. The production statistics are evidence of Lupino's remarkable management and cinematic skills. According to Hal Roach Studios' Production Report, she finished fifty-seven script scenes, 34¼ pages, and 105 setups in four days, completing the trailer on December 19. Lupino shot 12,460 feet of film, using just over forty-six crew hours. Like Ray and Aldrich, Lupino shot in 35 mm. Her episode cost $50,591, with below-the-line services at $28,768 and above-the-line at $21,823, with the cast alone accounting for $11,053.[18]

Lupino's story is about a young deaf woman who runs a small tourist camp, Deep Lake Cabins, with her father. As the episode begins, a shot of the swinging sign at the camp's entrance immediately conveys that it is too isolated—a noir staple—with the word *deep* triggering subconscious unease. The camp might be a place of refuge from the city, out of the way and peaceful—Lupino's thematic city-country contrast—but we understand that Lupino's main character, Mary (played by Wright) is vulnerable in this setting. The camera then pans to the densely shadowed exterior of the tourist camp's office. The cinematographer—Paul Ivano—used classic noir lighting, creating moments of chiaroscuro that enhance Lupino's disquieting setting. As Barney (Talman) enters the room, he is in shadow, dramatically contrasting with Mary. A generous

HAL ROACH STUDIOS
PRODUCTION BUDGET

SERIES Screen Director's Playhouse DAYS 4 DATE December 7, 1955

TITLE "Number 5 Checked Out" NUMBER 9647 TIME

		BUDGET		NOTES:
118-01	STORY	3177	00	
118-02	SUPERVISION	1925	00	
118-03	CAST	11853	00	
118-04	S.D.G.	3000	00	
118005	AMORTIZATION	1000	00	
118-29	COMP. INSURANCE	145	00	
118-30	PAYROLL TAXES ETC.	723	00	
	TOTAL ABOVE LINE	21,823	00	
118-10	PRODUCTION STAFF	1530	00	
118-11	WARDROBE	475	00	
118-12	MAKEUP-HAIRDRESS	475	00	
118-13	SET DESIGNING	425	00	
118-14	SET CONSTRUCTION	3945	00	
118-15	SET STRIKING	390	00	
118-16	SET DRESSING	1730	00	
118-17	SET OPERATION	2377	00	
118-18	ELECTRICAL	735	00	
118-19	CAMERA	1307	00	
118-20	SOUND	1200	00	
118-21	OPTICAL EFFECTS	300	00	
118-22	FILM & LABORATORY	3750	00	
118-23	BACK PROJECTION			
118-24	EDITORIAL	1575	00	
118-25	PREVIEW EXPENSE			
118-26	TRANSPORTATION	1040	00	
118-27	LOCATION	954	00	
118-28	MUSIC	300	00	
118-29	INSURANCE	346	00	
118-30	PAYROLL TAXES & FRINGE BENIFITS	2185	00	
118-31	STUDIO CHARGES	3030	00	
118-32	LABOR IMPOUNDS	699	00	
	TOTAL BELOW LINE	28,768	00	
	TOTAL ABOVE LINE	21,823	00	
	T O T A L	50,591	00	

Hal Roach Studios' production budget for "No. 5 Checked Out."

and kind spirit, she is brightly lit. We understand that Barney is a criminal—conflicted, but still a criminal.[19] As her name suggests, Mary is a virginal presence. She desires love, but consummation is impossible because her disability makes her undesirable. Having given up on relationships, Mary exudes a pervasive melancholy. She uses her deafness as a protection against loss and danger. The lack of open communication between Mary and Barney on the conscious level, with a deepening understanding between them on a deeper level, creates a sense of unrequited love that links the episode to film noir.[20]

Lupino cast Peter Lorre as Willy, Barney's partner. Lorre, a classically trained actor of Austrian-Hungarian descent, was indelibly linked to noir through repeated typecasting as a foreign, sinister presence. Audiences particularly identified him with his role in Fritz Lang's *M* (1931), in which he plays a serial killer who preys on little girls.[21] Lupino uses that baggage deftly, imprinting the suggestion in viewers' minds that real horror is to come. In "No. 5 Checked Out," he is yet again a psychopathic monster, completely devoid of empathy, which differentiates him from Barney. Whereas Barney is the getaway driver in a heist gone bad, Willy is a killer who needlessly murders a young man during the robbery. As Lupino had done in *The Hitch-Hiker*, she developed her characters carefully, showing levels of corruption rather than good-versus-evil binaries. This allows the audience to develop some empathy for Barney while rightly fearing the vicious Willy. The way Lorre handles his cigarette between his thumb and forefinger, his offhanded gun wielding, and his hypnotic twirling of his watch fob all contribute to his layered performance. These bits of stage business, which Lupino may have given to Lorre to add reality to his character, help create a subtle portrait that pushes against the melodramatic mode.

Lupino used costuming to define her characters. Willy, always in black, is deadly—an irredeemable criminal. Barney, in beige or light-checkered flannel, is a reluctant one. In another context, he might have loved the outdoors, wildlife, and living in a bucolic environment. He could, we surmise, live happily ever after with Mary, whose innocence and, particularly, deafness have initiated Barney's newfound moral awareness. The voice-over that introduces the episode hints at the stakes for Mary: "Tonight, *Screen Directors Playhouse* proudly presents Miss Ida Lupino, renowned for her direction of *The Hitch-Hiker* and *The Bigamist*. For this evening, Miss Lupino brings us the searching story of a deaf girl and the man she is afraid to love, entitled 'No. 5 Checked Out.'" By setting Willy's murderous disregard for life against Barney's hope for a new life with Mary, Lupino invoked a gripping dread that escalates until the very end.

As the action starts, Lupino's camera follows Mary as she moves through the office to the bedroom, where she is packing her father's suitcase (again, independent activity) in preparation for his trip to visit an ailing relative. As Mary and her father discuss his uneasiness at leaving her alone, Lupino avoids shot–reverse shots, using two-shots and close-ups, keeping the beat simple, subtle, and clear. The scene is fluid and efficient, with the cuts unnoticed. The thoughtful construction produces an emotionally moving exchange between father and daughter. After her father leaves, Mary sits alone. She places her hands on the radio beside her, which she can't hear. She concentrates on the speaker's vibrations while a slowly swinging instrumental number plays, as if the pulsing might give her a new life. Lupino communicated not only the intensity of Mary's desire to hear but also, perhaps, her sexual frustration in three subtle shots.

Lupino's camera cuts again to the ominously dark exterior as a black car drives up the dirt road outside the office. Barney pulls up, leaves the car, and walks to the office door, accompanied by the music from Mary's radio. Viewers who had seen Talman in *The Hitch-Hiker* know immediately that he is a threat to Mary's well-being. This economic sequence conveys the richness of classic black-and-white noir photography even in the restricted frame. Lupino's camera is filming for the small screen but employs the painterly composition that she had imposed on the big screen. The viewer senses life beyond Lupino's frame. The dense darkness of the cabin's exterior at night is an obvious contrast to the bright light that illuminates the daytime scenes, especially as Mary and Barney spend a sweetly romantic morning fishing by the lake. (Lupino shot the scene at Malibu Lake in the Santa Monica Mountains.)

Talman's character is introduced in much the same way that his character was introduced in *The Hitch-Hiker*. As Barney walks up to the office, low-key lighting puts his face half in shadow, but the brighter lighting in subsequent scenes suggests that he isn't the cold-blooded killer of *The Hitch-Hiker*. Lupino was intent on creating a nuanced picture of criminality and showed Barney as surprised and a little hopeful by the psychological change he is undergoing. Casting Talman as a redeemable criminal rather than a murderer confused viewers' expectations, increasing the tension they experienced as they watched Lupino's triangle of characters: the psychopathic Willy, the confused and anxious Barney, the guarded and vulnerable Mary. These gray areas of humanity are essential film gris.

Lupino foreshadowed death in a dramatic exterior shot of the cabin. First, we see a white number 5, which stands out from the deeply shadowed wall. The camera pans to the cabin's mullioned windows, where Talman stares out, visibly upset.[22] He draws the blinds. Lupino's camera cuts to the interior of the cabin, where Barney is reading aloud from a newspaper story about a robbery to a man sitting in a leather wing chair, whose face is hidden from the camera. The camera stays on Barney in a wide shot that shows only the man's left hand and the cigarette he holds. Its smoke swirls above the arm of the leather chair as the second man speaks. The audience can't see his face, but they would immediately recognize Lorre's sinister voice. Barney is agitated and scared because Willy murdered a man during this robbery. "You said there wasn't going to be any shooting. That's what you said!" Barney exclaims. "Says here the guy was only twenty-eight years old. Married, two kids!" Lupino took as much advantage as she could of Lorre's "bad guy" baggage. When she cut from a medium shot of Barney to a medium shot of Willy, she was playing on Lorre's fame as the self-satisfied child killer in Lang's *M*. Unconcerned, Willy replies, "Oh no. Oh that's too bad. Boys or girls?" It is a moment of Lupinian dark humor, which is underlined when Barney barks, "It's no joke," and Willy responds, "Am I laughing?"

This is essentials-only filmmaking. In six shots, Lupino gave us all the dramatized exposition we need. She continued this alchemical synthesis to the end of the episode. As in Ray's *On Dangerous Ground* (1952), in which Lupino had played a blind woman, the woman's disability marks her as a possible victim. Compromised by her deafness, Mary is in great danger. In this Lupinian world of masculine threat, the safety promised by the bucolic, isolated setting is an illusion.

Mary's deafness, however, has made her strong, giving her control of her environment, whereas Barney becomes increasingly uncertain and unmoored. This reflects Lupino's sympathy for bewildered characters—what Therese Grisham and Julie Grossman refer to as her "cinema of empathy"—as well as her sensitivity to women's issues.[23] Lupino's bewildered people are outsiders, but they are also tough noir figures. This is evident at the ending of "No. 5 Checked Out." As Mary gazes at the stillness of the lake, waiting for Barney to return, Barney and Willy exchange gunshots on the hillside right behind her. The camera focuses on Mary as she floats in a mental world, far away from the reality of a place that cannot sustain her and completely unaware of the violence that she cannot see or hear. Willy collapses, and Lupino's camera cuts to a three-shot looking down the hillside. Near the top is Willy, dead; at the bottom is Mary, sitting silent at the lake's edge. Between them, Barney crawls toward Mary, who is oblivious to his desperate attempt to reach her. In a final effort, Barney weakly tosses his car keys toward her with a bloodied hand. Lupino's final shot, before the screen goes black, is of the keys lying in the dirt. Barney's hope for a different future has been lost, and Mary's isolation is complete. The episode ends in satisfying ambiguity as Mary's story remains with us, unresolved. The last scene is an eerie set piece, beautifully wrought and incredibly spare, like a tone poem. Lupino's half hour is jam-packed.

Unlike Lupino, Bob Aldrich got his start not as an actor but as an assistant director in Hollywood's Poverty Row boot camp. Like Lupino, however, Aldrich was part of the guerrilla alliance that moved between film and television productions. A versatile director, Aldrich could film television episodes in three to four days as well as direct Academy-nominated and award-winning films.[24] Aldrich, like Lupino, used noir motifs and expressionistic lighting, but unlike Lupino, he was a favorite of the New Wave critics, earning the badge of auteur. His work was surveyed in *Les Grande Créateurs du Cinéma*, a series of monographs on film directors that was published by the Club du Livre de Cinéma in Brussels.[25] Like Lupino, Aldrich avoids strict binaries such as good versus evil in his explorations of morality and creates stories that are ambiguous, with characters who struggle internally. The characters of both directors are trapped, sometimes in their past, sometimes within their own obsessive, controlling needs. Aldrich's genres of choice—noir, psychological melodrama, and the neo-gothic—are another commonality with Lupino. Aldrich's noir style can be seen in the five episodes he made for *Four Star Playhouse*, including "The Bad Streak."[26]

"The Bad Streak" (January 14, 1954), starring Charles Boyer and Virginia Grey, is a drama about gambling, losing, and starting over with nothing.[27] The photography was by George Diskant, who worked with Lupino on her independent film *The Bigamist*; her directed television episode for *Dante* (NBC), "Opening Night" (October 10, 1960); and several episodes in which she acted, including five for *Mr. Adams and Eve*. Diskant worked with Ray on *They Live by Night* and *On Dangerous Ground*, the latter of which starred Lupino—more collaborations within the guerrilla alliance. The story is straightforward: Renneck, Charles Boyer's character, owns a casino that is experiencing a bad streak—the business has been losing money. One night his grown son, David (played by Robert R. Arthur), whom he has never met, walks in and begins to win steadily, threatening to break the casino's bank. Renneck confronts his son, and they agree to have one last game: blackjack. Renneck wins back the casino's money, but then he secretly puts it into a trust for his son, bankrupting his business. Now broke, Renneck and his girlfriend start over.

The episode opens with archival black-and-white exterior footage of flashing neon signs. The most prominent proclaims that Reno is "The Biggest Little City in the World." This, plus the pulsing music, establishes the tone of the episode in seconds, which is vital for the run time of about twenty-five minutes. Aldrich's camera cuts to Boyer; he knew from his many live dramas that it's important to show the star as soon as possible. Aldrich used only three interiors—a bar, a gaming area, and Renneck's office in the casino—and kept the frame tight, engaging his audience with a variety of shots and realistic,

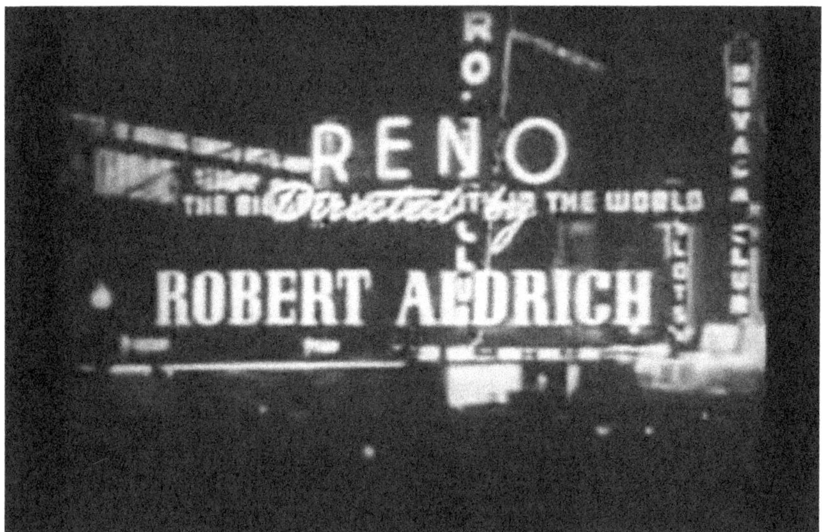

Opening credits for "The Bad Streak," establishing a pre–Rat Pack Reno location and tone for the Robert Aldrich–directed episode about gambling.

subtle performances. As the action starts, Virginia Grey, playing Angela, wears a light-colored dress, while Boyer wears a black suit and is shot with his face half in shadow. These were common noir codes, well understood by audiences of the time.

Aldrich had studied the acting techniques of Sanford Meisner, which helped him tailor his shots to his actors' choices of independent activities and thus to their performances.[28] Close-ups widen out to deeper focus, allowing Angela to walk up to and away from Renneck in a fluid sequence in which the camera remains invisible. The repeated shot of Angela approaching Renneck sends a subtextual message that she wants something from the casino owner. She is concerned and needy, while he suppresses his feelings, deep in thought. Aldrich placed Renneck in shadow to reflect his worries about his business. Aldrich blocked out his angles well in advance, as Lupino often did, and he chose subtlety over exposition, transcending conventions not only of genre but of the television medium overall. For example, as Renneck and Angela argue, they turn their backs to the audience, demonstrating their alienation from each other as the audience listens to them quarrel.

In noir and crime dramas, Aldrich often combined strong side lighting with close-ups of the protagonist, and although he liked unusual framing and high- and low-angle shots, neither he nor Lupino shot from these angles unless it supported the narrative and the genre. Both Lupino and Aldrich were always prepared but at the same time open to considering actors' ideas, as long as filming kept to the schedule.

As the action continues, Renneck confronts his son, David, on the casino floor, where David is making a killing—a symbolic patricide. Renneck and David move away from the roulette table; the frame is cluttered with the crowd of gamblers in the background. This contrasts with a triangulated shot during the father and son's final game of blackjack, in which Aldrich's blocking focuses as much attention as possible on the drama unfolding within the frame. A high-angle shot shows the abandoned son and misunderstood father facing each other across the table. When Renneck decides to place his winnings in trust for his son, everyone, including Angela, is in black, reflecting the death of Renneck's business.

In 1977–1978, Aldrich visited a directing class at the American Film Institute. During his presentation, he reflected on his work in television and noted that directing is a craft. He continued, "You have to practice that craft. Television offered that practice."[29] In "The Bad Streak," Aldrich offset the limitations of working with only three interiors, finding various ways to shoot the same settings, filling the frame and layering the background. He used alternating blocking and deep focus to suggest crowds where he had none and low-key and side lighting to emphasize character. The spare dramatic overhead shot emphasizes the gravity of the final card game, in which Renneck must make a difficult choice. If he keeps his winnings, he can finance his casino, but if he doesn't help his son, he will have abandoned him once again. It is Renneck's second chance at fatherhood. This ending, like many of Lupino's, is ambiguous and bittersweet.

This comparative look at Lupino's "No. 5 Checked Out" and Aldrich's "The Bad Streak" demonstrates thematic and stylistic similarities between these two directors for hire. The solutions Aldrich and Lupino found within the limitations of television directing were on a par. Both directors used framing and lighting not only to realize the text but also to complete the psychology of their main characters. Their feature films may have had much bigger budgets and far more generous schedules, but their work for television revealed the skill, experience, and flexibility of both directors. Their sheer know-how is evident in both media.

Lupino and Hitchcock

Alfred Hitchcock admired the work that Lupino—his female counterpart—created for television.[30] Both directors shared a love for suspense and action, which created continuity between their directed feature films and television episodes. The themes of Hitchcock's television episodes relate directly to his larger works, as film scholar Steve Mamber has noted that closer scrutiny of these small movies could give us even more information about Hitchcock the artist. The same is true for Lupino, whose television brand is consistent with that of her independent films. In both media, she explored gender confusion for women in a dangerous, masculinist world; sympathized with her marginalized characters; and experimented with genre hybrids. Director Barry Jenkins has pointed out that there are many women today who direct television well because they have been making small, independent films for years.[31] Lupino immediately became part of a select group of skilled directors in demand who could turn out high-quality television within a rigorous, three-to-four-day shoot.

Lupino directed two episodes of *Alfred Hitchcock Presents*. The first was "Sybilla" (December 6, 1960), for which Hitchcock had offered Lupino the title role. Lupino chose to direct instead. The teleplay was written by Charlotte Armstrong, based on a story by Margaret Manners, and produced by Joan Harrison. Cinematographer John Warren and editor Edward W. Williams were on Lupino's above-the-line crew. The episode stars Barbara Bel Geddes and Alexander Scourby, with Bartlett Robinson, Madge Kennedy, and Gordon Wynn. The darkly comic introduction to the episode shows Hitchcock standing in front of a sign that reads "Lovers' Leap." We watch a young couple walk up a slope behind him, arms around each other's waists, toward the cliff that we understand is just outside the frame. The suggestion is that they plan to take the leap together . . . until the lady returns alone, meets another man, and kisses him with familiarity. Hitchcock used the unseen cliff as a cliffhanger, and this wry comment on love is carried through in the episode that follows.

We meet the two main characters, Sybilla Meade (played by Bel Geddes) and her husband, Horace (Scourby), just after they married. It is clear from the outset that this is not a typical newlywed relationship. Sybilla says everything a subservient wife should, but we understand quickly that she has another agenda. Grisham and Grossman note that the psychology of this episode is "in keeping with Lupino's penchant for dissecting matrimony" and that Lupino investigates one of her favorite ideas: "Sybilla is a provocative figure who sets off men's insecurity and projection," a femme fatale who forces men "to reveal their own neuroses."[32]

Lupino's second episode was "A Crime for Mothers" (January 24, 1961). Henry Slesar wrote the teleplay, which was based on his story by this title in *Alfred Hitchcock's Mystery Magazine*.[33] The episode was again produced by Joan Harrison. It starred the strong character actress Claire Trevor, whom Lupino had directed a decade earlier in *Hard, Fast and Beautiful*. Trevor had received rave reviews for her portrayal of a morally ambivalent tennis mother who pushes her daughter to win at all costs. In "A Crime for Mothers," Trevor plays

Title card for Lupino's Hitchcock series episode "A Crime for Mothers," starring Claire Trevor.

Mrs. Meade, an alcoholic who had given up her infant daughter, Eileen, who is now turning seven years old. Having fallen on hard times, Meade blackmails the young couple, the Birdwells (an ironic Hitchcockian name), who have lovingly raised the girl. Eileen was never formally adopted, so Meade threatens to take back the child unless she is paid. The ending is a double twist that has the iconic suspense and dark humor for which Hitchcock and Lupino are known.

The episode opens with a domestic scene in which Jane and Ralph Birdwell (played by Patricia Smith and Robert Sampson) are discussing a gigantic doll that Jane has purchased for Eileen's birthday. It is a happy domestic scene, if darkly comic. The doll is ridiculous in its overly large size, but its artificiality suggests that it will come alive at any moment—a tried and true horror cliché, but here with a happy-face twist. A knock on the door brings a different scare, however. Jane opens the door, and we see Meade posed in the doorway like a movie star. Lupino's camera depicts her as a beautiful, glamorous woman from a completely foreign world; she is the antithesis of the motherly domesticity emphasized in the opening. Obviously drunk, Meade enters without an invitation, disrupting the family's comfortable morning routine. She walks past Jane into the house, looking around the Birdwells' living room with appreciation. Lupino's famously mobile camera is efficient and alive, following Meade with a moving one-shot as she turns and strolls toward the bright sunlight of the patio, then turns back toward the camera. After playing with the doll, which Jane takes away, Meade plops down on a couch and starts to shrug off her coat. She seems to be making herself at home, further alarming the young couple.

Lupino's work with Trevor in this sequence creates a tour de force introduction into the Birdwells' home.

Throughout the episode, Lupino took great care with the contrasts that underline the difference between the kind and loving Birdwells and the dissolute Meade. For Trevor's character of the bad mother, Lupino costumed her in fur, with heavy makeup and jewelry. Mrs. Meade is the stark opposite of the good mother, Jane Birdwell, whose simple dress with its Peter Pan collar emphasizes her innocence. The Birdwells live in a comfortable middle-class home that suggests a happy family life; Meade's apartment is run-down and unkempt, indicating her moral laxity.

Like Lupino's independent feature films and many of her episodes for television, "A Crime for Mothers" is a slyly provocative piece that reflects a contemporary social issue. In 1960, psychiatrist Marshall D. Schechter published a study claiming that adopted children were one hundred times more likely than their nonadopted counterparts to show up in clinical populations.[34] Debate ensued about adopted children's risk factors for mental illness, and studies proliferated around children and various adoption practices, as well as the potential and real abuse suffered by adoptees.[35] Lupino's episode asks these pointed questions: What if a birth mother changes her mind and wants her child back? Is the mother's claim always stronger than that of the adoptive parents?

Meade, who is desperate for money, is approached by a private investigator, Phil Ames (Biff Elliot), who suggests a plot to extort a huge sum from the Birdwells: Meade will abduct and ransom her own child. Because Meade is the birth mother, Ames says persuasively, she technically won't be kidnapping. Meade, however, has not seen the child since birth, so she unwittingly plays into a reverse sting. Ames is Ralph Birdwell's friend—and Meade is caught in her own trap. The child, it turns out, is the detective's daughter. The Birdwells have not put an innocent child in jeopardy, and Meade is now guilty of kidnapping. Ames, backed up by an FBI agent, exposes the con to Meade and threatens to arrest her if she ever bothers the Birdwells again.

This double twist is as surprising as it is suspenseful, a combination that is tricky to realize effectively, but Lupino successfully created both suspense and surprise in "A Crime for Mothers." In a presentation in 1970, Hitchcock discussed the difference between surprise as in a mystery, an "intellectual process," and suspense, "an emotional process."[36] Suspense creates fear in the audience, which must lead to a revelation and thus relief.

Lupino employed deft camera work, choosing particular angles for Meade, Ames, and the child, to emphasize their very different personalities. The discrete selection of angles and lenses was also vital to Hitchcock. Lupino incorporated elegant pans and lens-perfect movie star close-ups, especially of Meade, and she used her camera to contrast Meade, who is devoid of domestic instincts, with household items in the apartment. One of Lupino's—and Hitchcock's—hallmarks was the use of ironic inserts that advanced the narrative by focusing on objects in juxtaposition. As the "wrong" child jumps on the couch in Meade's apartment, for example, Lupino's camera frames the child's bouncing feet, which jar a liquor bottle from its hiding place beneath a pillow.

The double twist that ends "A Crime for Mothers" and the episode's subversive domestic context are pure Lupino, but they are also pure Hitchcock, as seen in the Hitchcock-directed "Lamb to the Slaughter" (April 13, 1958), an episode of *Alfred Hitchcock Presents*. From a story by Roald Dahl, who also wrote the teleplay, is quintessential Hitchcock. The episode stars Barbara Bel Geddes as Mary Maloney, the sweet—and pregnant—wife of a cop. In the twenty-six minutes and eleven seconds of run time, Hitchcock turns the submissive Mary into a darkly comic killer who, in the last scene, visually anticipates *Psycho*'s Norman Bates.

The story begins as Mary tidies up the couple's living room, preparing for the return of her husband, Patrick (played by a hulking Allan Lane), from work. The furnishings are fussy, implying that the home is a domestic trap. As Patrick strides in, we see he is a uniformed cop twice Mary's size. He pushes past Mary, ignoring her kiss on his cheek. He takes a few stiff drinks and informs Mary that he is leaving her. She can keep her baby when it is born, but he wants out. He has fallen in love with someone else.

In the first suggestion that Mary is psychotic, she decides that dinner will help change Patrick's mind. She wanders into the garage and opens the deep freezer. A bright, otherworldly light blasts up into her face, like a sign from hell, and she pulls out a leg of lamb and carries it into the kitchen. Mary begs Patrick to stay, but Patrick, his back toward Mary as he stands in the living room, prepares to leave for good. Mary exclaims, "I won't let you," and Patrick replies, "Try and stop me!" As he turns around, Mary walks into the living room, the leg of lamb still in her hand. She hits Patrick hard over the head with the frozen meat, killing him instantly. Mary makes a phone call to establish an alibi and then, in an economical sequence, leaves the house, goes to the market, comes home, and drops the grocery bag and her purse just inside the doorway. Groceries roll across the living room floor. Mary then ransacks the room to make it look like the scene of an attack. Finally, she remembers the frozen lamb, putting it in a pan and roasting it in the oven.

The remainder of the half-hour episode is a police procedural. Both uniformed cops and suit-and-tie detectives swarm the house, checking the body, dusting for prints, looking around the property for the murder weapon, and asking Mary a lot of questions. The lead detective, played by character actor

Harold J. Stone, does not believe there was a scuffle: there are no marks on the body, and Mary's husband was hit from behind. Stone concludes that his attacker was someone he knew because he hadn't pulled his gun. Hitchcock's camera focuses on the detective's discussion of the weapon as the lamb cooks. Mary suggests that the police stay and eat the meat; it will go to waste otherwise. The camera pans away from the detectives at the dining room table as they eat the lamb, leaving only the bone in the center. In the background, uniformed cops sit on the staircase, eating off plates held in their hands.

Like Lupino, Hitchcock used suspenseful inserts, such as the stove and the oven's control knob; dissolves from Mary's earnest face, urging the detectives to eat, to a shot of them around the table, consuming the murder weapon; and a mobile camera panning around the living room to show the police at work. The watercolors of birds that decorate Mary's walls reappear in *Psycho* and also in the Birdwells' home in Lupino's "A Crime for Mothers." Hitchcock's blocking is complex, accommodating the many men who assemble in Mary's living room. All are tall and meaty actors who wear heavy coats and hats and bear lots of paraphernalia. Their intimidating presence overshadows the "smallness" of the pregnant Mary, yet she remains in full control of the investigation, eventually getting away with murder.

Hitchcock placed the sociopathic Mary within the trappings of an *Ozzie and Harriet* existence. His framing is precise, inducing a claustrophobic atmosphere. He used specific camera angles for Mary and framed her against domestic backgrounds, illuminating her softly with low lamplight. As the episode ends, Hitchcock's camera shows Mary's final break with reality, using a long tracking shot to zoom in as she sits alone in the living room. Realizing she has committed the perfect murder, she smiles and erupts into a quiet giggle. As the camera moves into a close-up, we see the same deranged grin that two years later will belong to Norman Bates. We then hear Hitchcock's voice-over: "As for Mary Maloney, she would have gone scot free if she hadn't tried to do in her second husband the same way. Unfortunately, he was the forgetful type and had forgotten to plug in the freezer. The meat was as soft as jelly. Speaking of plugs, that is precisely what our sponsor wants to do for his product."[37]

Lupino's Other Episodes

Lupino directed notable episodes for many other television series besides Hitchcock's, including *The Twilight Zone* and *Sam Benedict* (NBC, 1962–1963), a legal drama starring Edmond O'Brien. Comparisons between her work and the work of another TV director for each of these two series demonstrates how Lupino elevated the art of television directing. Lupino, who was the only woman to ever direct for Rod Serling's *The Twilight Zone*, filmed one episode, "The Masks." Don Siegel directed two episodes, "Uncle Simon" (November 15, 1963), starring Cedric Hardwicke and Constance Ford, and "The Self-Improvement of Salvadore Ross" (January 17, 1964). Siegel directed dozens of films over his long career, including *Private Hell 36* (1954), produced by Lupino's Filmakers, and classics like *Dirty Harry* (1971). Despite his reputation as a director of hard-boiled action adventures, Siegel's camera in his *Twilight Zone* episodes is static. Lupino's camera work in "The Masks," in contrast, is dynamic, providing more energy to every scene. Siegel's direction is straightforward, his blocking is stagy, and the performances are weak. Consequently, his episodes are rigid, while Lupino's are fluid. Jack Edmund Nolan, writing in *Films in Review*, notes that "The Masks" is "vividly directed."[38] Lupino's episode is considered one of the finest in the series.[39]

A comparison of one of Lupino's episodes for *Sam Benedict*, "Sugar and Spice and Everything . . ." (February 6, 1963), with an episode by Don Medford, "Hear the Mellow Wedding Bells" (November 3, 1962), is also illuminating. Medford, a prolific television director, was hired to direct two *Sam Benedict* episodes.[40] His direction of "Hear the Mellow Wedding Bells" is stagnant and dull, relying on wide, establishing static shots. Lupino, in contrast, used slow, imperceptible dolly tracks and sweeping views of exteriors and interiors, and she drew deep performances from her actors. The financial disparity between the two episodes is instructive. Medford's budget for his episode was $120,900, with another $26,001 for casting. He exceeded both budget lines, the former by $6,905 and the latter by $6,001. This is unexpected because his setups were minimally complex. Lupino had the same budget for her episode, $120,900, but a lower casting budget, at $21,523. When she wrapped her episode, she was only slightly overbudget, by $1,000, and her expenditure for her cast was underbudget by $123. Yet her shot list comprises an extraordinary twenty-three complex setups, a remarkable accomplishment, particularly in light of Medford's work. Medford was paid $3,131 to direct; Lupino received $2,865. Lupino delivered an episode that was essentially on budget, and her shots were more interesting. The estimate for Lupino's art director, set decorator, set designer, and set totaled $2,301. Medford's set design and artwork were only budgeted at $1,814.[41] The assistant director for both episodes was Erich von Stroheim Jr.

Siegel and Medford were veteran directors, but Lupino's episodes for *The Twilight Zone* and *Sam Benedict* are more complex and more engaging, not only because of her skill with the camera but also because of her more cinematic, modern, and realistic performances.[42] Because of her long career and her experience as a working actress, Lupino had a deep understanding of authentic acting. She could elicit fine performances from her entire cast, whether she was working with principal actors or day players.[43] Her episodes are full of noir references and impressive camerawork. She found new ways to shoot that elevated her productions from what might have been static to something fresh and exciting.

A good example is a scene at the end of "Sugar and Spice and Everything . . ." We see a close-up of feet dancing around a transistor radio on the floor, which is patterned by noir shadows from prison bars. In the courtroom, expert witnesses discuss the details of gun markings—another instance of Lupino's brand of docudrama and painterly crosscutting. The episode ends with a twist, as the lawyer for the defense asks the defendant, "Did you kill your husband?" and she responds, "Yes I did." Lupino's camera wipes to black and then opens slowly on a reel-to-reel tape recorder. An unreliable narrator asks, in voice-over, "Who really is guilty, and what happened to Amy Vickers?" With her trademark brand of ambiguity, Lupino once again leaves the audience wondering.

Chapter 9

PATTERNS AND STRATEGIES IN LUPINO'S TELEVISION DIRECTING

Darling, we have a three-day schedule. There is no time to do anything but to do it.

Ida Lupino in Wheeler Winston Dixon, "The Hitch-Hiker," *Senses of Cinema 50*, April 2009

Over her long career, Lupino's use of genre, the way she moved the camera, her lighting style, her expert use of lenses, and her nuanced and subtle direction of actors combined to make her an acknowledged creative force. When she moved into television, she continued to film suspense narratives, but she also widened her range to a variety of hard-hitting action dramas. Lupino's work in this genre prefigured the later work of Kathryn Bigelow, who was the first woman to win an Academy Award for Best Director, in 2010 for *The Hurt Locker* (2008). Because of Lupino's restrained modernist hybrid style, distinct voice, and exemplary skill set, she was asked to return to some of the most popular and more complex action series, including *The Untouchables*, *The Fugitive*, *Thriller*, *Have Gun—Will Travel*, *Hong Kong*, *Mr. Novak*, and *Breaking Point*.

The patterns and strategies in Lupino's work for television warrant deeper analysis. Much of this work—including her role in *Mr. Adams and Eve*—was influenced by her independent films. Her half-hour and one-hour westerns, dramas, and action and suspense thrillers, made on microbudgets with four- to five-day shoots, represent the best of classic television. Her flexibility during this period remains unexplored, especially in relation to her roles as mother and wife and her direction of actors, the latter of which is particularly under-researched. A close reading of her authorship during this formative time in the television industry offers a better understanding of American film and television history and honors her work as an art form.

Lupino transitioned from acting in film to acting and directing in 1949. About seven years later, she made a second transition, from television acting into acting and directing. After she began directing television episodes, her appearances on television became rare, and most roles were in neorealist or suspense dramas about aging within the film business. As a director, Lupino continued to take on provocative subjects about marginalized characters.

Watching Lupino's and Duff's star turn in *Mr. Adams and Eve* reveals that Lupino drove the satiric story to create once again an unusual genre hybrid: part comedy, part exposé. The series comments on stardom in an ironic fashion, producing a narrative that is more complex and intimate than much of what was available on television at the time. Most television performances in the 1950s were, as Christine Becker notes, "part of a constructed strategy born of the specific industrial, cultural and programming catalysts that formed the medium."[1] Many critics thought a move from film to television sounded the death knell for a star's career, but this was not the case. As Hal Humphrey, a popular television critic, pointed out, simply and correctly, stars like Ann Sothern and Joan Crawford were not has-beens: "The medium's rekindling of these old celluloid luminaries has caused some of Hollywood's so-called elite or upper crust to dismiss TV as the place where the old-timers crawl off to die. . . . Actually, in many instances, it's been a case of TV proving that the movie studios had scrapped actors whose talents were far from being played out."[2] The Hollywood brand of glamour was increasingly seen as inauthentic and outdated. Instead, the intimacy of television promised its viewers authenticity.

Mr. Adams and Eve was the modern choice for television viewers, contradicting the happy nuclear family that was the focus of other postwar series. Most sitcoms in the 1950s were about ordinary people, so it was highly unusual to develop a series around a glamorous Hollywood couple. But Lupino, a real-life film actress, screenwriter, and film and television director, was in no way ordinary. She became Eve Drake, a fictional movie star, complicating her already complex image. Unlike the characters who portrayed ideal housewives, Eve Drake escapes the drudgery of the home because she is a famous movie star. To twist the narrative further, Eve is a success in Hollywood, but she is a failure in the home. Her husband, Howard Adams—played by Howard Duff, Lupino's real-life husband—is the straight man for her comic entanglements. Although their onscreen relationship resembled that of star couples Desi Arnaz and Lucille Ball and George Burns and Gracie Allen, the tone of *Mr. Adams and Eve* was completely different. In a 1957 *TV Guide* article, Robert Johnston argued that Lupino and Duff "were putting on the funniest documentary on TV."[3]

The series satirizes the outmoded movie star system. Vastly different from *I Love Lucy's* screwball figure American audiences knew, Eve Adams is a hard-driving, hyper-focused veteran with no patience for any sort of unprofessionalism. Lupino was a tough perfectionist who successfully acted in opposition to her television image—exactly like the real-life Lucille Ball. In an episode titled "The Life Story of Eve Drake and Howard Adams" (November 1, 1957), the scriptwriters can't reconcile the many versions of the characters' biographies with the premise of the comedy: that the glamour of stardom is inauthentic, and that stars' personalities are vacuous and ultimately disappointing. Another episode in the same vein, "Academy Award" (March 22, 1957), emphasizes the studio-contrived lives behind the camera and the conflicts that ensue. Although *Mr. Adams and Eve* reveals an aspect of Hollywood reality, it contains no truthful revelations about the Lupino-Duff marriage; indeed, they separated soon after the series ended.

Lupino, because she was fluid across media, was the perfect anomalous mix for a sitcom that ironically jeered at "Hollywood star lives" while acknowledging the new blurring of film and television personalities. At the same time, Lupino's multifaceted identity as wife, mother, writer, director, and producer could be exploited. In an episode titled "Howard and Eve and Ida" (April 22, 1958), Lupino, as herself, is hired by an unnamed studio to shoot a star vehicle for Howard Adams and Eve Drake.[4] Eve is jealous because Lupino and Adams had a former relationship. In the opening shot of the episode, Adams talks directly to the audience: "Over here is Eve Drake, and over here is Ida Lupino. Stick around and see how it turns out." At the end of the episode, Adams looks back at the television audience and says, "Now my problem is, which one do I go home with?" Howard puts his arms around both women, and they all walk off together: he takes home both versions.[5]

Popular with many audiences, *Mr. Adams and Eve* received consistently good reviews, and the industry nominated Lupino for an Emmy in 1957 for Best Actress in a Comedy Series. Although she was not nominated for writing or directing, a production fragment from a *Mr. Adams and Eve* script provides evidence of her involvement with different aspects of production. The script contains suggestions, new dialogue, and cuts in Lupino's hand, as well as notes on the script's title page also in Lupino's handwriting: "Bring 2 trays," "Bring tux shirt," "Bring two pairs of loafers, and a pants shirt." The penciled notes show that Lupino was involved in aspects of production other than acting, including set design and writing. Although she may not have received credit for all she did, she constantly collaborated with the writer, Sol Saks, on every sequence of the episode.[6]

In a chaotic and contradictory media world, *Mr. Adams and Eve* offered a fresh narrative and was an unusually sophisticated sitcom. Taking risks by being different, and full of self-mockery, it continually lampooned star images and the rigid studio system. The show exhibited the qualities that were becoming necessary for the more modern celebrity and represented the 1950s diaspora from film to television. The sponsors used Lupino and Duff—and their guest stars, such as Robert Cummings and Alfred Hitchcock—to natively advertise Camel cigarettes, Lustre-Creme shampoo (the "Hollywood" shampoo), Lustre-Net hair spray, American Express, and a variety of other products. Viewer resistance to the products could be quelled by allowing the stars, who were perfectly situated as television sponsors, to do the product promotion. And of course, they could do it much better. Lupino and Duff were even invited to the White House by President Lyndon Johnson to greet Eisaku Satō, the Japanese prime minister. Satō liked the show, which was popular in Japan.[7]

Television, where jobs for Lupino were easily available to her, gave her the opportunity to create multiple meanings as she worked with rich texts that attracted large and devoted audiences in a rapidly changing media culture. Her successes with science fiction fantasy (*The Twilight Zone*) and gritty westerns (*Have Gun—Will Travel*) were widely recognized by her colleagues in the television industry. As crime and action dramas and thrillers proliferated in the late 1950s and early 1960s, Lupino was asked to direct for the most widely watched and prestigious of these series: *The Untouchables*, *The Fugitive*, and *Thriller*.

The Untouchables

The Untouchables (ABC, 1959–1963), like all the series with Lupino-directed episodes, was one of the most popular on television.[8] This crime drama was based on the memoir of Eliot Ness, a federal crime fighter in Prohibition-era Chicago, whose agents were picked for their moral incorruptibility. The series, produced by Desilu Productions, was narrated by Walter Winchell, American journalist and powerfully influential gossip columnist. Each hour-long show comprised a teaser and four segments. Winchell's opening voice-over gave background and a who's who of the characters and added drama and suspense to the documentary style of the series. Robert Stack, who starred as Ness, won an Emmy for Best Actor in 1960. Each week, Stack costarred with Paul Picerni, Nicholas Georgiade, Abel Fernandez, and Steve London.

Lupino directed three episodes of *The Untouchables*: "A Fist of Five" (December 4, 1962), "The Man in the Cooler" (March 5, 1963), and "The Torpedo" (May 7, 1963), all of which aired during the show's last season. In "The Man in the Cooler," written by John Black, convict Al Remp (played by J. D. Cannon) agrees to work undercover for Ness in exchange for guaranteed early parole. Ness's target is Remp's old boss, bootlegger Fat Augie Strom (Peter Whitney). A deal with the feds is struck, but Remp remains dazzled by "the life" and grapples with the choice of returning to it or honoring his commitment to Ness. After Winchell's introduction, the first segment opens with a dialogue sequence that is typical of the show's format. As Ness makes his offer to Remp, Lupino's camera films their conversation with a noirish series of shots inside a dark jail cell. Behind them, shadows from the cell bars cross against a stark white background.

After the commercial break, documentary footage of the Chicago stockyards rolls on the screen as Winchell states that Fat Augie operates his illegal enterprise from a cooler in his legitimate business, a meatpacking plant. As the action continues, Lupino's camera employs complex cross blocking and close-ups to establish the main characters in Augie's operation: Bitsy (Eddie Firestone), Augie's lieutenant; Pete (I. Stanford Jolley); and Augie himself. As Augie enters the plant, the camera moves out wide, panning across the interior, which is filled with workers who are cutting and carrying bloody slabs of beef. The camera then moves in on the fat mob boss as he uses a delicate but sharp knife first to open a letter and then to threaten Pete for making a mistake. In a shot that intensifies the undercurrent of threat, Lupino's camera keeps the knife near the center of the frame. She instructed Whitney, "Peter, darling, hold the knife this way," adding (undoubtedly to her cameraman, Charles Straumer), "and make sure we see that sweet meathook."[9] Augie slams Pete against a wall, just missing the empty hooks that are waiting for slabs of beef, and laughs. As the scene ends, the camera moves in close as Fat Augie eats a chunk of sausage cut with the same knife, connecting the character to gluttony and greed as well as insanity.

We see Remp again as the camera cuts from the exterior of a train to its interior, then closes in on a two-shot of Remp and his wife, Marcie (Salome Jens). As they talk about their life together, an old woman standing behind them listens to their conversation, forming a triangle that emphasizes the connection between the two lovers. Lupino foregrounded youth in this scene, as she did consistently in her films. Remp leaves the train, and the camera cuts to a sequence of shots on the street outside Pete's apartment. With the camera positioned at the top of a short set of steps, we watch from the gunman's point of view as Pete exits his car, starts up the steps, and is shot point-blank. The camera moves to a close-up of the gloved hand that holds the gun as Pete collapses behind it. It follows the killer, Bitsy, as he casually walks down the steps, putting the gun in his pocket, then pans down to rest the focus on the dead man. The camera then actively cuts to Ness and his crew as they wait for a meeting with Remp, establishing their location in a swish pan that takes in the dark street. At the commercial break, Ness and Agent Hobson (Paul Picerni) walk away with their backs to the camera. This shot is employed in every episode.

The next scene opens at the meatpacking plant. As Remp walks into the cooler, the camera shows Fat Augie's narcissism and suggests his distrust of Remp by filming his reflection in a mirror. Augie watches in the mirror as Remp enters, then the camera cuts to a close-up of Remp. The sequence is repeated—the crime boss in the mirror, a close-up of Remp—to underline Augie's wariness. Remp gets the job, but Fat Augie gives him a test first: as Augie stabs his knife into the table, the camera cuts to the blade quivering between Remp's thumb and forefinger. It is a near miss, but Remp doesn't flinch.

Lupino made excellent use of her sets, which included Remp's apartment and a busy arcade, in addition to the meatpacking plant. Her framing was exquisite as she moved quickly, capturing emotions in close-ups and cutting out seamlessly. In a style that is reminiscent of director Max Ophüls, she sometimes allowed minor characters and elements of the set to block her main characters and her mobile camera as it dollied by. This required a complex setup, particularly for television. No one ever simply sat in a Lupino-directed show: they slouched, leaned on a desk, crouched, or knelt. She often began a sequence with a three-shot, followed by a two-shot and then a single, ending with a telling close-up on a character. After Marcie is introduced, for example, close-ups emphasize her as the moral center of the film. As a pure innocent who goes crazy with grief and anger, she exemplifies the type of character that Lupino, and Ray as well, filmed with empathy.

At the climax, a shootout occurs, in which Remp and Harry (another of Augie's gangsters, played by Steve Gravers) are killed. Lupino's camera visually layers the characters as the action rapidly unfolds, moving between Ness and Hobson, whose faces are partially lit, and Harry, who is hidden in the shadows of a dark alley. Ness and Hobson walk out of the alley together in the requisite two-shot, their backs to the camera. The coda is an ambiguous Lupinian note about Marcie's character, delivered by Winchell: "She lost herself in the limbo of her own loneliness." As one reviewer noted about "The Man in the Cooler," Lupino took a fairly generic plot and infused it with "Murnau-ish touches."[10]

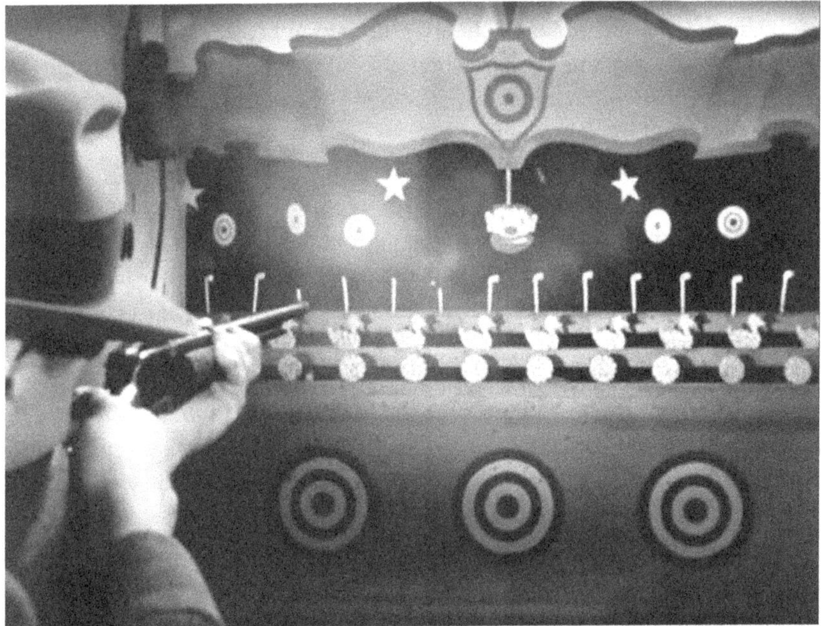

Robert Stack, in a kids' shooting gallery, starring in the Lupino-directed episode of the series The Untouchables, *"The Man in the Cooler."*

The Fugitive

The Fugitive (ABC, 1963–1967), which starred David Janssen, was a crime thriller classic extremely popular with viewers. Created by Roy Huggins, the series ran for four seasons, airing a total of 120 episodes.[11] Lupino directed three episodes of *The Fugitive*: "Fatso" (November 19, 1963), for which she was nominated for an Emmy for Best Director; "Glass Tightrope" (December 3, 1963); and "The Garden House" (January 14, 1964). David Janssen, like Richard Boone and Robert Stack, often asked for Lupino.

In December 2016, I talked with Pippa Scott, one of the stars of "The Garden House." When I asked about Lupino's working methods, she described a director who was always in control but who admired and understood actors:

> Scott: Ida was incredibly efficient, organized. You know what's expected of you, you have rehearsal. She rehearses enough—a good deal—especially for the time, when there wasn't a lot of rehearsal devoted to [television] production. She knew what she wanted. She was elegant and calm about it all—the sign of a very smart person . . . She wasn't

bossy, but she was forceful when she needed to be, you know. It was a good time. I was interested in where she put the camera. She had an air of independence about her . . . [She knew] what she wanted of you and then watched the take carefully.

Seros: Was she easy to be with? Relaxed, or more formal?

Scott: We had a few conversations. It was kind of formal. She wanted to know what I had recently done and what I had enjoyed. She was gentle but firm. A great, wonderful four days. David Janssen—he came and went.[12]

An experienced actress, Lupino knew the value of rehearsal, and she managed to incorporate rehearsal time into the fast, four-day shoot of "The Garden House." Although Scott appreciated the opportunity to rehearse, some actors, such as Richard Boone, the star of *Have Gun—Will Travel*, did not. Lupino had to be flexible from series to series.

Narrator William Conrad introduces the action in a recurring opening that reminds the audience of the story of Dr. Richard Kimble (Janssen), who has been wrongfully accused of killing his wife. Each episode of *The Fugitive* places Kimble in a new location and a different dramatic adventure, as he searches for the real killer while trying to evade a federal manhunt. "The Garden House" is divided into four acts with an epilogue. In this episode, Janssen is working as a temporary caretaker on a ranch in Connecticut that is owned by newspaper heiress Ann Guthrie (Peggy McCay), who lives with her husband, Harlan (a villainous Robert Webber), and her sister, Carol (a sexualized Pippa Scott). Ann is the sole benefactor of her father's estate, but she believes Carol should share her wealth. Carol, however, is having an affair with Harlan. Carol and Harlan plot to kill Ann, take her fortune, and blame it on the caretaker, whom Carol has recognized as Kimble from a back issue in the newspaper's morgue. Carol is a photographer on the newspaper, and her still camera figures prominently in the plot. Carol's skillful ease with a camera reflects Lupino's own.

Lupino's shot lists for the episode demonstrate how she clarified meaning and introduced innuendo through her camera work. She was careful to establish several areas of the ranch: the exterior of the main house with its rock facade; the house's large living room; the diminutive garden house with its claustrophobic interior, designed for a child and occupied by dolls; the corral and the riding trail between the main house and the garden house. Lupino shot other contrasts as well: the jeep used by Kimble and the late-model Thunderbird convertible driven by Harlan and Carol.

Lupino's two-shots move seamlessly into close-ups, and her lens choices are always beneficial to the actors and to establishing their characters. Her choices

David Janssen as Richard Kimble in "The Garden House" episode of The Fugitive. *Lupino's use of lighting created this Sirkian, godlike shot.*

of angles, like Hitchcock's, support the script and the characters. Lupino used dissolves with skill throughout the episode, maintaining a seamless visual narrative, such as when Carol discovers Kimble's identity, dissolving from a shot of Carol with her camera to the newspaper story that identifies him. Kimble is asexual and almost godlike in his intelligence and quiet demeanor, so Lupino shot him from below, as if he is spiritually above the others.

Ann, earnest, innocent, and not sure of herself, is filmed head-on, with an emphasis on her open face. The two villains, the gorgeous but bad Carol and the unfaithful and treacherous Harlan, are often shot from the side. Lupino used the staircase of the main ranch house for entrances by Ann and Carol. Early on, Carol walks down the stairs as the camera sweeps left from Kimble, bringing first Carol and then Ann into the shot. In the scene where Harlan reveals his true feelings to Ann, Lupino started by focusing the camera on Harlan's hand as he picks up his gun, panning up to show his face, then sweeping right to show Ann walking down the stairs. These shots allow characters to join the scene without cutting away. This fluidity is employed throughout the episode, giving it momentum. The hour-long episode unfolds quickly, encouraging the audience to remain engaged with the program during the commercial breaks, which was a primary concern for the producer and the sponsors.

The final scene takes place in the garden house, and here Lupino exploited the grotesque aspects of the location to add a touch of Lupinian madness, building suspense. Once Ann's childhood playroom, the garden house is now her refuge, where she retreats when her insecurities overwhelm her. The room is filled with Ann's mementos: a music box with a dancing ballerina, childish drawings on the walls, half a dozen dolls carefully arranged on the wicker garden furniture. The score makes use of flutes and piccolos to emphasize the surreal nature of the room. The need to return to one's childhood to escape the real world is one of Lupino's themes.

The suspense of the climax is heightened by Lupino's noir textures and angles. Harlan walks down through deep shadows toward a dramatically lit garden house; inside, he waits for Ann, gun in hand, behind a wicker screen that throws shadows across his face. Lupino's camera then cuts, and suddenly we see the door from Harlan's perspective as he waits for Ann to enter. This shot, through a wicker screen and angled toward the floor, is partially impeded by the creepy profile of a doll that sits on one of the wicker chairs. As the door starts to open, we can see only the feet of the woman who enters. The camera cuts to Kimble, running toward the garden house, and we hear a gunshot. Kimble bursts through the door and attacks Harlan, who is kneeling by a body with the gun in his hand. Lupino handled the fight scenes realistically, and Janssen excelled here. As Ann opens the door and turns on the light, we see that it is Carol who is dead, mistaken by her lover for Ann. Harlan tries to convince Ann he is a good man, but he lunges for the gun as Kimble knocks him out. The dolls are the witnesses in this chilling combination of homicide and domesticity.

Kimble has saved a life, but he must move on or be captured. The episode concludes with the narrator's wrap-up: "Tomorrow the *Westbourne Clarion* will have a new editor. One of the paper's first editorials will be a plea for innocent men pursued by the furies, men such as Richard Kimble . . . The Fugitive!"

Thriller

Lupino's interest in suspense and the grotesque is on display in the episodes she filmed for *Thriller* (NBC, 1960–1962), an anthology series hosted by Boris Karloff. She was hired to direct "Trio for Terror" (March 14, 1961) and "Mr. George" (May 9, 1961) in the first season and went on to direct seven more episodes in the second, the series' final season. Originally launched in 1960 as a mystery series, *Thriller* had an inauspicious beginning despite the solid presence of Boris Karloff as the show's host. Producer William Frye was quickly brought in. He hired new talent with impressive credentials and steered the series toward the gothic horror episodes for which it is best remembered. The episodes were greatly enhanced by the music of Jerry Goldsmith and Morton

Stevens, as well as Pete Rugolo, who composed the main theme. *Thriller*'s style, both aural and visual, shows the influence of Hitchcock's *Psycho*.[13] Stephen King called *Thriller* "probably the best horror series ever put on TV" and noted that the show's evolution owed much to its writers:

> One of the most significant things about the *Thriller* series from the standpoint of the horror fan was that it began to depend more and more upon the work of the writers who had published in those "shudder pulps" . . . the writers who, in the period of the twenties, thirties, and forties, had begun to guide horror out of the Victorian-Edwardian ghost-story channel it had been in for so long, and toward our modern perception of what the horror story is and what it should do.[14]

These writers included Cornell Woolrich, whose stories were adapted three times. Alan Warren states that Lupino's fourth episode, "Guillotine" (September 26, 1961), is "the finest adaptation of Woolrich ever filmed."[15] Adapted for television by Charles Beaumont, the episode is set in France in 1875, during the French Revolution. The story revolves around a condemned man, Robert Lamont (played by Alejandro Rey), who is awaiting his execution. He hopes to evade death through a national tradition: if the executioner dies, the next person scheduled to be guillotined will be pardoned. Lamont asks his wife, Babette (Danielle De Metz), to poison the executioner, Monsieur de Paris (Robert Middleton). Because it is Babette's unfaithfulness that has led to Lamont's sentence—Lamont was convicted of murdering her lover—she agrees. Her plan to poison de Paris succeeds, and the executioner dies just as Lamont's head is secured in the guillotine's lunette—the opening where the neck of the prisoner rests. Lamont screams, "I win, I win," but when the prison doctor, who has lifted the executioner's hand to check his pulse, releases it, the dead man's hand drops onto the iron handle that controls the blade, and Lamont is decapitated in midscream. Lupino's direction is full of nuance, with an emphasis on suspense and the macabre, and ending with her signature twist—suspense and surprise.

Each episode of *Thriller* opens with an initial sequence, then the camera cuts away to horror maestro Karloff, who introduces the story in a darkly humorous monologue. For "Guillotine," he discusses the episode's theme while standing next to a working model of the machine. Appropriately, he introduces each of the three main characters as decapitated heads, which he lifts from the basket below the blade. The writer of Karloff's introductions was never credited, but the weekly monologues were particularly creative and incorporated early special effects. *Thriller*'s title design is distinctive and modern, with animated thick, white stripes (recalling the work of graphic designer Saul Bass) forming an angular web that enmeshes the type. Each episode was shot in black-and-white and printed in 35 mm, and each was about fifty minutes long.

Lupino opened "Guillotine" with a decidedly documentary-like sequence that functions as a how-to manual for guillotine operation. It shows not only how the guillotine works, with the lethal blade falling swiftly to its terminus with an ominous, slicing thunk, but also how well it worked to create fear. In his introduction, Karloff gives us another demonstration, carefully placing an apple in the lunette and dropping the blade. The segment ends with Karloff thoughtfully chewing on a half of the cut apple, musing that the old ways were so . . . "quaint."

Rather than the shot–reverse shot sequence that was ubiquitous in television dramas, Lupino employed two-shots throughout to emphasize relationships between characters. Babette's seduction of de Paris, for example, plays out over a long sequence in which Lupino's camera incorporates shots that frame them together along with close-ups, which always offer insights into a character's emotions or motivation. Mirror shots provide additional information about a character's state of mind, including de Paris's pleasure at the attention he has received from Babette.

The impact of the episode depends on the audience's understanding that the terror inspired by the guillotine was very real, so Lupino carefully integrated several more docudramatic scenes that show the guillotine in use as Lamont awaits his fate. De Paris has a Stanislavskian moment with his blade, which he keeps in a specific pristine, black leather case made for such blades. Executioners were expected to dispatch condemned prisoners quickly and cleanly, and they took great care with their equipment. De Paris runs his finger along the blade with satisfaction, as he anticipates the execution and the opportunity to enact power over another's mortality. Lupino's camera pans to his empty breakfast plate: the headsman has little time to live.[16]

Lupino's masterful use of intercutting emphasizes connections between characters and clarifies the timeline of the narrative. Lupino's cuts work like glue. For example, when she economically cut from Babette's lace dress to her lace handkerchief, and then to the next day, she elegantly made a time cut as well. Her linkages between scenes are exquisite because they are imperceptible. Moving from an over-the-shoulder shot of the prison director reading the execution decree to de Paris, Lupino zooms in on the headsman, who asks the prison director for the date of Lamont's execution. Lupino's camera cuts immediately to a close-up of Lamont grasping the bars of his cell. He seems to answer de Paris's question: "I don't know the date." But as the camera zooms out to a two-shot, we see that Lamont is speaking to Babette. She must discover

A Lupinian, docudramatic opening shot of an actual guillotine for The Thriller *series episode "Guillotine," hosted by Boris Karloff.*

the date if Lamont's plan is to succeed: "Do you remember the guard? Find out from him." Warren observes that this sequence shows the essential connection between the executioner and the condemned man, "even though they do not actually meet until the very end."[17] Another intercut deftly handles one of the complexities of the narrative. In the first scene, the story unfolds simultaneously in two locations: Lamont's cell and de Paris's home. Lupino's camera time cuts from Madame LeClerc (Janine Grandel) handing Babette her recipe for pancakes to Lamont receiving Babette's note that she has successfully poisoned de Paris.

Lupino also used inserts for emphasis, which add not only to the suspense but also to the grotesque character of the episode. Inserts of a dead cockroach, of Babette preparing the poison, and then of her mixing it smoothly into the pancake batter have enough reality to scare us and, oddly, to help us empathize with the executioner. Lupino's camera cuts from an insert of the executioner's watch, which shows us that only fifteen minutes remain before Lamont is to be beheaded, to a shot of the prison director checking his watch. In this way, she continued to delay beats to add suspense within the scene, as well as within the larger sequence.

The remainder of the episode alternates beats of Lamont with de Paris's agonizing walk to the square where the guillotine waits on its elevated platform. Lupino's camera shadows the executioner as he doggedly keeps moving, racked with pain from the poison he ingested in his morning pancakes. Lupino's skillful direction of "Guillotine" is enhanced by Jerry Goldsmith's outstanding score, which employs brass and percussion that together create a military tone. A musician herself, Lupino took full advantage of the music's death knell.

In the final sequence, Lupino slowed the pace, stretching out the time even more as de Paris struggles to reach the guillotine by dawn and drawing out the action to a suspense-filled climax. De Paris collapses at the foot of the platform's steep steps that lead to the guillotine, and Lupino's camera cuts to a painterly three-shot as Lamont implores the crowd to recognize his right to be pardoned. Another cut reveals that the executioner, in agony, is slowly crawling up the steps. The crosscutting escalates the tension until the last moment: the unexpected death of both prisoner and executioner. The final moment is stingingly ironic. As the obsessively careful executioner dies, his hand is dropped onto the lever by an official, releasing the blade. This complex and complicated sequence was painstakingly organized, shot, and edited. The shots described and illustrated here represent only a small number of the shots that Lupino executed for "Guillotine," but they are representative of her astonishing skill set, which allowed her to craft a complex narrative over a four-day shoot.

A Modernist TV Director

This consideration of Lupino's television work reveals that she was a standout director whose work was at an explicitly higher level than that of many of her colleagues. Moreover, she was often involved in rewriting, set design, art direction, music, and overall production values—what is now regarded as an auteurist collaborator. Although in many cases she went uncredited, Lupino honed her teleplays in a way that makes them recognizably hers in tone, genre, and impact. When Kathryn Bigelow does some rewriting today, she is credited for it; Lupino was not always given the same consideration.[18]

Lupino was asked to direct multiple episodes of series because her work was distinctive, styled in a way that other directors could not match. Therese Grisham and Julie Grossman write that Lupino was one of the professionals "who, given their influence on actors and scripts as well as their directorial choices during production, have had a decided impact on television episodes."[19] Lupino's television work is filled with noir futility, trauma, isolation, alienation, and dark humor—the same themes, motifs, and concerns that distinguish her independent films.

Often television directors are defined only as directors for hire, and they are thus without agency. Lupino, however, had a strong reputation for excellence and control, subtle and realistic performances, and advanced technical skills. A careful review of all her episodes shows clearly that she had a consistent style that employed a signature economy, and this consistency constitutes trademark auteurism. Her two-shots saved time on set, and her efficient technique worked because she could elicit excellent performances from both actors at the same time. These shots are blocked creatively, recognizing the confines of the set and the expectations associated with the genre. The shot–reverse shot is not interesting to watch but was used frequently by directors such as Jack Webb, who could not get the performances his show needed. To replace the ubiquitous, static establishing shot, Lupino used a mobile camera. Economy had a role, but because Lupino's mobile camera was efficient, she could use it to further delineate her characters and provide details within her mise-en-scène. Jack Edmund Nolan, a columnist for *Films in Review*, summarized her directorial style: "She's especially fond of the slow ease-in shot and of sweeping views of a set or an exterior, a rarity in US TV films. She almost never uses odd-ball framing or other gimmicks merely for virtuosity's sake. They say she stays within budget and finishes on time. She occasionally does a little scripting."[20]

Lupino's distinctive and identifiable style was a product of her expertise with camera, lenses, genre, lighting, and performance. She used specific angle shots to define her characters and her themes for the audience, and her use of lenses and lighting was formidable. Actors such as Richard Boone, David Janssen, Robert Stack, Gena Rowlands, and Claire Trevor succeeded in their television performances because of Lupino's understanding of close-ups and the nuances of behavior. Lupino employed crane and overhead shots carefully. Never gratuitous, they are always in service to the script, but they adhere to Lupino's particular style. Her crosscutting and dissolves, essential to economy, were seamlessly timed, demonstrating her ability to create and maintain suspense. When she wrote the scripts herself or gave notes on an existing teleplay, her agency increased. She often chose the script for her episodes, which gave her greater scope to create a recognizable Lupinian production. Lupino embodied auteur values that give her directed work for television a dynamism that is uniquely hers. Her recovery today is a phenomenon, as she endures without the help of an archive or self-promotion. She endures because she is exemplary.

Conclusion

LUPINIAN COLLABORATION, THE NEW AUTEURISM

I played Steve McQueen's mother, but I was only twelve years older than him, and he complained to Sam [Peckinpah, the director]. He said, "What's going on here? How can I look at Ida and think of her as my mother?" I said, "That's good, because when I look at you, I'm not thinking of you as a son."

Ida Lupino on her *Junior Bonner* costar, in Wheeler Winston Dixon, *Senses of Cinema 50*, April 2009

In Charlie Kaufman's film *I'm Thinking of Ending Things* (2020), a character the screenplay called only Young Woman (played by Jessie Buckley) and Jake (Jesse Plemons) drive through a snowstorm to Jake's parents' house, discussing and dissecting cinema on multiple levels of scholarship. Jake invokes the richness of John Cassavetes, someone he admires but whom quintessential critic Pauline Kael famously disdained. The Young Woman immediately quotes from Kael's review of Cassavetes's *A Woman under the Influence* (1974), a sentence assessing the performance of Gena Rowlands, Cassavetes's wife: "Conceivably, she's a great actress, but nothing she does is memorable, because she does so much."[1]

In a way, Kael was commenting on the pixelated nature of Rowlands, which some believe was Lupino's problem as well. On December 10, 1998, three years after Lupino's death, Rowlands was the presenter when New York Women in Film and Television gave Lupino a posthumous Muse Award.[2] The famously reclusive Rowlands also had appeared in an A&E documentary about Lupino's life. In Rowland's first segment, she stated, "I was crazy about Ida. Ida Lupino was something. She liked to shake things up!" Later, she commented on Lupino's career, offering a hint as to why Lupino had been overlooked for so long: "No one ever thought of the progression from actress to director to producer. It was not seen."[3] Lupino had a similarly high regard for Rowlands, calling her "the greatest living film actress."[4] She had directed Rowlands in a memorable *Breaking Point* episode, "Heart of Marble, Body of Stone" (ABC, December 23, 1963), portraying an actress in the throes of a mental breakdown. The teleplay, chosen by Lupino (like those for most of her directed episodes), reflected her interests in the power of madness and the fear of infertility. Both Lupino and Rowlands were anomalies, both uncategorizable, both unique.

Lupino's pixelated image might have been clarified by the film and television projects that she considered but never realized. In the 1960s, Lupino and Duff attempted to form another production company, Stanley Productions, with television executive Fred Hamilton.[5] The new company was named for Lupino's father, Stanley. Lupino outlined some of her plans for the new company, saying that she and Duff were "highly encouraged by the fact that the money men and producers seem to want to keep production here in the States and are willing to put up money for low-budget pictures. The story is the thing. . . . We bought a couple of books, including one called 'The Plotters,' which we hope to get into production in June of this year." She noted, "I'll direct some of these pictures."[6] In 1967, she reported that she was writing an original screenplay, a suspense story titled "Murders and Minuets." "When I'm satisfied with the script, I'd like to direct it," she said, adding, "That's what we [the Filmakers] did for a decade and that's what I'd like to do again."[7] In 1982, she told Luaine Lee of the *Chicago Tribune* that she was planning a comic western for television—and that she had just completed an autobiography, tentatively titled "Laugh like Hell."[8] As Barbara Scharres, director of the film center at the Art Institute of Chicago, commented in 1997, "It's a shame she didn't go on to make more films for theatrical release that might have covered the subject matter she gravitated toward on television. I think we might have seen a whole new, amazing Ida Lupino."[9]

In the 1970s, Lupino considered optioning the autobiography of Frances Farmer, *Will There Really Be a Morning?* The project was an overtly feminist conception in having an all-female above-the-line group. Farmer, a talented actress of the mid-1930s who didn't fit Hollywood's expectations for its stars, was to be a consultant and coproducer. Glenda Jackson was to star, and a female-driven company was to handle distribution of the film.[10] *Boxoffice* noted that the biopic would be "the first major movie to be made with women occupying the top production chairs."[11] Lupino likely identified with Farmer, who clashed with her bosses at Paramount because she wanted better roles with more substance, just as Lupino did a few years later. Farmer left Hollywood to join the Group Theatre in New York City, but her career faltered, and in the mid-1940s, she found herself in a "personal hell"—the kind of entrapment or prison that so many of Lupino's characters experienced.[12]

Another project that was ultimately a missed opportunity was Lupino's last film, *The Trouble with Angels* (1966), which she made for Columbia Pictures. Had Lupino been given creative control, had she been able to infuse the film with her restrained narrative and give it an innovative ending, the film might have been a career changer. Her independent sensibility, had she been allowed to employ it, could have resulted in a different type of film, one that would have broken through the mediocrity of studio fare.[13] A truly Lupinian film could have generated an opening for more women to move into above-the-line industry work at that time. Lupino came from a comedy background, and *Angels* should have been a vehicle for showing her expertise in yet another genre.

A teen rite-of-passage film set in a convent, *Angels* starred Hayley Mills as Mary Clancy, a student at the convent's high school, and Rosalind Russell as Mother Superior. The screenplay by Blanche Hanalis was based on Jane Trahey's 1962 memoir, *Life with Mother Superior*. The project started when Lupino was in the throes of forming Stanley Productions. Lupino owned or had optioned three properties, and she was negotiating with Columbia Pictures for a multipicture distribution contract.[14] Columbia held the film rights to Trahey's story and slated William Frye to produce what was initially titled "Mother Superior." Frye had worked with Lupino on *Thriller* and *Alfred Hitchcock Presents*, and he smartly tapped Lupino to direct.[15] Lupino acknowledged that it would be a departure from her independent films, noting, "The picture will be warm and funny. And it's such a nice change—no blood spilled at all, darling."[16] Filming began in the summer of 1965, nearly twelve years after the release of *The Bigamist*. As columnist Peter Bart described it in a *New York Times* article:

> Tomorrow morning one of television's most successful directors of blood-and-guts detective stories and Westerns will move into a small convent near Ambler, Pa., to start shooting a lighthearted motion picture titled, "Mother Superior," starring Rosalind Russell. A convent may be an incongruous place to find a blood-and-guts TV director but the director in question specializes in incongruity. The director, to begin with, is a woman, and a glamorous woman at that. Her name is Ida Lupino—a name that should conjure up memories for movie buffs. Twenty years ago she was a movie star who happened to hate stardom, a glamour queen who loathed glamour. So . . . she shed her unwanted roles in a typically unorthodox way: she became a director. Over the

last decade she has become, in fact, television's most successful woman, renowned for her ability to spill blood with the best of them.[17]

Under Lupino's direction, Russell received some of the best reviews of her career from critics writing for the *Hollywood Reporter*, *Motion Picture Daily*, *Film Daily*, and *Variety*. The reviewer for the *New York Times* noted, "Rosalind Russell plays so graciously and with such an air of serene composure that you'd never think she once went wild as Auntie Mame."[18] Mills, in one of her earliest post-Disney films, was a hit with critics as well as audiences. *Angels* had a respectable run and brought in good reviews, and it received support from the Catholic Church, undoubtedly because, in a surprise twist, Mills's character chooses to become a nun and stays to begin her novitiate as the movie ends. For the independent Lupino, though, the film felt like a failure. She had no creative control, and several scenes that she fought for were cut from the release. For a director who was used to shaping her films to her vision, this was a devastating blow. She was an innovator, not a studio hack, and she had an artistic obsession to create. Lupino did earn a "substantial sum" for her directing, apparently her only consolation.[19]

Despite Lupino's frustrations with the film, her sleight of hand is evident throughout. The audience understands that this will be an uncommon comedy as soon as the film begins. The opening credits, a hand-drawn animation sequence produced by DePatie–Freleng Enterprises (of *The Pink Panther* fame), introduce the main characters and the essence of the plot: the clash of wills between Mary and Mother Superior. In a reference to the extraordinary number of women in the cast, the animated Mary slams an arch-shaped door, shutting out the credits for the male cast members, who are listed as "The Outsiders" (with possibly two women who are not living at the convent).[20] As the sequence ends, a feather flies gracefully offscreen in a nod to Lupino's famous feather touch as a director.

The film's sardonic humor, which is pure Lupino, is evident in the provocative casting, which includes former stripper Gypsy Rose Lee as the school's exuberant dance instructor and fashion model Camilla Sparv as one of the nuns. Mary's observation that Sparv is "a flawless beauty" must have been added by Lupino when she decided to cast Sparv. There is no doubt that Lupino did some of the rewriting, as directors often do. Although it is not possible to know which lines she contributed, the celebrity name-dropping for comic effect—mentions of Kim Novak, Rock Hudson, and Jack Lemmon—recalls *Mr. Adams and Eve*, as do the references to beacons of high fashion such as Dior and Saks Fifth Avenue. Lupino draws on her impeccable comic timing, a genetic gift she shared with Stanley Lupino and Lupino Lane. One reviewer notes that the comic turns were managed "without resorting to cloying sentimentality, mean-spiritedness, vulgarity, or the kind of over-the-top slapstick that bogged down the 1968 sequel, *Where Angels Go . . . Trouble Follows*."[21]

Although the studio may have made cuts that upset Lupino's original editing design, her skillful camerawork and the subtlety of her directorial voice are evident throughout the film. As the action begins, Lupino's camera establishes the restorative, contemplative setting of the school with a slow pan of statuary, including the figure of St. Francis, fronting a peaceful lake. The bus that delivers the new students recalls the buses in *Not Wanted* and *The Bigamist*, which promise transportation from lives of entrapment and unhappiness to opportunities for freedom and fulfillment. Lupino's efficient dissolves are particularly important in *Angels* because the unwieldy narrative spans four years.

Cuts are unobtrusive, and blocked two-shots are varied and imaginative. Those featuring Mills and Russell strengthen their roles as antagonists and set up the ending of the film. Mary outwardly disdains the pious life of the nuns, yet she is confused and curious, intrigued by the nuns' pure unselfishness and unwavering patience. In the second half of the film, Lupino inserted several ambiguous moments that indicate the change that Mary is experiencing, but they are not obtrusive or expositional. In a pivotal moment, she watches quietly as Mother Superior mourns the death of a sister, one who was particularly full of life. Mary is moved by what she witnesses, and the audience watches as her defiance begins to evolve into understanding. Although the ending departs from Lupino's signature ambiguity, these beats resonate with the uncertainty and vulnerability that are hallmarks of her independent films. Occasionally, Lupino's camera fills an opening frame with a single vibrant image—red roses (recalling the white gardenias in *Never Fear*), a Pollock-like oil painting—then pulls back, inviting the viewer into the shot. Sometimes her shots are filled with people. The narrative foregrounds youth and de-emphasizes adulthood, and in this the studio film is consistent with Lupino's independent films.

Even though she lacked the creative control she wanted, Lupino made *Angels* her own. The notion of a child who is not wanted is reflected in the character of Mary, a young girl whose parents have died, leaving her in the guardianship of a wealthy, womanizing uncle who is uninterested in taking care of her. His neglect is the source of Mary's disruptive acting out. The pool sequences in *Angels* have a documentary feel that is similar to the pool scenes in *Never Fear*, which were filmed with nonactors. Even the brief scene in which a nun explains to Mary that she is leaving St. Francis Academy to teach children with leprosy highlights a theme of an earlier film: the idea that disease, whether leprosy or polio, can be managed with professional care and empathy. *Angels* can even be seen as another of Lupino's prison films: the girls, who live highly regimented lives inside a fortress-like building, are trapped.

Angels also continues the exploration of mother-daughter relationships that

Lupino began in her first film, *Not Wanted*. The disapproving mother in *Not Wanted* has a minor role, but her character is essential as an unhappy, weary, trapped post–World War II housewife who tries to warn her daughter not to make the same mistake she did. The daughter, who is pregnant but unmarried, fears both childbirth and motherhood, and she ultimately succumbs to guilt after making the traumatic decision—in a remarkably moving Lupinian monologue—to give her child away. The camera holds on her face as she goes from being ecstatically happy, as she sees her just-born baby, to devastated, as she acknowledges the cruel truth that she is unable, emotionally and financially, to take care of her child. Lupino shot this moment with restraint, pushing in slowly with her camera. The two main characters in *Hard, Fast and Beautiful* are caught in a complex and tragic mother-daughter relationship that is the product of the mother's inflexible determination to see her daughter succeed. In "A Crime for Mothers," the negligent mother who abandoned her daughter at birth returns, only to demand money to disappear again. In *The Bigamist*, the main character, Eve, is tormented by her infertility and her gnawing desire to conceive. Her character also reveals flashes of Lupino's dark humor: Eve is a refrigerator saleswoman whose house is immaculate—oblique references to frigidity and sterility.

These repeated expressions of the fears and desires shared and contested by mothers and daughters are threads that are braided throughout Lupino's work. They reflect the persistent issues and problems that women faced after World War II, when they were often silenced by society's expectations. In *Angels*, Lupino rejects the good-versus-evil construct, opting to instill levels of compassion, austerity, tolerance, and kindness that offer a more nuanced depiction of motherhood. Therese Grisham and Julie Grossman note the silent interactions between Mary, who is an orphan, and Mother Superior over the course of the film and point out that Mary's "abiding feelings of abandonment" are answered by the devotion of Mother Superior to her calling and the love shared by the nuns.[22]

During the filming of *Angels*, Gypsy Rose Lee (with the help of at least one assistant) used an 8 mm camera to shoot silent footage of Lupino and her cast and crew. The footage offers a fascinating and rare glimpse of the quiet, restrained director in the process of working with her actors on set.[23] Lupino's physical direction is precise and specific. For a sequence depicting a modern dance class, for example, she demonstrates a balletic arm movement to Lee. Cigarette in hand, she repeats the gesture over and over again, all the while consciously turning away from Lee's camera. The footage also includes an action beat of Hayley Mills and costar June Harding (as Rachel Devery) jogging through the asbestos that stands in for snow, while Lupino and others wear makeshift masks.[24] Lupino is always low-key and professional in the footage, but at times she seems slightly annoyed by the camera's intrusion. We see her smile only once, during a birthday party for Harding. Lee also took a moment to document the sign that was placed at the entrance to the set. Commanding the top line is "Mother Superior," the original title of the film; at the bottom is a caution to visitors to "*Please* Smile Quietly."

Russell, who was initially unsure about working with Lupino, acknowledged the director's professionalism, saying, "She knows what she wants, and knows how to do it. She is clear, concise and has a sense of humor. Above all she has vitality and enthusiasm."[25] Hayley Mills discussed Lupino's direction with Randy Haberkamp in a November 2020 video that was curated by Lynne Kirste and features a portion of the footage that Lee shot on the *Angels* set. Mills related how unusual it was to have a female director, especially one who had been an actress. Lupino "saw what [the actors] brought and then made suggestions," giving them room to experiment, but she also knew what she wanted. This unusual combination gave Mills confidence. "I trusted her," she said. "Oh, and she insisted we all call her Mother. She changed my perspective. She didn't try to be manly. She was just herself, sweet, and clever." Because everyone on the set had mothers, "you sort of had to be respectful." Mills observed that although Lupino never challenged the actors, she did challenge the status quo. It was all done from a fully female, Lupinian point of view. The young actress felt comfortable with a female-centric production. "You had three remarkable women," Mills noted. "Rosalind Russell, Gypsy Rose Lee . . . and Ida Lupino."[26]

Angels is notable and rare because it was adapted by a woman from a book by a woman, had women working in all the leading roles and nearly all the minor ones, and was directed by a woman. A lighthearted anecdote in a pressbook for the movie, titled "Director's Delight," describes a moment of camaraderie on set and also underlines the unique position that Lupino still held in the mid-1960s:

> As Ida Lupino, Hollywood's only woman director, was busy filming scenes with Rosalind Russell and Hayley Mills on "The Trouble with Angels," . . . her visitors were mostly male—and all of them directors. One day Blake Edwards was an engrossed onlooker, watching Miss Lupino's directorial technique in action. Another day Billy Wilder came to call as did also Norman Jewison. Also a visitor was David Swift, who had directed Miss Mills in "Pollyanna" when she was a child. Swift watched with horrified eyes as Miss Mills puffed on a cigarette in a scene as the rules-breaking convent school student.

"Look what she's doing," he exclaimed. "She's smoking!"

"You forget, dear, like all teens, Hayley has come of age," replied Miss Lupino sagely. "Feeling old, David?"

Swift had to admit he did.[27]

Lupino's commitment to independent filmmaking sent her down a path filled with obstacles, but her skills and professionalism helped her succeed on her own terms. Making independent films gave her creative control, and though it was difficult financially, these films ultimately were more satisfying emotionally and artistically.

Being an independent filmmaker also allowed Lupino to battle for diversity, although she had to be subtle. In a 1950 article, she discussed her aversion to racial prejudice, saying that there would be "no stereotyped roles for any nationality group—especially Negro" in the films produced by the Filmakers. She pointed to two characters in *Outrage*—a Black policeman and a white shoeshine boy—as characters who defied Hollywood's expectations.[28] When she scripted *Not Wanted*, she wanted it to reflect the reality of hospitals like St. Anne's, which sheltered women of all ethnicities and races. She reported that when a financial backer informed her that her heroine couldn't be "in the same room with a Negro girl and a Spanish girl and a Chinese girl," she did what she could: "I managed to sneak a Chinese girl into that scene. I got a stiff letter from the man, but it was too late then to re-shoot and he had to stuff it down his pipe!"[29]

Lupino's regard for the country and culture of Mexico, usually "othered" in films of the era, is clear in *The Hitch-Hiker*. She chose to have Gil Bowen (Frank Lovejoy) be bilingual, an especially modern decision in 1953. The scenes in which Gil converses in Spanish with Mexican characters are an important element of the tension that increases steadily throughout the film. The killer, Myers, who cannot speak Spanish, becomes suspicious and agitated when Gil talks freely with a gas station attendant. Myers fears, and the audience hopes, that Gil is engineering an escape. These exchanges are not subtitled, but Lupino's direction allows the viewer to understand the narrative without having to understand the language. This adds to the docudramatic feel of the film and contributes to the building suspense. The audience is aware that as the drama unfolds in the Mexican desert, the Mexican police are working with the FBI to find the three men. In fact, the Mexican police are the real heroes of the narrative. Also notable is the love shown between a Mexican shop owner and his young daughter in a brief scene that underlines the importance of family in Mexican culture. Their strong tie contrasts with the killer's childhood trauma of being abandoned as well as with Gil's and Roy's disregard for their families, whom they in effect abandon when they change their plans. As R. L. Armstrong notes in a 2002 article on *The Hitch-Hiker*, "If Mexico is traditionally regarded in Hollywood films as the wilderness beyond the suburbs, liminal space to which Americans go to resolve personal conflicts, think, or get stinko, here the country comes into its own. The script shows genuine respect for ethnicity."[30]

Additionally, Lupino infused Mexican culture into *Never Fear*, which features John Franco's optimistic song "Guaymas," performed by Franco during the picnic scene, and she had planned to do a film about "what the press calls zoot-suiters."[31] This script, titled "Pachuco," was about "the trials and tribulations and adventures of young Mexicans in America."[32]

Lupino continued to challenge stereotypical and misogynistic representations that were prevalent in the 1950s as she moved into television. Asian influences are seen particularly in her episodes for *Have Gun—Will Travel* and the action series *Hong Kong*. Her exploration of gender representation, a hallmark of her independent films, expanded dramatically. As white women began to work outside the home, white female characters became more independent as well. Lupino's choice of television episodes often reflected her determination to portray strong female characters. In "Sybilla" (December 6, 1960), her darkly comic drama for *Alfred Hitchcock Presents*, a kind and generous wife subverts her controlling husband. "The Lady on the Wall" (February 20, 1960), one of Lupino's eight episodes for *Have Gun—Will Travel*, is a portrait of a vigorous woman who sustains the elderly residents of an entire town. And in "A Very Special Girl" (March 11, 1962), one of six episodes Lupino directed for *General Electric Theater*, a young, female, and very successful reporter would like to marry, but unfortunately no man meets her or her mother's standards.

Maggie Hennefeld argues that feminist film history is accomplished only by rewriting the past from the perspective of women, pointing out that the work of women filmmakers has "too often been erased or sidelined in dominant narratives of the history of cinema."[33] Claire Johnston states that sexist film ideology often "places man inside history, and woman as ahistoric and eternal."[34] Pushing against this narrative requires women to be anchored to history and considered in terms of their "place, production, creativity, labor and artistic expression."[35] These are the gender considerations that have informed this study of Ida Lupino. She was a famous actress, and her gendered celebrity diffused her accomplishments, creating obstacles to the recognition of her authorship that were not encountered by her male peers. Despite this, and owing to her careful management of her rebranded persona, she developed a sort of standout power as she became established in television, just by virtue of her consistent and voluminous work. Johnston, in her 1979 essay "Women's

Cinema as Counter-Cinema," was one of the earliest scholars to call attention to Lupino's accomplishments, and Lucy Ann Liggett Stewart, in her assessment of Lupino's independent features published in 1980, might have been the first to identify Lupino as an auteur.[36] Other scholars and critics have followed their lead, yet Lupino's authorship is still not fully recognized. It is for this reason that I call her an "auteur-in-waiting."

The debate about auteurism, a concept identified with French film criticism and the men writing for *Cahiers du Cinéma*, has always been contentious, and the opinions of Andrew Sarris, the foremost American promoter of "auteur theory," were countered by critics and scholars from the beginning.[37] Kael, writing in *Film Quarterly* in 1963, dismissed Sarris's definition of the auteur as masculinist, sexist, and privileging technique over entertainment, and Roland Barthes and Michel Foucault thoroughly dissected notions of the auteur, authorship, and auteurism in essays written a few years later.[38] Lupino's way of working aligns with C. Paul Sellors's recent reconceptualization of auteurism, which positions filmmaking as a collaborative endeavor, in which the question of authorship embraces more than a single forceful personality.[39]

By these measures, Lupino's authorship is undeniable. As a film director, she managed the Hollywood system in order to make the films she wanted to make, and as a television director, she understood that the new industry was the future of entertainment. Collaboration was always an essential element of Lupino's working style, whether she was forming her production companies, directing her early independent films, filling multiple roles in her work on *Four Star Playhouse*, or building the network of filmmakers that she cultivated over her long career. These were all *family* relationships, alliances that functioned as collaborative authorship. Lupino was a facilitator, managing her films and television episodes as if she were a showrunner in today's television landscape. She was a modern auteur, the collaborative author whose product is ultimately defined by everyone who has a causal role in its creation.

Within these family structures, Lupino created an astonishingly wide range of work: she produced, wrote, directed, designed sets, and composed scores. She became involved in every industrial aspect of radio, film, and television. She was a stylist, authoring her social problem pictures, exploitation films, and documentary hybrids from a spare and modern point of view. She was neither fragile nor passive, and she was definitely not an anti-feminist. Her point of view wasn't about gender, as some feminists expected or wanted; rather, she explored the imbalance of power between men and women that was prevalent during the disruptive transitional period that followed World War II. Scharres points out that "any woman director who manages to make her career in Hollywood, especially at that time, is by virtue of that a feminist."[40]

Ronnie Scheib argues that Lupino "belongs to that generation of modernist

Lupino with her Moviematic 16 mm cine camera, ca. 1938.

filmmakers" that includes Nicholas Ray, Robert Aldrich, and Sam Fuller.[41] David Thomson, too, has compared Lupino's films to Sam Fuller's, noting that they are "as tough and quick" as those of the older director.[42] Ginger Varney recognizes this, but she identifies an important distinction between the two directors: when Lupino began directing, Fuller was "already hacking away at this country's hide-bound sense of satisfaction with itself." Lupino had a different point of view, portraying "the victims of that satisfaction rather than the rebels against it."[43] The brutality of *The Hitch-Hiker*, for example, is filmed not only with implacable resolve but also with emotional and psychological sensitivity. Lupino's films evoke empathy for the most compromised of her characters because she finds the loneliness within each of them. As Martin Scorsese has observed, "There's a sense of pain, panic and cruelty that colors every frame. . . . Far in advance of the feminist movement, [Lupino] challenged the passive, often decorative images of women then common in Hollywood. What is at stake in Lupino's films is the psyche of the victim."[44]

There was no one like Ida Lupino. Although she never won an Oscar, she did receive various tributes, including the Muse Award from New York Women in Film and Television for her lifetime achievements and a New York Film Critics Circle Award for Best Actress, and she has two stars on the Hollywood Walk of Fame, one on Vine Street for film and one on Hollywood Boulevard for television.[45] On November 17, 1993, the New York chapter of the American Federation of Television and Radio Artists (AFTRA) presented Lupino with its second annual WIN Award.[46] Elaine Le Garo, then chair of AFTRA's Women's Committee, noted, "Lupino is a major force and an inspiration to all women by breaking barriers, setting precedents and being responsible for advancements by women in the entertainment arts. She won't be able to pick up her prize in person; she's asked Mala Powers, who starred in Lupino's 1950 *Outrage*, to accept the honors for her."[47]

Ida Lupino successfully navigated the film industry as a feature director during a period of extreme marginalization for women. She helped usher in independent cinema with her distinctive brand of Poverty Row and B-movie hybrids. She cannily worked with—and around—the PCA censors to ensure that her provocative genre films would be made. She worked steadily, producing, writing, directing, and acting, even during the industrial transition from film to television. Any one of these accomplishments would mark her as exceptional and exemplary.

Ultimately, as a reluctant star who chose to be a director, she quietly, without fanfare, challenged what it meant to be an auteur. And although she would not have recognized her career as unparalleled or revolutionary, it was. Her films, television movies, and episodes presented a woman's point of view to millions of film and television viewers during a period when women's issues were usually defined by the men in power. She was a champion of women's rights in service to a woman's point of view. She was at the center of a cultural and industrial change, which she transcended. Lupino's career sheds new light on the film industry's transitional contexts between 1933 and 1968. She was mother to the guerrilla alliance of directors, writers, cameramen, editors, and musicians who worked in film and television, and she repeatedly declared that she loved "being called Mother."[48] As mother to all her film and television families, Lupino was the face of a new, collaborative auteurism.

ACKNOWLEDGMENTS

I have many people to thank for helping me discover and recover this rare woman who could do anything, yet was misunderstood, mislaid, and almost forgotten. Professor Kathleen McHugh generously gave me new points of view and original thoughts about how to define and then find Lupino, and Chon Noriega, in his orchestral style and with few words, focused me and gave me the confidence to start and finish this book. Steve Mamber elevated Lupino in my work, pushing me to juxtapose her with Alfred Hitchcock. Ellen Scott mentored me in the use of diverse female voices and Janet Walker encouraged me to shine a light on Lupino's vast television work, vital to Lupino's story. Jasmine Trice focused me on the importance of motherhood and female labor, and Vivian Sobchack tried to help me become a better writer. Colin Gunckel gave me pages of ideas for restructuring my use of the archival images I had collected. Elissa Tognazzi, tough, smart, and kind, was available always with Italian language answers as I researched Lupino's ancestors from Naples, Italy: eccentric dancers, acrobats, and clowns. John Caldwell saw Lupino as uniquely current, referring to her as a *media strategist*, which made her spirit come alive.

Librarians and archivists are indispensable to any written work. From my first query at UCLA's Archive and Study Research Center, Mark Quigley, the John H. Mitchell Television Curator for the UCLA Film & Television Archive, was always and forever an incredible scaffold, introducing me to Lupino's television work and helping me find the video documents I needed to contrast her skill with that of the many male filmmakers and television directors working alongside her. Mark pushed me to talk about her, to keep searching the archives; he has been a real force behind this project. Diana King, master librarian and ruler of UCLA's Arts Library, a place where I could find the impossible, was ever-present and incredibly generous with her time. The Margaret Herrick Library is a gold mine; everyone there is knowledgeable, helpful, and full of encouragement. The late film historian and librarian Ned Comstock located a boxload of MGM TV day-to-day production sheets for the USC Cinematic Library, which gave me real data to prove that Lupino showed complexity within her TV episodes while making them for less money than the male directors working on the same series. It was Maya Montañez Smukler, head of the UCLA Film & Television Archive Research and Study Center, and my friend, who gave me the cover photo of Lupino I used for this book—what a gift! New York's Museum of Modern Art (MoMA) and the Mary Pickford Center for Motion Picture Study in Los Angeles hold 8 mm buried treasure of Lupino caught on film directing *The Trouble with Angels*, shot by Gypsy Rose Lee—whom Lupino had cast, ironically, as a nun. Virginia Steel, the former Norman and Armenia Powell University Librarian at UCLA, and Stephanie Kimura, executive director of development for the Charles E. Young Research Library, helped me transfer the Sally Forrest Archive into UCLA's Special Collections; I owe both women a real debt. May Hong HaDuong, together with Mark Quigley, has effected the restoration of Lupino's first teleplay and directed episode for *Screen Directors Playhouse*, "No. 5 Checked Out" (1956), which I sponsored, and Michelle (Miki) Bulos, Performing Arts Curator, has worked hard and fast to ready "No. 5" by the end of this year, 2024. Steve Wilson, the Robert DeNiro archivist at the Harry Ransom Center, graciously helped me find rare articles, images, and marginalia about Lupino housed there, an incredible archival repository not to be missed.

If not for my friend Mary Gaffney, who knew Sally Forrest, I would not have met the generous and intuitive Sharon Dunham, Forrest's niece, who graciously donated her aunt's archive to UCLA's Special Collections. Their contribution is enormous. I want to thank my great women friends, all hardworking mothers as well: Adriana, Andrea B. and Andrea H., Cindy C. and Cindy F., Danielle, Eileen, Gail, Alejandra Sr. and Alejandra Jr., Karen, Ki-'Ok, Lianne, Lisa, and Nina. A special thanks to Don and Ralph, two men who are true guardians of health. And to my assistant, Genesis: I appreciate her loyalty and bravery, and am in awe of her fast computer skills.

Richard Stern, artist, writer, and comic genius, has patiently advised me from beginning to end, and web designer Scott Citron guided Richard and me as we created idalupino.com, a place to see more images of Ida than even she might have imagined. Wayne Alexander, entertainment attorney, musician, and cyclist, provided legal and aesthetic guidance. Dr. Katie Marpe's belief in my project is unwavering. Chris Moore has been thoughtful and supportive as I made a sudden left turn, skidding into a PhD. I am indebted to Rebecca Frazier, a strong-voiced editor, who made compelling changes but never altered my meaning. She's born to the work! My friend and colleague Tom Strickler, iconoclast, agent extraordinaire, extreme sportsman, and wise world traveler, saw my manuscript first; he's a prodigious reader, and I depended on his taste and reflections.

I want to thank the gracious and professional senior editor Jim Burr, at the University of Texas Press at Austin. Jim supported me at every juncture, as I moved through the intricate publishing process, always available, smart, and kind. I loved working with Jim and with his discerning colleagues, including Derek George, whose design work and font choices created an elegant cover that reflects Ida's restraint; Mia Uribe Kozlovsky and Danni Bens, who both helped me by answering a lot of questions; freelance copy editor Joyce Bond, who was supremely knowledgeable and roadrunner-fast; and the patient and crystal-clear Lynne Ferguson, senior manuscript editor and a mother, who put all the pieces back together again!

All gratitude to my wildly talented father, George Seros—artist, political strategist, athlete, and comedian—whom I miss every day. Charismatic and indelible, he died too young, but left us with his immense creative legacy. My mother, Edith Seros (Aida was her given name, but her birth certificate, oddly, said Ida), who lived more than 109 years with grace and wisdom, taught me to be tough but thoughtful, direct but kind; I could not have had a more balanced role model. My big brother, Michael Seros, schooled me in progressive jazz with blindfolded tests from *DownBeat* magazine; he was the epitome of cool, but of course never defined himself as such. He let me hang onto his leg when he went to see foreign language and experimental movies, including those at L.A.'s Toho La Brea Theatre, where I saw Toshiro Mifune perform a samurai sword ritual for *Throne of Blood*—live. My magical son, Bruno, who always surprises me, is the most hilarious person I know, the definition of emotional intelligence and critical thinking on top of having a magnetic presence and a profound soul. And finally my husband of forty years, Walter Francis Ulloa, a unique and pivotal figure in Latino media, died too young, like my father—but not without amplifying many voices that might never have been heard.

NOTES

Preface

1. Carlo Ginzburg, *Clues, Myths, and the Historical Method*, trans. John Tedeschi and Anne C. Tedeschi (Baltimore: Johns Hopkins University Press, 1989), 97.

2. Amy Taubin, "Why Settle for Less?," *Film Comment* 54, no. 4 (2018): 59.

3. Ginzburg was referring to the witch trials in Modena, Italy. From traces in the archive, he tried to "hear" the voices of the women accused of being witches.

4. Amelie Hastie, *Cupboards of Curiosity: Women, Recollection, and Film History* (Durham, NC: Duke University Press, 2007), 17.

5. Ginzburg, *Clues, Myths*, xi.

6. Only a few of the 250 images that I have collected could be included in this volume. As an addendum to the manuscript, please access idalupino.com throughout your read for more archival images, photographs, and other ephemera and memorabilia.

7. Michael Paulson, "Giving a Hand to Parents in Theatre," *New York Times*, November 10, 2018, AR6.

8. Paulson, "Giving a Hand." Ryder Farm in Brewster, New York, a small village fifty miles north of Times Square, is one of a few residency programs that allow children to accompany their parents. The children are exposed to many role models, not just their parents, and all are engaged in creative work. They experience what it actually means to be a working artist, whether the artist is writing, painting, acting, or directing.

9. Paulson, "Giving a Hand."

10. Susan Sontag, *On Women*, ed. David Rieff (New York: Picador, 2023), 75.

11. Silvia Federici, *Wages against Housework* (Bristol, UK: Power of Women Collective and Falling Wall Press, 1975).

12. Amelie Hastie, *The Bigamist* (New York: Palgrave MacMillan, 2009), 4.

Introduction. Ambiguity and Paradox in Ida Lupino

1. *This Is Your Life* ran on TV from 1952 to 1961, and after being revived for a couple of seasons in 1971 and 1983, it aired as specials in the late 1980s and early 1990s.

2. Lupino acted in, directed, and produced *The Bigamist*. She also did a little writing, but she is not credited. See idalupino.com career charts.

3. See chapter 1 for a discussion of feminist critiques of Lupino's work.

4. The labor organization was founded as the Screen Directors Guild in 1936. In 1960, it merged with the Radio and Television Directors Guild and was renamed the Directors Guild of America.

5. See "*The Hitch-Hiker*," Rotten Tomatoes, https://www.rottentomatoes.com/m/the_hitch_hiker_1953. The Library of Congress lists *The Hitch-Hiker* as an example of the "film noir," "road films," and "thrillers" genres. See https://www.loc.gov/item/mbrs00047382/.

6. See chapter 3 for a discussion of Lupino's independent films.

7. Amelie Hastie, *Cupboards of Curiosity: Women, Recollection, and Film History* (Durham, NC: Duke University Press, 2007), 9.

8. As Michele Hilmes has noted, archiving is a feminist issue, given the relative absence of texts that are traditionally coded as feminine in publicly accessible archives, and she tasks archivists and historians with addressing this absence. Michele Hilmes, "Is Archiving a Feminist Issue? Historical Research and the Past, Present, and Future of Television Studies," *Cinema Journal* 47, no. 3 (2008): 156.

9. Giuliana Bruno, *Streetwalking on a Ruined Map: Cultural Theory and the City Films of Elvira Notari* (Princeton, NJ: Princeton University Press, 1993), 132.

10. Isabella Rossellini, *Some of Me* (New York: Random House, 1997), 21.

11. William Donati, *Ida Lupino: A Biography* (Lexington: University Press of Kentucky, 1996), 2.

12. In a telephone conversation with the author on November 5, 2018, Lupino Lane's granddaughter related that the Lupino family, including Ida, descended from puppeteer Giorgio Luppino (1632–1693). Georgio fled the Duke of Naples's court and settled in England in the seventeenth century, perhaps for political reasons. He is buried in East London. Other sources state that Ida is descended from George Hook, who was not related to Giorgio Luppino but worked with the Luppino family and took their name.

13. Donati, *Ida Lupino*, 2, gives an interview with Francine Parker as the source for this statement. Archival pictures in the Cineteca di Bologna, Italy, show two diagrams hand drawn by George's nephew Lupino Lane, titled "How to spin on head" and "How to twist round the neck." Both seem to have been impossible for anyone to execute except Lupino Lane and Stanley Lupino. Lupino Lane, *How to Become a Comedian*, 3rd. ed. (London: F. Muller, 1946). (Although Grimaldi and Stanley Lupino look very much alike, I was told during the conversation in note 12 that Grimaldi had no children, so I think it might be the Hook side of the family from which Lupino had descended.)

14. Richard M. Roberts, "Lupino Lane, Music Hall Comedian," *Classic Images* (October 1996), 22. An international star of stage and cinema, Lane was featured in two-reel comedies during the 1920s. He is credited with acting in close to eighty movies, including films with Ernst Lubitsch, plus twenty-eight as director. "Lupino Lane," IMDb, accessed January 11, 2024, https://www.imdb.com/name/nm0313449/. Working with Ernst Lubitsch in the film *The Love Parade* (1929) gave Lane more credibility in the film world. Lupino Lane is sometimes said to be Ida's uncle, but I conclude based on my research that Lane was Ida's father's cousin.

15. Elia Kazan, *Kazan on Directing* (New York: Vintage Books, 2010), 239.

16. She may have been thirteen; sources differ on the dates of her birth and early work. On *This Is Your Life*, Lupino says that she was fourteen when she was cast in *Her First Affaire*.

17. Between the time when Lupino left for Hollywood and Warner Bros. fired her, she had made a slew of forgettable movies, just as other classic actors had done in the 1930s and 1940s, including Katharine Hepburn, Humphrey Bogart, and Cary Grant. Lupino was often suspended—at the time, without pay—for turning down unimaginative roles offered to her or for asking for character rewrites in an effort to avoid copying herself.

18. Lupino was popular not only in Europe and Asia but also Peru, Brazil, and Mexico. Several articles from South American and Latino periodicals about Lupino can be found in the Billy Rose Theatre Division of the New York Public Library. Her last acting role was on *Charlie's Angels*. See idalupino.com for charts of her television work. Episodes include the pilot for *Holloway's Daughters*. Between 1933, the year the Screen Actors Guild was established, and 1938, Lupino completed several less-than-successful movies. During that

same period, she wrote a number of musical compositions, including *Aladdin Suite*, which was performed by the Los Angeles Philharmonic.

19. The Filmakers Inc. was established in 1949 as Emerald Productions, after Connie Emerald, the stage name of Lupino's mother. When Anson Bond left the trio and Malvin Wald came on as a writer, the company changed its name to the Filmakers.

20. Lupino had known Hughes since she was in her teens, and after the financial success of *Not Wanted*, Hughes became interested in Lupino's company. Before Hughes decided not to distribute *The Bigamist*, RKO had distributed three of Lupino's movies: *Outrage*, *Hard, Fast and Beautiful*, and *The Hitch-Hiker*.

21. Ida Lupino, "Me, Mother Directress," *Action* 2, no. 3 (1967): 14. A later version appeared as Ida Lupino, "Ida Lupino—Just Plain Mother to Camera Brood," *Los Angeles Times*, June 18, 1967, C7.

22. James Naremore, foreword to *Orson Welles in Focus: Texts and Contexts*, ed. James N. Gilmore and Sidney Gottlieb (Bloomington: Indiana University Press, 2018), vii.

23. For a wheel chart comparing Lupino's and Welles's article types and output, see idalupino.com. Notable from the titles alone is that the articles about Lupino were written to feminize her, whereas those about Welles have a purely masculinist perspective. Hitchcock transitioned from film to television, but he was primarily a host of his own series, and he was never more than a bit actor, with no speaking lines, in a few of his films.

24. Library of Congress records include books, articles, web pages, recordings, and photos.

25. See idalupino.com for wheel graph comparison between Lupino and Welles.

26. From a conversation between Lupino and author Marjorie Rosen in June 1973. Marjorie Rosen, *Popcorn Venus: Women, Movies, and the American Dream* (New York: Avon, 1973), 403.

27. James Robert Parish and Don E. Stanke, *The Forties Gals* (Westport, CT: Arlington House, 1980), 132.

28. Ronnie Scheib, "Round Table: Ronnie Scheib," *Screening the Past*, November 2016, http://www.screeningthepast.com/issue-41-ronnie-scheib-dossier/round-table_ronnie-scheib/; first published in *Metro*, no. 109 (1997): 3–12.

29. Michel Mourlet, "In Defense of Violence," in *Cahiers du Cinéma*, vol. 2, *The 1960s (1960–1968): New Wave, New Cinema, Reevaluating Hollywood*, ed. Jim Hillier, trans. David Wilson (Cambridge, MA: Harvard University Press, 1986), 134; first published as "Apologie de la violence," *Cahiers du Cinéma* 107 (1960).

30. Jacques Rivette, "Notes on a Revolution," in *Cahiers du Cinéma*, vol. 1, *The 1950s: Neorealism, Hollywood, New Wave*, ed. Jim Hillier, trans. Liz Heron (Cambridge: Harvard University Press, 1985), 95; first published as "Notes sur une revolution," *Cahiers du Cinéma* 54 (1955): 18–19.

31. Francine Parker, "Discovering Ida Lupino," *Action* 2, no. 3 (1973): 21.

32. Richard Schickel, *Conversations with Scorsese* (New York: Alfred A. Knopf, 2011), 151.

33. The RKO collection at UCLA contains the scripts for *The Hitch-Hiker*, *Never Fear*, *Hard, Fast and Beautiful* (earlier titled *Mother of Champions*), *Outrage*, and *The Bigamist*, as well as fragments of *Not Wanted*. The collection is woefully incomplete because of Lupino's disregard for her potential legacy. This is something I like about Lupino: she was focused on her work rather than her legacy. Script for *The Hitch-Hiker*, RKO Collection Scripts Files, RKO Radio Pictures, series P, box 0205, RKO Radio Pictures Studio Records (collection PASC 3), UCLA Library Special Collections, Charles E. Young Research Library, University of California, Los Angeles (hereafter cited as RKO Records).

34. Donati, *Ida Lupino*, 202.

35. Therese Grisham and Julie Grossman, *Ida Lupino, Director: Her Art and Resilience in Times of Transition* (New Brunswick, NJ: Rutgers University Press, 2017), 11.

36. Martin Scorsese, "Ida Lupino: Behind the Camera, a Feminist," *New York Times Magazine*, December 31, 1995, sec. 6, p. 43. *The Man I Love* (1947), a noir musical in which Lupino stars as a torch singer, may have been a model for Scorsese's 1977 film *New York, New York*. See J. [James Lewis] Hoberman, "Ida Lupino, a Woman of Spine on Both Sides of the Lens," *New York Times*, November 24, 2016, https://www.nytimes.com/2016/11/24/movies/ida-lupino-a-woman-of-spine-on-both-sides-of-the-lens.html. The article was written in conjunction with the release of Blu-ray editions of *On Dangerous Ground* (1951), directed by Nicholas Ray, and *Road House* (1948), directed by Jean Negulesco.

37. Annette Kuhn, ed., *Queen of the 'B's: Ida Lupino behind the Camera* (Westport, CT: Greenwood, 1995); Hastie, *Bigamist*; and Lucy Ann Liggett Stewart, *Ida Lupino as Film Director, 1949–1953: An Auteur Approach* (New York: Arno, 1980).

38. C. Paul Sellors, *Film Authorship: Auteurs and Other Myths* (London: Wallflower, 2010), 127.

39. For collaborative authorship, see Sellors, *Film Authorship*.

40. For visual representations in chart and graph form, see idalupino.com.

41. The Production Code Administration was established in 1934 by the Motion Picture Producers and Distributors of America to enforce the Motion Picture Production Code through censorship.

42. "Wearing Mother's Clothes," *TV Guide*, May 14–20, 1960, 8–9.

Part I. Auteur-in-Waiting

1. Transcript of *The 39 Steps*, The Hitchcock Zone, accessed January 12, 2024, https://the.hitchcock.zone/wiki/The_39_Steps_(Lux_Radio_Theater,_13/Dec/1937). DeMille was a founder of the motion picture industry and a highly successful commercial director and producer. He is well known for his religious epics, including *The King of Kings*, *Samson and Delilah*, and *The Ten Commandments*.

Chapter 1. A Star Study

1. For example, Lupino was never interested in collecting clippings and other scrapbook memorabilia to curate her legacy.

2. Richard Dyer, *Heavenly Bodies: Film Stars and Society* (New York: Routledge, 2004), 17.

3. Francis Ford Coppola, "Playboy Interview: Francis Ford Coppola," interview by William Murray, in *Francis Ford Coppola: Interviews*, ed. Gene D. Phillips and Rodney Hill (Jackson: University of Mississippi Press, 2004), 39.

4. Although her overarching identity as an actress was of the strong, bad object, or femme fatale (in, for example, *The Man I Love* [1947] and *Road House* [1948]), she also played the "good girl" (*High Sierra* [1941]), and she could excel in comedy as well as in family drama.

5. Hoberman, "Ida Lupino."

6. David Thomson, *The New Biographical Dictionary of Film*, 5th ed. (New York: Alfred A. Knopf, 2010), 605.

7. Frieda Zylstra, "Ida Lupino Likes Role in Kitchen," *Chicago Daily Tribune*, April 11, 1958, 38; Johna Blinn, "Ida Lupino's Scrambled Egg Act," *Los Angeles Times*, April 17, 1975, H28; and Dinah Shore, *The Celebrity Cookbook* (Los Angeles: Price Stern Sloan, 1966).

8. Christopher Anderson, *Hollywood TV: The Studio System in the Fifties* (Austin: University of Texas Press, 1994).

9. The episode, which aired on January 2, 1957, is available at https://www.youtube.com/watch?v=pgcRec3H3w0. It was Collier Young's idea to create the show.

10. See idalupino.com for her film and television credits in chart and graph form.

11. Wheeler Winston Dixon, "Lupino, Ida," *Great Directors*, no. 50, Senses of Cinema, April 2009, https://www.sensesofcinema.com/2009/great-directors/ida-lupino.

12. Scheib, "Round Table." See also Ronnie Scheib, "Ida Lupino: Auteuress (1980)," *Screening the Past*, accessed January 9, 2024, http://www.screeningthepast.com/issue-41-ronnie-scheib-dossier/ida-lupino-auteuress/; first published in *Film Comment* 16, no. 1 (1980): 54–64, 80. Scheib (1944–2015) belongs to the generation of American film critics who wrote for the journal *Film Comment*. In the 1960s and 1970s, these critics drew a clear line of continuity from the tradition of American film criticism in the 1930s and 1940s to their work, extending the criticism of Otis Ferguson, James Agee, and Manny Farber with their own voices and making the work of the earlier generation fuller, stronger, and more informed. Scheib made vital contributions to film criticism and research from the mid-1970s through early 1980s on a diverse set of subjects, including animation; public film collections and facilities; Hollywood émigrés; films such as Samuel Fuller's *Shock Corridor* (1963) and Alfred Hitchcock's *Shadow of a Doubt* (1943); and filmmakers like Wim Wenders, A. I. Bezzerides, and Ida Lupino. She prepared a commentary for Kino Lorber's *Ida Lupino: Filmmaker Collection*, released in 2019; it contains *Not Wanted*, *Never Fear*, *The Hitch-Hiker*, and *The Bigamist*.

13. Barbara Koenig Quart, *Women Directors: The Emergence of a New Cinema* (New York: Praeger, 1988), 27.

14. Haskell's and White's critiques are discussed by Pam Cook in "*Outrage* (1950)," in Kuhn, *Queen of the 'B's*, 59.

15. Molly Haskell, *From Reverence to Rape: The Treatment of Women in the Movies* (Harmondsworth: Penguin, 1974), 201.

16. See, for example, Carrie Rickey, "Lupino Noir," *Village Voice*, October 29–November 4, 1980, 43–45; and the essays in Kuhn, *Queen of the 'B's*.

17. Carol Clover discusses this in Kuhn, *Queen of the 'B's*, 64–69; Cook, "*Outrage* (1950)," 57–72.

18. Hastie, *Bigamist*, and Stewart, *Ida Lupino as Film Director*.

19. Therese Grisham and Julie Grossman, *Ida Lupino, Director: Her Art and Resilience in Times of Transition* (New Brunswick, NJ: Rutgers University Press, 2017), 207–208n19.

20. In many ways, Lupino's story resembles that of Elvira Notari (1875–1946), about whom little is known. Notari, who was born in Salerno, was Italy's earliest and most prolific female filmmaker, having made over sixty feature films and about one hundred documentaries. Her features were often based on Neapolitan dramas and shot on the streets of Naples, using nonprofessional actors. In this, she was a precursor to Italy's neorealist movement. Lupino admired her empathetic characterizations of the "bewildered people." Though Notari was an influential female director of her time, history has forgotten her accomplishments. Her archive, like Lupino's, is notable for its lacunae: only three of Notari's sixty full-length features remain, and they are not complete. Notari and Lupino were similarly focused on stories of ordinary people in crisis. As only fragments of Notari's films exist today, Giuliana Bruno discusses Notari's contributions to early Italian cinematography by examining the cultural context in which she worked. Bruno's emphasis is a woman's point of view on love, violence, poverty, and death. Bruno, *Streetwalking on a Ruined Map: Cultural Theory and the City Films of Elvira Notari* (Princeton, NJ: Princeton University Press, 1993), 132. Bruno's filmmaking reminds me of John Cassavetes's, with his use of his own house and stolen shots on Los Angeles streets, used as sets, and his anarchic use of nonactors to support his performance-based and improvised—yet finalized to script—narratives.

Cassavetes followed Lupino into television, both acting and directing. Lupino also directed Cassavetes's wife, Gena Rowlands, who was an early and ardent supporter of Lupino as a director as well as an actress. Lupino directed a television episode of *Breaking Point*, starring Rowlands as an alcoholic actress pressured by her father to keep working, perhaps mirroring some aspect of a troubled Lupino.

21. Mary Desjardins, *Recycled Stars: Female Film Stardom in the Age of Television and Video* (Durham, NC: Duke University Press, 2015).

22. Martin Scorsese and Francis Ford Coppola, "A Conversation with Martin Scorsese and Francis Ford Coppola," interview by Geoffrey Gilmore, *USSB Hollywood Insiders*, 1997, YouTube video, July 24, 2013, https://www.youtube.com/watch?v=uJE3Zqb9zXY.

23. Sol Saks, interview by Bill Freiberger, Television Academy, May 21, 2009, https://interviews.televisionacademy.com/interviews/sol-saks#interview-clips.

24. Judith Mayne, *Directed by Dorothy Arzner* (Bloomington: Indiana University Press, 1944). Like Arzner, Lupino was often defined by her relationships to men: her father and directors who were assumed to be influences, like Raoul Walsh and William Wellman.

25. Mary Celeste Kearney and James M. Moran, "Ida Lupino as Director of Television," in Kuhn, *Queen of the 'B's*, 137.

26. Christine Geraghty, "Re-examining Stardom: Questions of Texts, Bodies, and Performance," in *Stardom and Celebrity: A Reader*, ed. Sean Redmond and Su Holmes (Los Angeles: Sage, 2007), 106.

27. Louise Heck-Rabi, *Women Filmmakers: A Critical Reception* (Metuchen, NJ: Scarecrow, 1984), 250; Parker, "Discovering Ida Lupino," 14.

Chapter 2. Certain Women of Post–World War II

1. This is well documented in the Motion Picture Association of America Production Code Administration Records, 1927–1967, Collection 102, Margaret Herrick Library, Academy of Motion Picture Arts and Sciences, Los Angeles (hereafter cited as PCA Records). Many of the documents, including correspondence between Lupino and the PCA for *Not Wanted*, *The Hitch-Hiker*, and *The Bigamist*, are also in the Margaret Herrick Library Digital Collection, https://digitalcollections.oscars.org/digital/collection/p15759coll30 (hereafter cited as PCA Digital Collection). The Production Code Administration (PCA) was established in 1934 to administer the Motion Picture Production Code. Joseph Breen, a Catholic and an intellectual, headed the office from 1934 to 1954. Because the PCA's decisions were considered binding, Breen controlled Hollywood's output, combing through every script before production could begin.

2. Kristin Ross, *Fast Cars, Clean Bodies: Decolonization and the Reordering of French Culture* (Cambridge, MA: MIT Press, 1995).

3. In California, the demand for housing for the white middle and upper-middle classes resulted in projects such as real estate developer Joseph Eichler's tract houses and architect Gregory Ain's modular Park Planned Homes in Altadena. Architectural taste here paralleled that of German Mexican architect Max Cetto, who often collaborated with Luis Barragán in Mexico City. The postwar California modern style employed post-and-beam construction, glass walls, and open floor plans. The one-story structures fit organically into their rocky, cactus-filled environments, exploiting the natural contour of the terrain, with the glass walls bringing the outside in.

4. See William H. Whyte, *The Organization Man: The Book That Defined a Generation* (Philadelphia: University of Pennsylvania Press, 2002); first published 1956 by Simon and Schuster (New York).

5. Whyte, *Organization Man*.

6. Emily Carman, *Independent Stardom: Freelance Women in the Hollywood Studio System* (Austin: University of Texas Press: 2016), 75.

7. Whyte, *Organization Man*, 16.

8. Whyte, *Organization Man*, 213.

9. Keith Eggener, "Good Neighbors Make Glass Houses: Design Dialogues in Mexico City and Southern California, c. 1940–1960," in *Found in Translation: Design in California and Mexico, 1915–1985*, ed. Wendy Kaplan (Los Angeles: Los Angeles County Museum of Art, 2017), 274.

10. Thomas H. Hutchinson, *Here Is Television: Your Window on the World* (New York: Hastings House, 1948), ix.

11. Kathleen Anne McHugh, *American Domesticity: From How-To Manual to Hollywood Melodrama* (Oxford: Oxford University Press, 1999), 6.

12. Philip Wylie, *Generation of Vipers* (New York: Rinehart, 1955), 184.

13. Gypsy Rose Lee's footage, including nine reels of behind-the-scenes material, was found and cataloged in 2017. Digital Video Disk – Recordable, ID number M1285538, AFA Compilation, Mary Pickford Center for Motion Picture Study, Academy of Motion Picture Arts and Sciences, Los Angeles.

14. Chon A. Noriega, Mari Carmen Ramirez, and Pilar Tompkins Rivas, *Home—So Different, So Appealing* (Los Angeles: UCLA Chicano Studies Research Center Press, 2018), 25.

15. Scheib, "Ida Lupino." Scheib notes that the feminist critics laud Dorothy Arzner for her "De Mille-ish class consciousness, runaway idealism, and about as much visual excitement as a shoebox," which are taken as "signs of genius when in the lip-service of a committed feminism." She goes on to say that Arzner's films are of "sociological interest" and have an "often fascinating contradictory play between premise and realisation," but that "women can and have done much better. Ida Lupino has."

16. *The Moon Is Blue* was banned or had audience restrictions imposed in cities and states across the United States. Rather than damaging the film's box office, the controversy piqued viewers' interest, and this film was the fifteenth highest grossing in 1953. Preminger and United Artists had appealed decisions in Maryland and Kansas that upheld the ban, and their appeal in Kansas reached the U.S. Supreme Court in 1954. In *Holmby Productions v. Vaughn*, 350 U.S. 870 (1955), the court struck down the bans. The trend away from film censorship in the United States had been marked a year earlier by a landmark decision by the court, in which the justices unanimously recognized film to be an artistic endeavor and thus protected by the First Amendment. The decision, *Joseph Burstyn, Inc., v. Wilson*, 343 U.S. 495 (1952), concerned the Italian film *Il miracolo* (1948, directed by Roberto Rossellini), whose distribution license had been revoked by the New York Board of Regents. Burstyn, the film's distributor, had sued to have the board's ruling overturned. Laura Wittern-Keller, *Freedom of the Screen: Legal Challenges to State Censorship, 1915–1981* (Lexington: University of Kentucky Press, 2008); and "The Moon Is Blue," Turner Classic Movies, August 25, 2010, https://admin.tcm.com/tcmdb/title/83928/the-moon-is-blue#articles-reviews?articleId=338705.

17. Sherman also directed Lupino in *The Hard Way* (1943), for which she won a New York Film Critics Circle Award for Best Actress.

18. Ginger Varney, "Ida Lupino, Director," *LA Weekly*, November 12–18, 1982, 12, box 107, Personality Clipping File Collection, Cinematic Arts Library, University of Southern California, Los Angeles.

19. During the late 1940s and early 1950s, female writers—and female audiences—were drawn to crime, pulp, and noir fiction in a reaction to the social, sexual, and emotional limitations placed on them during this period. Noir was valorized, but women also authored an extraordinary amount of crime fiction during this period.

20. Brian Yecies and Aegyung Shim, "The Rise of the Female Writer-Director and the Changing Face of Korean Cinema," chap. 9 in *The Changing Face of Korean Cinema*,

1960–2015 (London: Routledge, 2015); Hyon Joo Yoo, ed., *South Korean Film: Critical and Primary Sources*, vol. 3 (New York: Bloomsbury Academic, 2021), 427n8.

21. The data design shown in appendix 6 at idalupino.com visualizes Lupino's connections that are best known. The names listed on the left are only some of Lupino's artistic colleagues.

22. IMDb lists him as the cinematographer for ninety episodes of *Four Star Playhouse* and director of photography for another twenty-four, nearly every episode of the series.

23. See, for example, David Thomson, *The New Biographical Dictionary of Film* (New York: Knopf, 2010), 605. Critic J. Hoberman notes in "Ida Lupino" that she was said to have "supervised" several scenes.

24. Bernard Eisenschitz, *Nicholas Ray: An American Journey* (Minneapolis: University of Minnesota Press, 1996), 157–158.

25. Weiner asked Lupino if she had seen the films of Dorothy Arzner or Elaine May. Lupino replied that she had not seen Arzner's work, but she had seen May's: "I think it's excellent." Debra Weiner, "Interview with Ida Lupino," in *Women and the Cinema: A Critical Anthology*, ed. Karyn Kay and Gerald Peary (New York: E. P. Dutton, 1977), 170.

26. See appendixes at idalupino.com. Charts demonstrate the number and nature of Lupino's various accomplishments: her acting work from her first performance on film, in 1931, to her last, in 1978, and all of Lupino's work behind the camera.

27. See "Comprehensive Credits List" at idalupino.com. Lupino's career crisscrossed all media, and her linkages were a hallmark of her lengthy career.

28. "The Bad Streak" is discussed in chapter 8.

29. For *Cahiers du Cinéma*'s annual lists of best films, see Jim Hillier, *Cahiers du Cinéma*, vol. 1, *The 1950s: Neo-Realism, Hollywood, New Wave*, trans. Liz Heron (Cambridge, MA: Harvard University Press, 1985), 284–288.

30. Film historian Raul Haid notes that *Kiss Me Deadly* was praised by the critics of *Cahiers du Cinéma*: "François Truffaut gave Aldrich a lengthy interview, lavishing praise on the film; and Jacques Rivette saw in the film a new realism rendered from the destruction of the morality that he saw all around him." Raul Haid, "Kiss Me Deadly (Robert Aldrich, 1955)," Senses of Cinema, March 2019, https://www.sensesofcinema.com/2019/cteq/kiss-me-deadly-robert-aldrich-1955/. *Vera Cruz* was also praised by Truffaut, who noted that it is "a dazzling lesson in story construction" and that "each scene would justify a film all by itself." Francois Truffaut, *The Films in My Life* (New York: Simon and Schuster, 1985), 95, 97. In 1999, *Kiss Me Deadly* was selected for preservation in the Library of Congress National Film Registry; films selected for the registry are considered "culturally, historically, or aesthetically significant." "Preserving the Silver Screen," *Library of Congress Information Bulletin* 58, no. 12 (December 1999), https://www.loc.gov/loc/lcib/9912/nfb.html.

31. Godard's regard for Fuller is discussed in "Director's Cut: Samuel Fuller and the French Connection," *New Yorker*, November 17, 2002, https://www.newyorker.com/magazine/2002/11/25/directors-cut. This anonymous article recounts that Jean-Luc Godard asked Fuller "to answer . . . some questions about his art." Asked to "define the cinema," Fuller said, "'A film is like a battleground: it has love, hate, action, violence, death—in one word, emotions,'" which "brought tears to Godard's eyes."

32. James Naremore, *More Than Night: Film Noir in Its Contexts* (Berkeley: University of California Press, 1998), 45. Naremore remarks that "the affinity between noir and modernism is hardly surprising," noting that "melodramatic literature and movies" were increasingly influenced by modernist art. As a result, "narratives and camera angles were organized along more complex and subjective lines; characters were depicted in shades of gray or in psychoanalytic terms; urban women became increasingly eroticized and dangerous; endings seemed less unproblematically happy; and violence appeared more pathological" (45). The

European talent who emigrated to the United States after the war also contributed to this new modernism in film. Nick Pinkerton points out that directors in the 1970s erroneously thought modernism had come from Europe, when European filmmakers "had been learning from the experimentation of Hollywood" since the 1940s. Nick Pinkerton, "Changing the Narrative," review of David Bordwell's *Reinventing Hollywood*, *Film Comment* 53, no. 5 (2017): 78.

33. Christoph Huber, "Mother of Us All: Ida Lupino, the Filmaker," *Cinema Scope*, no. 65 (2015), https://cinema-scope.com/features/mother-of-all-of-us-ida-lupino-the-filmaker/. Siegel was another favorite male action director who went on to a long career, working often with Clint Eastwood and touted by critics in Hollywood and France.

34. Weiner, "Interview with Ida Lupino," 171–172.

35. Lee Grant, interview for "Ida Lupino: Through the Lens," produced and directed by Torrie Rosenzweig, written by Gidion Phillips, narrated by Peter Graves, *Biography*, A&E, March 24, 1998.

Chapter 3. Six Movies, Five Years

1. Joel W. Finler, *The Hollywood Story*, 3rd ed. (London: Wallflower, 2003), 40.

2. For the purity of poverty, see Kazan, *Kazan on Directing*, 279–280.

3. Poverty Row films were the original low-budget film form, which was exploited in the 1960s by Roger Corman. Poverty Row is an underresearched area of film studies.

4. Dixon, "Lupino, Ida."

5. Scheib, "Round Table."

6. Critic Todd McCarthy has compared Hungarian-born John Alton to Swedish-born Greta Garbo; both reached the top of their professions, and both disappeared of their own volition. Todd McCarthy, introduction to *Painting with Light*, by John Alton (1949; repr., Berkeley: University of California Press, 2013), ix. Alton stated in a short documentary by Howard Schuman that he left Hollywood for South America because he wanted to live. Studio work wasn't worth it. Jorge Velez, "John Alton Documentary," YouTube video, December 12, 2013, https://www.youtube.com/watch?v=zJYXAxLeXM4. Alton's *The Big Combo* (1955), directed by Joseph H. Lewis, is often cited as the most beautifully lit noir film. Indeed, Alton wrote the first book about cinematography, *Painting with Light* (1949). Alton won an Oscar for his color work on Vincent Minnelli's *An American in Paris* (1951) for the one sequence he shot.

7. Imogen Sara Smith, "The Lost Land," *Film Comment* 55, no. 1 (2019): 49.

8. Kathleen McHugh demonstrates how exemplarity is often denied to women and people of color in the theorizing of independent cinema. Kathleen Anne McHugh, "Miranda July and the New 21st Century Indie," in *Indie Reframed: Women's Filmmaking and Contemporary American Independent Cinema*, edited by Linda Badley, Claire Perkins, and Michele Schreiber (Edinburgh: Edinburgh University Press, 2016), 239–253.

9. The Italian director's influence can be traced through Lupino's genre hybrids, some of which just skirt melodrama.

10. Jacqueline Levitin, Judith Plessis, and Valerie Raoul, *Women Filmmakers: Refocusing* (New York: Routledge, 2003), 445. While I agree with Cixous in general, I argue that Lupino was not the eccentric, lone woman; she was exemplary, working as part of a significant cultural movement: the great shift from B movies to television.

11. Scorsese, "Ida Lupino." A chamber piece, "also known as *chamber film* or *chamber drama*," is "a film involving a small number of characters interacting over a short period of time in a limited environment." "Chamber Piece (Definition)," Wonderful Cinema, accessed January 13, 2024, https://wonderfulcinema.com/chamber-piece-definition/.

12. Hedda Hopper, "Ida Lupino Pushes Hunt for Talent: Ability Rather Than Names to

Be Sought by Actress-Producer," *Los Angeles Times*, September 4, 1949, D1. Lupino's motivation for hiring new talent came from her experiences with producer Mark Hellinger, who cast her in *High Sierra* (1941) and *Moontide* (1942); she costarred with French noir actor Jean Gabin in the latter. Lupino was also influenced by Hellinger's insistence on realistic narratives and location shooting.

13. See Dixon, "Lupino, Ida." Dixon notes that Francine Parker and Ronnie Scheib each made this observation, but without attribution. Much the same speculation has been put forth with respect to male auteurs: Toshiro Mifune and Akira Kurosawa, Robert DeNiro and Martin Scorsese, Sergio Leone and Clint Eastwood.

14. Huber, "Mother of All of Us."

15. Ida Lupino, "Interview with Ida Lupino, Los Angeles, September 1974," by Patrick McGilligan and Debra Weiner, in *Film Crazy: Interviews with Hollywood Legends*, by Patrick McGilligan (New York: St. Martin's, 2014), 228.

16. James Naremore, "American Film Noir: The History of an Idea." *Film Quarterly* 49, no. 2 (1996): 12–28.

17. Naremore, "American Film Noir," 12. As Naremore argues, film noir might be one of the most misunderstood and overused genres in film. He explores the origin of noir as an idea, noting, "Noir is almost entirely a creation of postmodern culture, popularized by cineastes of the French New Wave, appropriated by reviewers, academics, and film-makers, and then recycled on TV" (14). Alain Silver and Elizabeth Ward assert that noir began in 1927 and list more than five hundred pictures with various characteristics and descriptions, but Naremore believes those listed are not the most representative of the noir mode. Alain Silver and Elizabeth Ward, eds., *Film Noir: An Encyclopedia of the American Style* (New York: Abrams, 1993).

18. Paul Schrader, "Notes on Film Noir," in *Film Genre Reader*, ed. Barry Keith Grant (Austin: University of Texas Press, 1986), 167–182; Foster Hirsch, *The Dark Side of the Screen* (New York: A. S. Barnes, 1981); Andrew Spicer, *Film Noir* (London: Taylor and Francis, 2002); Raymond Borde and Etienne Chaumeton, *Panorama du film noir americain, 1941–1953* (Paris: Editions du Minuit, 1955); and Raymond Durgnat, "Paint It Black: The Family Tree of Film Noir," *Cinema*, nos. 6–7 (1970): 49–56.

19. Pam Cook, *The Cinema Book*, 3rd ed. (London: BFI, 2007), 306.

20. Naremore, *More Than Night*, 26.

21. Naremore, *More Than Night*, 223.

22. Grisham and Grossman, *Ida Lupino, Director*, 218n17.

23. Mike Davis, *City of Quartz: Excavating the Future in Los Angeles* (New York: Verso, 1990), 41.

24. Douglas Sirk is the filmmaker probably most often associated with melodrama. He, too, has been compared to Lupino, although he cultivated the melodramatic mode and its excess.

25. Frédéric Bonnaud, "Radical Kindness," trans. Jonathan Robbins, *Film Comment* 48, no. 2 (2012): 25.

26. Shonni Enelow, "The Greatest Love of All," *Film Comment* 54, no. 3 (2018): 59.

27. Grisham and Grossman, *Ida Lupino, Director*, 86.

28. Tom Dewe Mathews, "The English Jean Harlow," *Guardian*, April 22, 2002, https://www.theguardian.com/film/2002/apr/22/artsfeatures2, quoted in Donati, *Ida Lupino*, 146. Donati notes that this comment made a "profound impression" on Lupino.

29. Lupino has often been quoted as having empathy for people who were lost and confused, whom she described as "bewildered." One example is the mother figure in *Hard, Fast and Beautiful*, who pushes her daughter to be a professional tennis player. She wants only the best for her daughter and is completely bewildered by her daughter's rejection, drawing the empathy of the audience. The seemingly happy ending for the daughter, who is to be

married, contrasts with the mother's dashed hope that her daughter will escape domestic entrapment. Lupino presents domesticity and marriage as a career ender that kills female ambition and talent: marriage is a trap that promises so much and delivers so little.

30. The opening of *Not Wanted* offers a comparison to the desolate volcanic landscape of Rossellini's *Stromboli*. Lupino shot the first scene on Bunker Hill, a prominent natural landmark in downtown Los Angeles that had long been considered an area of urban blight. Beginning in the 1960s, Bunker Hill became the site of aggressive and ongoing redevelopment schemes, and it no longer bears any resemblance to the neighborhood that appears in the film. In both *Not Wanted* and Rossellini's original cut of *Stromboli*, the wounded female protagonist finds a path to healing, but where that path will ultimately lead is left in question.

31. Dassin, Polonsky, Enfield, Rossen, and Losey were all called to testify by HUAC. Dassin and Losey left the United States and continued their successful careers in Europe.

32. Thom Andersen, "Red Hollywood," in *Literature and the Visual Arts in Contemporary Society*, ed. Suzanne Ferguson and Barbara S. Groseclose (Columbus: Ohio State University Press, 1985), 142–196.

33. Charles J. Maland, "'Film Gris': Crime, Critique, and Cold War Culture in 1951," *Film Criticism* 26, no. 3 (2002): 1.

34. Thom Andersen discusses the blurred boundaries between "enterprise" and "criminality" and between corrupt cops and a corrupt legal system in Joshua Hirsch, "Film Gris: Reconsidered," *Journal of Popular Film* 34, no. 2 (2006): 82. It can be argued that Lupino's film *The Bigamist* moves Andersen's 1951 boundary for film gris out to 1953, the year it was released. See also Andersen, "Red Hollywood," for excellent examples of directors, actors, and writers who in some cases were destroyed by the blacklist. Andersen particularly sets John Garfield apart, calling him, in Godard-like fashion, "the first axiom of film gris" (184). See also Maland, "'Film Gris.'"

35. Lupino's correspondence with the PCA and production fragments used in this book can be found in PCA Records and the PCA Digital Collection; UCLA Special Collections; the University of Southern California cinema library; the New York Public Library's scrapbook collections, marginalia, and various screen magazine articles about Lupino; and Nicholas Ray's storyboards and correspondence, housed at the University of Texas at Austin's incredible Harry Ransom Center. See the bibliography for a complete list of collections consulted.

36. Martin Scorsese, *A Personal Journey with Martin Scorsese through American Movies*, part 3, and "The Director as Smuggler: Part 2," (British Film Institute, 1995), documentary film, quoted in Hastie, *Bigamist.*

37. Lupino, "Ida Lupino," C7.

38. David Bordwell discusses the creativity that directors like Lupino introduced to film structure in the late 1940s and early 1950s in *Reinventing Hollywood: How 1940s Filmmakers Changed Movie Storytelling* (Chicago: University of Chicago Press, 2017).

39. Jim Hillier, ed., *Cahiers du Cinéma*, vol. 2, *The 1960s (1960–1968): New Wave, New Cinema, Reevaluating Hollywood* (Cambridge, MA: Harvard University Press, 1985), 1–17. Women have been omitted in subsequent auteur (authorship) studies, and some feminist filmmakers reject the authorship identification in their work altogether. Consequently, the male-dominated, genius-designated auteur has remained a men-only club.

40. See the essays in Hillier, *Cahiers du Cinéma*, vol. 2, *The 1960s*; and Maland, "'Film Gris,'" 1–30.

41. Andrew Sarris, *The American Cinema: Directors and Directions, 1929–1968* (Boston: Da Capo, 1996), 216.

42. Mourlet, "In Defense of Violence," 134.

43. Mourlet, "In Defense of Violence," 134. Walsh's influence can be seen in *The*

Hitch-Hiker, where Lupino incorporates a Walshian portrayal of the "ratio of human emotion to physical landscape" that Marilyn Ann Moss describes: "Where does each stand in the frame? And, who moves whom? Walsh's *High Sierra* advances pictorially, be it the chase, the face of a character, the language in his or her demeanor. The dialogue is surpassed by the film's physical, visual language." Marilyn Ann Moss, "The Tough and Tender Sides of a *Mad Dog* Classic," *Cineaste* 36, no. 2 (2011): 11.

44. Hoberman notes that *The Man I Love* was a model for Martin Scorsese's *New York, New York*. Hoberman, "Ida Lupino," 2.

45. Varney, "Ida Lupino, Director."

46. See Rivette, "Notes on a Revolution."

47. François Truffaut, "A Wonderful Certainty," in Hillier, *Cahiers du Cinéma*, vol. 1, *The 1950s*, 105, first published as Robert Lachenay [François Truffaut], "L'admirable certitude," *Cahiers du Cinéma* 46 (1955); Jacques Rivette, "On Imagination," in Hillier, *Cahiers du Cinéma*, vol. 1, *The 1950s*, 105, first published as "De l'invention," *Cahiers du Cinéma* 27 (1953).

48. Angela Martin, "Refocusing Authorship in Women's Filmmaking," in *Women Filmmakers: Refocusing*, ed. Jacqueline Levitin, Judith Plessis, and Valerie Raoul (New York: Routledge, 2003), 31–32. See also Claire Johnston's comments on Lupino in "Women's Cinema as Counter-Cinema," in *Feminist Film Theory: A Reader*, ed. Sue Thornham (New York: New York University Press, 1999), 31–40.

49. Martin, "Refocusing Authorship," 31. In 1967, Roland Barthes examined and shattered the auteur theory by postulating that the birth of the reader is at the cost of the author in his groundbreaking "The Death of the Author." See Roland Barthes, "The Death of the Author" (1967), in *Image, Music, Text*, trans. Stephen Heath (London: Fontana, 1977), 142–148. I do not claim that Lupino was an auteur, but I do think that her work should have been considered in these discussions. Phrases used to describe women filmmakers when they are finally counted as film authors include "otherness," "short shrift," "a nod," "a footnote," "an exception," and "special mention."

50. Quart, *Women Directors*, 27.

51. Annette Kuhn, "Introduction: Intestinal Fortitude," in Kuhn, *Queen of the 'B's*, 5.

52. Richard Koszarski, *Hollywood Directors, 1941–1976* (New York: Oxford University Press, 1977), 371.

53. The series "Hard, Fast and Beautiful: The Films of Ida Lupino" was presented by the UCLA Film & Television Archive and the Hugh M. Hefner Classic American Film Program on April 6, 7, and 27, 2018; see www.cinema.ucla.edu/events/2018/hard-fast-beautiful-ida-lupino. The films were chosen by UCLA archivist Mark Quigley. I opened the series with a discussion of Lupino's acting and directing oeuvre.

54. See, for example, Jack Miller, "Lean and Mean: 2 Films by Ida Lupino," *A Place for Film* (blog), Indiana University Blogs, February 8, 2021, https://blogs.iu.edu/aplaceforfilm/author/jarymill/. Kino Lorber's *Ida Lupino: Filmmaker Collection*, released in 2019, contains *Not Wanted*, *Never Fear*, *The Hitch-Hiker*, and *The Bigamist*.

55. Hastie, *Bigamist*, 73.

56. See Grisham and Grossman, *Ida Lupino, Director*.

57. See Maya Montañez Smukler, "Working Girls: The History of Women Directors in 1970s Hollywood" (PhD diss., University of California, Los Angeles, 2014).

Part II. Case Studies: Three Independent Films

1. "Joseph L. Mankiewicz Wins Best Directing: 1950 Oscars," YouTube video, May 10, 2014, https://www.youtube.com/watch?v=JwSf-jk7r7g. I urge you to watch this incredible

moment. Lupino might have been referring to Aladdin's genie; she had written *The Aladdin Suite* for the Los Angeles Philharmonic in 1937.

2. The other nominees were Robert Rossen for *All the King's Men*, William Wellman for *Battleground*, Carol Reed for *The Fallen Idol*, and William Wyler for *The Heiress*. Lupino was extremely close to Wellman, who gave her the role in *The Light That Failed* (1939) that propelled her into Hollywood's elite group of young actresses with talent. The film showcased Lupino's ability to portray madness. Wellman appeared when Lupino was featured on *This Is Your Life*.

3. "Mankiewicz Wins Best Directing."

4. To watch the complete video, see idalupino.com.

5. When I look at this picture, I always wonder what she was thinking. Michael Musto, "Legend of Lupino," *Vanity Fair*, April 1996.

Chapter 4. *Not Wanted*

1. Lupino, "Ida Lupino," C7.

2. Weiner, "Interview with Ida Lupino," 177. *Not Wanted* was released on June 24, 1949, and Clifton died on October 15, 1949.

3. J. A. [Jack] Vizzard, PCA employee, "Memo for the Files," June 11, 1948, PCA Records and PCA Digital Collection, 102_074432_p002. Paul Jarrico was under HUAC investigation at the time; he was blacklisted in 1950. Enterprise Productions (also known as Enterprise Studios) was founded in 1946 by actor John Garfield and producers David L. Loew and Charles Einfeld; it folded in 1949. United States Pictures (also known as United States Productions) was an independent production company associated with Warner Bros. Sperling married Betty Warner, Harry Warner's daughter, c. 1939.

4. J. A. V. [Jack Vizzard], "Memo for the Files," December 10, 1948, PCA Records and PCA Digital Collection, 102_074432_p008. Jack Vizzard had been a Jesuit priest before he joined the PCA in 1944 and stated in his autobiography that "the role of the Deceivers"—that is, Hollywood—was "to carry on in the mode of the Temptor . . . and to present a glittering and seductive picture of the cities of this earth." Stephen Weinberger, "Joe Breen's Oscar," *Film History* 17, no. 4 (2005): 382.

5. J. A. V., "Memo," December 10, 1948.

6. Ida Lupino to Jack Vizzard, February 11, 1949, PCA Records (nd PCA Digital Collection, 102_074432_p019; and "Emerald Productions Presents 'Not Wanted,'" [1949], PCA Records and PCA Digital Collection, 102_074432_p037.

7. Lupino to Vizzard, February 11, 1949.

8. "George Fisher Broadcast 2-6-49 Over Station KNX, 5:45–6:00," February 6, 1949, PCA Records and PCA Digital Collection, 102_074432_p009. Fisher (1909–1987) reported on Hollywood gossip for a number of radio stations and was a columnist for the *Los Angeles Evening News*.

9. "George Fisher Broadcast," February 6, 1949.

10. "Lupino Trying Low Budget 'Unwed Mother' Film," transcript of article published in *San Diego Tribune-Sun*, February 9, 1949, PCA Records and PCA Digital Collection, 102_074432_p020.

11. "Lupino Trying Low Budget."

12. "A Degenerate Article about a Degenerate Industry," *Ashland (WI) Daily Press*, February 2, 1949. Lupino's response via Western Union Telegram is lengthy; see idalupino.com.

13. Ida Lupino, telegram to Joseph I. Breen, February 9, 1949, PCA Records and PCA Digital Collection, 102_074432_p017.

14. Diane Waldman, "*Not Wanted* (1949)," in Annette Kuhn, "Introduction: Intestinal Fortitude," in Kuhn, *Queen of the 'B's*, 6.

15. Review of *Not Wanted*, *Variety*, June 20, 1949.

16. Review of *Not Wanted*, *Hollywood Reporter*, June 20, 1949.

17. Review of *Not Wanted*, Picture-of-the-Week, London, *Daily Herald*, November 2, 1949, PCA Records.

18. Richard Brody, "Not Wanted," Movies, *New Yorker*, June 20, 2016, 17, https://www.newyorker.com/goings-on-about-town/movies/not-wanted.

19. J. A. V., "Memo," December 10, 1948.

20. Kuhn, Introduction, *Queen of the 'B's*,' 6.

21. "Lupino's strategy for obtaining PCA approval for Not Wanted was to negotiate personally, stress her cordial relations with industry censors and their constructive role in shaping the film, and to incorporate this into the film's promotion." Waldman, "Not Wanted," 23.

22. Parker, "Discovering Ida Lupino," 20.

23. Kristin Thompson and David Bordwell, "SIDE EFFECTS and SAFE HAVEN: Out of the Past," *Observations on Film Art* (blog), March 24, 2013, https://www.davidbordwell.net/blog/2013/03/24/side-effects-and-safe-haven-out-of-the-past/.

24. Parker, "Discovering Ida Lupino," 20.

25. The credits state "Photography by Henry Freulich." Freulich was known for his work as director of photography on Lon Chaney's *The Hunchback of Notre Dame (*1923), Frank Capra's *It Happened One Night* (1934), and over one hundred *Three Stooges* films.

26. Bars and restaurant counters are ubiquitous in Lupino's films; these are scenes from her past experience as an actress playing a femme fatale, but they also hold economic value in their immediate meaning for the noir viewer. In *Outrage*, we have no idea the rapist is the charming, jovial guy who serves breakfast every day until we see the hideous scar on his neck. Lupino shot that scene actively, as the coffee in its cup slides all the way down the counter in one dramatic move that grounds the first half of the film in her expert action technique. The coffee cup shot reflects an early scene in Vincent Sherman's *The Hard Way* (1943), for which Lupino won a New York Film Critics Circle Award for Best Actress.

27. Director Lucile Hadžihalilović used a similar setting for her film *Évolution*: "We shot in a real . . . hospital. I prefer to be in real spaces because you have more texture, more surprises, more gifts from the place." Lucile Hadžihalilović, interview by Nicolas Rapold, in Laura Kern, "The Miracle of Life," *Film Comment* 52, no. 3 (May–June 2016): 39.

28. Ziegler's editing of the Wimbledon tennis sequences in *Hard, Fast and Beautiful* was always well reviewed. These tennis sequences might be the first ever seen in a fictional film. Famously, Ziegler worked with Alfred Hitchcock on *Spellbound*, *Rope*, and *Strangers on a Train*. He also edited *The Music Man*, *My Fair Lady*, and *Auntie Mame*, to name just a few; he is credited with over one hundred films on IMDb. Ziegler was nominated for an Academy Award three times in his forty-five-year-long career. Like Lupino and Hitchcock, Ziegler also made the modern transition to television in 1953, though he was never an actor, producer, or writer. For his filmography, see https://www.imdb.com/name/nm0956155/.

29. Lupino used her personal doctor for this sequence, perhaps to save money; regardless, it enhanced the documentary-like feeling of this scene.

30. Huber, "Mother of All of Us."

31. Waldman, "Not Wanted," 31.

32. Grant, "Ida Lupino," gives a figure of $150,000 for the budget. Budgets for Poverty Row pictures ranged from $10,000 to $400,000, but most fell between $20,000 and $100,000.

33. Parker, "Discovering Ida Lupino," 2.

34. Grisham and Grossman, *Ida Lupino, Director*, 68–69.

35. For example, Louise Heck-Rabi says of an article published in the February 5, 1954, issue of *Films in Review* that "the tone of the criticism . . . is sexist and condescending." The review states in part, "Ida Lupino is developing into a capable director of minor pictures, and in this trifle about a traveling salesman whose good intentions land him in bigamy, her directorial skill saves a sudsy tale from some of its lack of substance." Louise Heck-Rabi, *Women Filmmakers: A Critical Reception* (Metuchen, NJ: Scarecrow, 1984), 237.

36. Thompson, who signed his early reviews in the *Times* as HHT, also praised Lupino's direction: "'The Bigamist' belongs to Miss Lupino, and in more ways than one. This fragile director keels [*sic*] the action with such mounting tension, muted compassion and sharklike alacrity for behavior detail that the average spectator may feel he is eavesdropping on the excellent dialogue." HHT, review of *The Bigamist* at the Astor, *New York Times*, December 26, 1953, 10.

37. Johnston, "Women's Cinema as Counter-Cinema," 30.

38. Kuhn, "Introduction," 4.

39. See idalupino.com for more on this image.

40. Wheeler Winston Dixon, *Lost in the Fifties: Recovering Phantom Hollywood* (Carbondale: Southern Illinois University Press, 2005), 140.

Chapter 5. *Never Fear*

1. Centers for Disease Control and Prevention, "Polio in the United States," last reviewed August 3, 2022, https://www.cdc.gov/polio/what-is-polio/polio-us.html.

2. M.-J. Freyche, A. M.-M. Payne, and C. Lederrey, "Poliomyelitis in 1953," *Bulletin of the World Health Organization* 12 (1955): 595–649, https://www.ncbi.nlm.nih.gov/pmc/articles/PMC2542300/pdf/bullwho00548-0107.pdf.

3. Lupino may have been traumatized by her bout with polio. At the time, everyone was frightened of two things: the atom bomb and waking up with polio.

4. Scheib, "Ida Lupino."

5. Lupino's docudramas included elements of real life. Both *Not Wanted* and *Never Fear* used nonactors in the background and incorporated actual second unit location work in, for example, hospitals, gas stations, and identifiable downtown Los Angeles exteriors like Bunker Hill. In *Outrage*, Lupino shot in a canning plant. For *The Bigamist*, she moved a satiric scene into an actual bus that toured movie star homes. *Hard, Fast and Beautiful* employed some real tennis footage as well as rehearsed tennis sequences. The true-story elements in the opening crawl of *The Hitch-Hiker* and real-life details throughout lend that film much of its gravitas.

6. The origin of the Kabat-Kaiser Institute dates to 1944, when Henry J. Kaiser's son was diagnosed with multiple sclerosis. MS is the most widespread disabling neurological condition affecting young adults worldwide, and Kaiser was determined to find a cure for his son. Lincoln Cushing, "Kabat-Kaiser: Improving Quality of Life through Rehabilitation," Kaiser Permanente, June 14, 2017, https://about.kaiserpermanente.org/who-we-are/our-history/kabat-kaiser-improving-quality-of-life-through-rehabilitation.

7. See, for example, Heck-Rabi, *Women Filmmakers*, 229; and Yvonne Tasker and Suzanne Leonard, eds., *Fifty Hollywood Directors* (London: Routledge, 2015), 160. Another film that addressed a similar topic at that time was *The Men*, directed by Fred Zinnemann, written by Carl Foreman, and starring Marlon Brando and Teresa Wright, which was was released on July 20, 1950. (Wright worked both with Hitchcock in *Shadow of a Doubt* [1943] and with Lupino in her first cowritten and directed half-hour teleplay for *Screen Directors Playhouse*, "No. 5 Checked Out" [1956]). It landed in theaters six months

after Lupino's film was released. Unlike Lupino, who filmed at actual locations, Zinnemann used Encino's Birmingham High School to front for a veterans' hospital; however, Brando famously lived with paraplegic vets for several months without being paid, and Zinnemann photographed actual vets, both of which brought a Lupinian docudramatic postwar reality to this shoot. Like Lupino, Zinnemann used the San Fernando Valley for many of his films' exteriors. It was important to both directors that their films reflect the postwar reality of physical and mental trauma.

8. Quoted in Cushing, "Kabat-Kaiser"; the source is not given.

9. Cushing, "Kabat-Kaiser."

10. Collier Young to Geoffrey Shurlock, August 9, 1949, PCA Records.

11. Collier Young to Joseph I. Breen, August 17, 1949, file #699 (*Never Fear*), PCA Records. These items and the answers submitted were as follows: 1. Name of releasing company: Eagle-Lion. 2. Number of feet in the picture: 7,733. 3. Classification: original screen story, Larry Marcus and Lou Schor. 4. Official credit sheet. 5. Brief synopsis of the story. *Hard, Fast and Beautiful* used an almost equal amount of film: 7,485 feet.

12. "Analysis of Film Content—Part One—General," November 25, 1949, file #699 (*Never Fear*), PCA Records.

13. "Cast of Characters and Synopsis Forms," November 10, 1949, file #699 (*Never Fear*), PCA Records.

14. "Analysis of Film Content," November 25, 1949.

15. Forrest kept this note in one of her scrapbooks along with her childhood drawings. The note is in pristine condition, an indication that she treasured her time with Lupino. Ida Lupino and Collier Young to Sally Forrest, September 20, 1949, Sally Forrest Collection, in processing, UCLA Library Special Collections, Charles E. Young Research Library, University of California, Los Angeles (hereafter Sally Forrest Collection). This collection had not been fully processed at the time of this writing. It will eventually be available to researchers as part of RKO Records.

16. Script for *Never Fear*, box 8, 07-AUH-9313, Hugh O'Brian Papers, 1949–1973, Collection 257, Performing Arts Special Collections, Charles E. Young Research Library, University of California, Los Angeles. The script is dated September 7, 1949, fourteen days before shooting began. In the 1960s, O'Brian endowed an annual acting award, the Hugh O'Brian Award, for undergraduates in the UCLA Department of Theater. To win the award was the desire of every undergrad actor in the Theater Department during the 1960s and 1970s.

17. Script for *Never Fear*.

18. The film was released with the title *Young Lovers*, and some home videos carry that title. The original posters however, use, *Never Fear*.

19. I have reverse-engineered Lupino's screenplay by following what is onscreen. I have not found a screenplay that fully correlates with Lupino's final version.

20. Scheib, "Ida Lupino," 44.

21. Scheib, "Film Comment," 59.

22. Dixon, "Lupino, Ida."

23. Tom Vallance, "Sally Forrest: Performer Who Made Her Name as a Dancer, but Found Real Fame in Ida Lupino's Taboo-Busting Films," *Guardian*, April 7, 2015, https://www.independent.co.uk/news/people/news/sally-forrest-performer-who-made-her-name-dancer-found-real-fame-ida-lupino-s-taboo-busting-films-a107826.html.

24. Fragment of an undated interview in the Sally Forrest Collection. Forrest had edited the fragment, redacting some portions. Later, in an article in the *Los Angeles Times*, Forrest speaks about working with Lupino. "She was electric," Forrest says. "She never had the popularity she should have had. She was a fine actress. She was beautiful. She had a

fabulous figure and was a great director. Maybe she was too strong for those days." She praises Lupino's direction of actors, saying, "She was so knowledgeable in every area. She was wonderful with actors. She was the best I ever worked with. She was completely understanding and knew exactly what she wanted and how to explain it." In the same article, film curator Andrea Alsberg notes that Forrest and actress Mala Powers "are interesting figures because they are [Lupino's] stand-ins. They really do resemble her in a way." Susan King, "A Very Independent Streak," *Los Angeles Times*, October 15, 2002, https://www.latimes.com/archives/la-xpm-2002-oct-15-et-king15-story.html. Forrest and Lupino worked together again, both acting in Fritz Lang's *While the City Sleeps* (1956).

25. See idalupino.com.

26. Scheib, "Ida Lupino," 58.

27. O'Brian alludes to his first major role in an article in *Cosmopolitan*: "Here's a list I settled with my landlady (four weeks back rent at $10. a week) put new tires on my old car, ordered flowers for Ida Lupino who was directing me in *Young Lovers*, took my girl and her Mom to dinner at Chasen's, then I thought I'd better not forget my agent—I got him a sweater. There was still fifty dollars left, so I put it into the church poor box." Anita Summer, "What Did You Spend Money on When You First Felt Rich?," Roundup, *Cosmopolitan* 182, no. 1 (1977).

28. Ronnie Scheib, "Never Fear," in Kuhn, *Queen of the 'B's*, 54.

29. Hausner had notable roles in Stanley Kubrick's *Paths of Glory* (1957) and Maxwell Shane's *The Naked Street* (1955), with Anthony Quinn and Anne Bancroft.

30. *Never Fear* put a new young, Mexican American composer, John Franco, on the path to success. He composed a haunting love ballad titled "Why Pretend" and a "rollicking novelty" called "Guaymas." "Announcement Page Features," page 14, Sally Forrest Collection.

31. Lupino managed it both ways in *Outrage*. Her pastorlike redeemer figure was both sexual, with "normal" urges and drives, and genderless or nonsexual, so that his healing ability would not be tarnished. The *New York Times Film Review* for October 16, 1950, commended Lupino's *Outrage* for its "restraint and a modicum of courage in jousting with another social problem," saying, "Its preachment is indeed honorable, but its execution lacks punch and conviction." Ultimately, despite Lupino's goals, the PCA softened the expressive blows that she tried to throw. Heck-Rabi, *Women Filmmakers*, 231.

32. Review of *Never Fear*, *Hollywood Reporter*, January 4, 1950.

33. Pressbook for *Never Fear*, Sally Forrest Collection.

34. Lupino's campaign for *Outrage* was similarly exploitative: "Victim of attack!" and "Her plight screams the shame of laws that fail to protect young girls from fiends on parole! See her sensational story! Blistering drama honestly told and fearlessly presented!" "Teen-Age Beauty Is Victim of ATTACK!" (flash promo). *RKO Radio Pictures* 1, no. 1 (September 27, 1950). In "Photographic Inventories," RKO Radio Pictures Photographs, Margaret Herrick Library, Academy of Motion Picure Arts and Sciences, Los Angeles.

35. "Why I Made 'Never Fear' by Ida Lupino," Sally Forrest Collection.

36. Huber notes the confusion caused by the title change, alluding to a "box-office disappointment." Huber, "Mother of All of Us."

37. *Christian Century*, April 5, 1950, 447, quoted in Heck-Rabi, *Women Filmmakers*, 229.

38. *Rotarian* 76 (May 1950): 41, quoted in Heck-Rabi, *Women Filmmakers*, 229.

39. *New York Times*, "2D Worst Polio Year; Record 598 Cases in 48th Week Help Bring Total to 31,989," December 13, 1950. (A screening of the film *Young Lovers / Never Fear* on TCM concluded: "Unfortunately it seemed that the prevalence of the polio contagion in the news kept audiences away, as they were tired of hearing about polio and wanted to escape the bad news. The year this film was released, 1950, there were approximately 33,000 reported cases of polio in the United States. This was the main reason this film flopped at

the box office.") The Turner Classic Movies website notes, "Selznick International Pictures picked up the original camera negative. ABC Pictures International bought the Selznick library in 1978 and donated its nitrate elements, including *Never Fear*, to the Museum of Modern Art. Since the film had been out of circulation for decades, the negative was still in good condition, making it relatively easy for MoMA to create a fine-grain master and 35 mm exhibition prints. *Never Fear* is the first feature-length film directed by a woman that MoMA preserved, and since that time, works by Shirley Clarke and Yvonne Rainer amongst other female filmmakers have been preserved." "Never Fear," Watch TCM, Turner Classic Movies, accessed January 20, 2024, https://www.tcm.com/watchtcm/titles/84699.

40. Scheib, "Ida Lupino."

41. Scheib, "Ida Lupino."

42. Scheib, "Ida Lupino."

43. Charles Silver, "An Auturist History of Film," Museum of Modern Art, November 6, 2012, https://www.moma.org/explore/inside_out/2012/11/06/ida-lupinos-never-fear-the-younglovers/. Silver, curator of film at MOMA, wrote the notes to accompany the screening of Lupino's *Never Fear* (*The Young Lovers*) on November 8–10, 2012.

44. Anne Morra, "Ida Lupino," in *Modern Women: Women Artists at the Museum of Modern Art*, ed. Alexandra Schwartz (New York: Museum of Modern Art, 2010), 237.

Chapter 6. *The Hitch-Hiker*

1. These two slugs (screenplay paragraphs) are my transcriptions of what happens on the screen in Lupino's two opening shots of *The Hitch-Hiker*, written in screenplay format. I was unable to find a screenplay that matched this opening in the RKO Records at UCLA. What I did find was a lengthy, two-page series of quick cuts in what is labeled as a "revised final" script dated June 5, 1952, including a paragraph of narration (dialogue), none of which wound up in the final cut of the movie. I have not found a script with a later date. This difference shows that Lupino drastically pared down the screenplay to the story's essentials, which ratcheted up the tension and possibly saved money. Lupino may have reworked this opening with her cameraman, Nicholas Musuraca, on set.

2. Italo Calvino, *Six Memos for the Next Millennium* (Cambridge, MA: Harvard University Press, 1988), 103. The qualities Calvino writes about, "lightness," "quickness," "exactitude," "visibility," and "multiplicity," can be easily applied to the aesthetic of Lupino's film oeuvre.

3. Rickey, "Lupino Noir," 43. In this interview, Rickey spoke with Clint Eastwood, who told her, "I believed that if an actress could become a director, it kind of made me think I could be a director." While Eastwood worked on the television show *Rawhide*, he reportedly watched Lupino direct *Have Gun—Will Travel* on the same lot. He saw her riding alongside Richard Boone one day to find a specific shot, and he was inspired by her ability. To watch his films is to see Lupinian, essentials-only filmmaking.

4. Production files for *The Hitch-Hiker*, prod. no. B774, box 1595S, RKO Records. *The Hitch-Hiker* began production on June 24, 1952, and the release date was March 20, 1953.

5. Barry M. Parker, "Newsreel: Lost Lupino," *American Film*, June 1,1981, 14. RKO promotional materials for *The Hitch-Hiker* featured Highway Patrol inspector M. P. Hebblethwaite, who cautioned, "Every person who drives a car should see this picture." "Campaign for *The Hitch-Hiker*," in "RKO 25 Years of Showmanship," prod. no. B774, box 1595S, RKO Records.

6. Cary O'Dell, "'The Hitch-Hiker': National Film Registry #10," *Now See Hear!* (blog), Library of Congress, November 22, 2018, https://blogs.loc.gov/now-see-hear/2018/11/the

-hitch-hiker-national-film-registry-10/; "The Hitch-Hiker," Library of Congress, accessed January 16, 2024, https://www.loc.gov/item/mbrs00047382/. A 16 mm print is held in the Archive Research and Study Center, UCLA Film & Television Archive.

7. "Feature Reviews: *The Hitch-Hiker*," *Boxoffice*, January 17, 1953. Brackets in original.

8. "Film Reviews," review of *The Hitch-Hiker*, *Variety*, January 21, 1953.

9. David Greven, "Ida Lupino's American Psycho: *The Hitch-Hiker* (1953)," *Bright Lights Film Journal*, February 27, 2014, https://brightlightsfilm.com/ida-lupinos-american-psycho-hitch-hiker-1953/#.YATTty1h3OR.

10. Scheib, "Ida Lupino."

11. Parker, "Discovering Ida Lupino," 20. *The Hitch-Hiker* has a harrowing precedent in Felix Feist's 1947 film, *The Devil Thumbs a Ride*, in which Lawrence Tierney plays a psychopath who goes on a similar rampage.

12. Hundreds of films and television episodes and countless commercials have been filmed in the Lone Pine area, including *Joe Kidd* (1972), with Clint Eastwood, and *The Lone Ranger* (2013), with Johnny Depp. Through the years, directors have also used the unique landscape for films other than westerns, including *Star Trek V: The Final Frontier* (1989), with William Shatner, and *Gladiator* (2000), with Russell Crowe. According to Wikipedia, "The most important movie filmed in and around Lone Pine is director Raoul Walsh's *High Sierra* (1941)," starring Ida Lupino as Marie Garson and Humphrey Bogart as Roy Earle. Wikipedia, s.v. "Lone Pine, California," last modified November 21, 2023, 19:40, https://en.wikipedia.org/wiki/Lone_Pine,_California. Bogart's performance in that film moved him from respected supporting player to leading man. Lupino's credit was above Bogart's.

13. Dixon, *Lost in the Fifties*, 142–143.

14. Musuraca worked with Tourneur on *Cat People* (1942), which was produced by horror master Val Lewton; the film was remade in 1982 by Paul Schrader. Musuraca was also director of photography for *The Blue Gardenia* (1953), directed by the remarkable Fritz Lang, and with skilled noir director Robert Siodmak on *The Spiral Staircase* (1946).

15. John D. Thomas, "Shelf Life," *Village Voice*, October 21, 1997, 90.

16. Mainwaring had a series of credits, including *The Big Steal* (1949), directed by Don Siegel, and *This Woman Is Dangerous* (1952), with Joan Crawford. He also wrote the original version of *Invasion of the Body Snatchers* (1956). As a novelist, Mainwaring wrote under the pseudonym of Geoffrey Homes, and he acted as a front for the blacklisted Paul Jarrico on Lupino's *Not Wanted* (1949), though in the end, Jarrico was credited on that film.

17. Peter Odens, "The Billy Cook Murders," *Calexico Chronicle*, August 18, 1991. Odens states that the two men may have been hunting, not prospecting. The two men are variously described in different accounts as prospectors, hunters, or engineers. Some contemporary accounts state that it was Santa Rosalia's police chief, Luis Parra, who captured Cook in Guaymas by simply walking up to Cook and pulling Cook's pistol from his pants. Others give the credit to Tijuana's police chief, Francisco Kraus Morales, relating that he recognized Cook from international wanted posters and arrested him without incident.

18. Frank Miller, "*The Hitch-Hiker*," Turner Classic Movies, June 28, 2004, https://www.tcm.com/tcmdb/title/78138/the-hitch-hiker#articles-reviews?articleId=78324.

19. The warden at San Quentin was Harley Teets, an empathetic warden who, during his term at San Quentin, gassed fewer than fifty inmates. See "Rider on the Storm," *Sword and Scale* blog, December 21, 2015, https://www.swordandscale.com/rider-on-the-storm.

20. Ben Cosgrove, "'I'm Gonna Live by the Gun and Roam': Portrait of an American Spree Killer," *Life*, April 1, 2014, http://time.com/3879488/billy-cockeyed-cook-portrait-of-an-american-spree-killer/, originally published January 1951.

21. See, for example, Cosgrove, "'I'm Gonna Live.'"

22. Cosgrove, "'I'm Gonna Live.'" This was before the release of Charles Laughton's *Night of the Hunter* (1955), in which Robert Mitchum's knuckles are tattooed with "Love" and "Hate."

23. Payroll cards, RKO Records, UCLA, April 11, 1952. Lupino was paid a flat fee of $1500 to write all drafts of "The Hitch-Hiker."

24. Equivalent fragments for Lupino's *Hard, Fast and Beautiful* can be found in RKO Records. For example, music files are carefully stored in archival box M316. Box 188 has call sheets, shooting schedules, and a cast sheet. Box 712 contains Lupino's lean budget, showing that she had few prop men but five grips, as usual; a seventeen-day shooting schedule; a daily talent requisition; transportation lunch sheets; central casting for day players; and several claims for adjustment. Box S/1592 holds all iterations of the scripts that are housed at UCLA, including three final scripts: April 19, 1950, 115 pages; May 9, 1950, 102 pages; and June 30, 1950, 104 pages with colored revisions, which might be the final script. Another document lists the cutting continuity: 5 reels, 9 sections, 7,025 feet, with a running time of 78 minutes, 3⅓ seconds. Generally, the film was released on 2,000-foot reels.

25. Other cues are titled "The Shotgun," "The Grocery Store," "The Hill Sequence," "The Roadblock Montage," "The Shaft Sequence," "The Newspaper Opening and Montage," and "Hop In." Box M512, RKO Records.

26. Parker, "Discovering Ida Lupino," 22.

27. Unsigned "Memo for Mr. Breen," with handwritten response by Breen, January 23, 1951, file #699, correspondence, *The Hitch-Hiker*, PCA Records and PCA Digital Collection, 102_074324_p001. Cook was not caught until 1951 and was convicted in 1952, when Lupino and Young secured Cook's signed release for his life story.

28. Unsigned "Memo for Mr. Breen."

29. Hedda Hopper, "Story of Captives Stirs Ida," *Los Angeles Times*, February 2, 1951, 6.

30. H. H. Z. [unidentified], "Memo for the Files, Re: Killer William Cook and the Two Hunters Kidnaped by Him and Held Prisoner for Eight Days in Baja California," February 2, 1951, file #699, correspondence, *The Hitch-Hiker*, PCA Records and PCA Digital Collection, 102_074324_p003–004.

31. H. H. Z., "Memo for the Files," February 7, 1951.

32. H. H. Z., "Memo for the Files," February 7, 1951.

33. James V. Bennett to Joseph I. Breen, March 31, 1952, file #699, correspondence, *The Hitch-Hiker*, PCA Records and PCA Digital Collection, 102_074324_p005.

34. Bennett to Breen, March 31, 1952.

35. Ida Lupino and Collier Young to James Bennett, April 10, 1952 (photostat), page 1, file #699, correspondence, *The Hitch-Hiker*, PCA Records and PCA Digital Collection, 102_074324_p011. The letter denies any trickiness or illegality in gaining Cook's life rights for their film.

36. Ida Lupino and Collier Young to James Bennett, April 10, 1952, page 2, PCA Digital Collection, 102_074324_p012.

37. Ida Lupino and Collier Young to James Bennett, April 10, 1952, page 3, PCA Digital Collection, 102_074324_p013.

38. James V. Bennett to Geoffrey M. Shurlock, April 11, 1952, file #699, correspondence, *The Hitch-Hiker*, PCA Records and PCA Digital Collection, 102_074324_p010.

39. Joseph I. Breen to William Feeder, May 21, 1952, file #699, correspondence, *The Hitch-Hiker*, PCA Records and PCA Digital Collection, 102_074324_p021–022.

40. Breen to Feeder, May 21, 1952. Note that Feeder's letter used a slightly different form of the movie title, omitting "Billy" Cook's first name.

41. Breen to Feeder, May 21, 1952.

42. Breen to Feeder, May 21, 1952.

43. Joseph I. Breen, letter to William Feeder, May 21, 1952, 8, 25, 34. The note about weapons is from special regulation 8, regarding the treatment of crime in motion pictures.

44. The censors of Lupino's era have been replaced by the studios, which now want blood, violence, and amorality because those movies sell better overseas. The notes that passed between Feeder and Breen are much like the notes screenwriters currently receive from the studios. Finding a way around studio notes is difficult and time-consuming, but it is important because the studio can easily destroy the central concept as they pull out parts of the script, essentially separating the writer from her unconscious. Today the studios might have fought over *The Hitch-Hiker* very differently—the more lurid and frightening, the better.

45. Greven, "Ida Lupino's American Psycho."

46. The Korean War "ended" in 1953. It was a war, like Vietnam, involving questionable motives by the United States. Only a few years after a devastating good-versus-evil World War II, vets returning from Korea were unsettled and not lauded as heroic.

47. Jean Baudrillard, *Le système des objects* (Paris: Gallimard, 1968), 94, quoted in Ross, *Fast Cars, Clean Bodies*, 19.

48. Scorsese reflects this frightening desert landscape in his *Casino* (1995), in which the desert dust signifies the American western, another genre that Lupino mastered after she began directing for television.

49. Second revised final script of *The Hitch-Hiker*, June 5, 1952, prod. no. B774, box 1595S, RKO Records.

50. The sheet music for the "One-Eyed Sleeper" cue is scored for violins, cello, and horns. M 31, box M512, RKO Records.

51. Lupino went on to use Edmond O'Brien in her next film, *The Bigamist*. He plays the bigamist, Harry Graham, who is a confused, passive, helpless organization man of the 1950s. During the 1960s, O'Brien hired Lupino to direct two of his *Sam Benedict* series episodes. O'Brien famously was cast in Sam Peckinpah's western film classic *The Wild Bunch*; Peckinpah himself was hired very early in his career by Lupino to write on her *Mr. Adams and Eve* series. Late in Lupino's and Peckinpah's careers, he cast her in *Junior Bonner*, which is being newly reevaluated and recovered as Steve McQueen's greatest acting performance and Peckinpah's best, and most subtle, western family drama.

52. Musuraca's geometric blocks of light and dark forms reflect his professional inspirations: constructivism, the Bauhaus School, and German expressionism. See Wikipedia, s.v. "Nicholas Musuraca," last modified September 22, 2023, 16:14, https://en.wikipedia.org/wiki/Nicholas_Musuraca.

53. Vivian Carol Sobchack, "*Detour*: Driving in a Back Projection, or Forestalled by Film Noir," in *Kiss the Blood off My Hands: On Classic Film Noir*, ed. Robert Miklitsch (Urbana: University of Illinois Press, 2014), 114.

54. "A beat," for the purposes of this discussion, is a unit that gives the audience some information through either an image or dialogue; it might be a twist in a discovery, an introduction of a new character, an event, or a crucial decision.

55. Scorsese made this point in his documentary *Val Lewton*. Lewton worked with Musuraca, another Lupino connection.

56. Greven, "Ida Lupino's American Psycho."

57. Rabinovitz, "*Hitch-Hiker*," in Kuhn, *Queen of the 'B's*, 92.

58. The original Arriflex 35 motion picture camera, released in 1937, was designed and developed by Arnold and Richter Cine Technik (ARRI) of Munich, Germany. The company, which manufactured film equipment, was founded in 1917, a year before Lupino was

born. The Arriflex 35 II was often used by French New Wave and Hollywood filmmakers, including by Delmer Daves for his *Dark Passage* (1947). Unfortunately, Lupino did not have access to this new, lighter camera, which might have altered her shot setups and made shooting easier, as it did for Godard and other filmmakers.

59. These challenges foreshadowed those of television productions, including the *Screen Directors Playhouse*, which began in 1955. Lupino's first written and directed movie for the *Screen Director's Playhouse* was "No. 5 Checked Out," which aired January 18, 1956, and is discussed in detail in chapter 8.

60. Tasker and Leonard, *Fifty Hollywood Directors*, 162.

61. Parker, "Discovering Ida Lupino," 23.

62. Barbet Schroeder, comment to author during his on-set shoot for *Single White Female* (1992) in Paris, France, in 1990.

63. Weiner, "Interview with Ida Lupino," 177.

64. Rhona J. Berenstein, "Acting Live: TV Performance, Intimacy, and Immediacy (1945–1955)," in *Reality Squared: Televisual Discourse on the Real*, ed. James Friedman (New Brunswick, NJ: Rutgers University Press, 2002), 26–27; and Scheib, "Ida Lupino."

65. Scheib, "Ida Lupino."

Part III. Television

1. Lupino directed one episode of *The Rifleman*, "Assault," which aired on March 21, 1961. Sam Peckinpah developed the series, and Joseph H. Lewis, director of *Gun Crazy* (1950), is credited as the director of over fifty episodes.

2. Rickey, "Lupino Noir," 43. Eastwood was filming *Rawhide* while Lupino was directing *Have Gun—Will Travel* on the same lot. To watch his films is to see spare, taut, essentials-only filmmaking. Arguably, both Lupino and TV itself were influences on Eastwood's style. See Ruthe Stein, "Mother Directs: Ida Lupino behind the Camera," *Eat Drink Films*, http://eatdrinkfilms.com/2015/11/19/mother-directs-ida-lupino-behind-the-camera/.

3. Richard Gehman and Michael McFadden, "The Golden Sex: They Use Beauty, Brains to Produce TV," *Los Angeles Herald Examiner*, May 14, 1963, B1, B8; Kearny and Moran, "Ida Lupino as Director," 142.

Chapter 7. Lupino and Early Television

1. John Cassavetes, yet another renowned, one-of-a-kind auteur, made that same transition, only later, after Welles and Lupino.

2. Kathleen L. Spencer, *Art and Politics in "Have Gun—Will Travel": The 1950s Television Western as Ethical Drama* (Jefferson, NC: MacFarland, 2014), 85.

3. Grisham and Grossman, *Ida Lupino, Director*, 134. Other female directors did enter television later and perhaps shot more cumulative shows as the medium expanded its reach. Among them is Beth McCarthy-Miller, who became *Saturday Night Live*'s staff director in 1995 after stints at MTV; she then moved to other popular formulaic comedies such as *Modern Family*. However, Lupino might still hold the record for her variety of shows and genres. Though a few women worked in TV in various roles, there were two who actually directed before Lupino: Thelma A. Prescott and Frances Buss. Sarah Arnold, *Gender and Early Television Mapping Women's Role in Emerging US and British Media, 1850-1950* (London: Bloomsbury Academic, 2021), 95. Other female directors came after Lupino, beginning in the late 1960s: Karen Arthur, Anne Bancroft, Joan Darling, Lee Grant, Barbara Loden, Elaine May, Barbara Peeters, Joan Rivers, Stephanie Rothman, Beverly Sebastian, Joan Micklin Silver, Joan Tewkesbury, Jane Wagner, Nancy Walker, and Claudia Weill. See Montañez Smuckler, "Working Girls," ii–iii. Again, most of these women had been actors.

4. Lynn Spigel, *Make Room for TV: Television and the Family Ideal in Postwar America* (Chicago: University of Chicago Press, 2013), 32.

5. The percentage is for 1959. Robert J. Thompson, "Television in the United States," *Encyclopaedia Britannica*, July 1, 2019, https://www.britannica.com/art/television-in-the-United-States.

6. Christine Becker, "Televising Film Stardom in the 1950s," *Framework: The Journal of Cinema and Media* 46, no. 2 (2005): 7.

7. Thomas Schatz, *The Genius of the System: Hollywood Filmmaking in the Studio Era* (New York: Pantheon, 1988), 318; and Cobbett Steinberg, *TV Facts* (New York: Facts on File, 1980), 235.

8. Today the storytelling on television is diverse, and it's common for professionals to work in both media. See *Vanity Fair*, Special Edition 2019 (https://archive.vanityfair.com/issue/20190215), which examines the vast power of television and how regard for the historically maligned medium has changed again.

9. "TV Film Employment: It's Going Up from Coast to Coast, Screen Actors Report," *Broadcasting*, December 13, 1954, 44, cited in Becker, "Televising Film Stardom," 7.

10. Becker, "Televising Film Stardom," 7. Rogers's show was not picked up.

11. A film star's fame could also sell television sets. Christine Becker, *It's the Pictures That Got Small: Hollywood Film Stars on 1950s Television (Middletown, CT: Wesleyan University Press, 2008)*, 215.

12. Becker, *It's the Pictures*, 108. Orson Welles famously told Cotten, "You're very lucky to be tall and thin and have curly hair. You can also move about the stage without running into the furniture. But these are fringe assets, and I'm afraid you'll never make it as an actor. But as a star, I think you well might hit the jackpot." "The Hosts: Open House on TV," *TV Guide*, February 4–10, 1956, 21. See also Joseph Cotten, "Orson and Me," *New York Daily News*, October 13, 1985.

13. This practice continued in talk shows hosted by Johnny Carson, David Letterman, Jay Leno, and Jimmy Kimmel, to name a few.

14. The show was retitled *Susie* when it moved to syndication. Ann Sothern subsequently starred in *The Ann Sothern Show* (1958–1961, CBS), in which she played the assistant manager of an upscale hotel.

15. Ernie Kovacs successfully pushed television's boundaries, however, presenting "some of the zaniest and most original comedy of his day" on *The Ernie Kovacs Show* (1952–1956). John Charles, "Ernie Kovacs: Biography," Turner Classic Movies, accessed January 9, 2024, https://www.tcm.com/tcmdb/person/105013%7C48853/Ernie-Kovacs#biography.

16. Although Reed played a prostitute in *From Here to Eternity*, which was released in 1953 concurrently with *The Hitch-Hiker*, she could not shake her good-girl image.

17. Becker, *It's the Pictures*, 173. The series was produced by Lupino and Duff's Bridget Productions. See Amelie Hastie, "The Trouble with Lupino," *Cinema Comparative Cinema* 4, no. 8 (2016): 53.

18. Kuhn, "Introduction," 3.

19. Grisham and Grossman, *Ida Lupino, Director*, 134.

20. Hastie, "Trouble with Lupino," 53.

21. Gwendolyn Audrey Foster, *Women Film Directors: An International Bio-Critical Dictionary* (Westport, CT: Greenwood, 1995), 223.

22. Louella Parsons and Harriet Parsons, "Ida Lupino, Rarest of the Rare," *New York Journal-American*, December 5, 1965.

23. Lupino, "Interview with Ida Lupino," 228.

24. Hastie, *Bigamist*, 13.

25. Peter Bart, "Lupino, the Dynamo," *New York Times*, March 7, 1965, X7, Personality Clipping File Collection.

26. *Four Star Playhouse* was the first series produced by Four Star Productions, formed in 1952 by Dick Powell, David Niven, Ida Lupino, and Joel McCrea. The company merged

with Four Star Films to become Four Star Television in 1958. It produced several other popular shows, including *The Dick Powell Show* (1961–1963).

27. Becker, *It's the Pictures*, 189.

28. Television also became a training ground for future generations of actors and filmmakers. Clint Eastwood started directing some of the *Rawhide* television episodes in which he had been acting from 1959 through 1965.

29. Today writer-creators are called showrunners and content creators, and episodes that once cost $50,000 to $127,000 now average $3 million for a one-hour scripted drama and $2 million for a cable episode. An episode of *Game of Thrones* cost $6 million during the first season and climbed to $15 million by the final season, while *The Crown* went from $7 million to $15 million.

30. Writers of noirish pulp fiction receive similarily poor pay, although some are now classics whose sales remain high today. These maligned objects are often the foundation of our most iconic and artistic works.

31. Becker, *It's the Pictures*, 176.

32. This episode is discussed in detail in chapter 8. For a detailed analysis of *Screen Directors Playhouse*, see Grisham and Grossman, *Ida Lupino, Director*, 124–133.

33. Horace Newcomb and Paul M. Hirsch, "Television as a Cultural Forum," in *Television: The Critical View*, ed. Horace Newcomb (Oxford: Oxford University Press, 1987), 571.

34. Roger Corman helped launch the careers of many actors and filmmakers, just as Hitchcock did. The Hitchcock talent team included, in his show's early seasons (beginning in 1955), novelists Philip Roth, John Cheever, Ray Bradbury, and Roald Dahl; iconic television writer Stirling Silliphant; screenwriters Adela Rogers St. Johns, Buck Henry, Ian McLellan Hunter (cover for blacklisted Dalton Trumbo and father of director Tim Hunter), and Evan Hunter; directors Stuart Rosenberg, Arthur Hiller, and Atom Egoyan; and actors Barbara Bel Geddes, Keenan Wynn, Fay Wray, Jessica Tandy, Cloris Leachman, Ben Johnson, Scatman Crothers, Claire Trevor, and Art Carney. Occasionally a writer/actor would emerge, as in the case of Garson Kanin, or an actor/director, like Paul Henreid. Later seasons included actors Peter Lorre, Steve McQueen, William Shatner, Beatrice Straight, James Franciscus, Dennis Weaver, Burt Reynolds, Harry Dean Stanton, Anne Francis, Rip Torn, Claude Rains, and the incomparable Jo Van Fleet, and the final seasons included actors Robert Redford, Robert Duvall, Sandy Dennis, Martin Sheen, Eli Wallach, and Joaquin Phoenix.

35. Aldrich's five episodes of *Four Star Playhouse* are "The Squeeze" (October 1, 1953), "The Witness" (October 22, 1953), "The Hard Way" (November 19, 1953), "The Gift" (December 24, 1953), and "The Bad Streak" (January 14, 1954).

36. "High Green Wall," which stars Cotten, was filmed for *General Electric Theater*, airing on October 3, 1954, and was rebroadcast on Cotten's anthology show on August 17, 1959. Lupino's episode, "The Trial of Mary Surratt," aired on November 23, 1956. Both episodes are discussed in detail in chapter 8. The series was initially titled *On Trial*, but Cotten became so closely linked to the show that the title was changed in February 1957 to *The Joseph Cotten Show: On Trial.* Tim Brooks and Earl Marsh, *The Complete Directory to Prime Time Network and Cable TV Shows, 1946–Present* (New York: Ballantine, 1995), 540.

37. Lupino's episodes were "Sybilla" (December 6, 1960) and "A Crime for Mothers" (January 24, 1961), discussed in chapter 8. Of the 268 episodes filmed for the series, Hitchcock directed 17.

38. Transcript from "Women Directing for Television," presentation as part of *She Made It: Women Creating Television and Radio*, Museum of Television and Radio, Los Angeles and New York, January 13–February 16, 2006. The presentation preceded a screening of "The Masks," directed by Lupino for *The Twilight Zone.*

39. Spencer, *Art and Politics*, 85.

40. Lupino could not use the word *rape* in her own film *Outrage*; even though it was a story about rape as such, the operative word was *attack*.

41. Spencer, *Art and Politics*, 85.

42. Television during the 1950s and 1960s had no "created by" showrunners. Depending on the show, the writers or lead actors might have shepherded the episodes. For *Have Gun—Will Travel*, Boone hired the directors and worked closely with the writers, so he had the weight of the show's success or failure on his shoulders. If he seemed impatient, that may have been the reason. In addition to "The Man Who Lost," Lupino directed "First, Catch a Tiger" (September 12, 1959), "Charley Red Dog" (December 12, 1959), "The Day of the Bad Man" (January 9, 1960), "The Lady on the Wall" (February 20, 1960), "Lady with a Gun" (April 9, 1960), and "The Trial" (June 11, 1960), all in the third season, and "The Gold Bar" (March 18, 1961) in the fourth season.

43. Erskine Johnson, 1961, quoted in Spencer, *Art and Politics*, 85n60.

Chapter 8. Across Media with Ray, Aldrich, and Hitchcock

1. "High Green Wall" was Ray's last work for television; see Eisenschitz, *Nicholas Ray*.

2. Welles directed Cotten in *Citizen Kane* (1941), *The Magnificent Ambersons* (1942), and *The Third Man* (1949).

3. Eisenschitz, *Nicholas Ray*, 221, 227–228.

4. Eisenschitz, *Nicholas Ray*, 227–228. Planer worked with Ray on *King of Kings* (1961). Planer shot over 130 films, including Max Ophüls's *The Exile* (1947), Robert Siodmak's *Criss Cross* (1949), William Wyler's *Roman Holiday* (1953), Edward Dmytryk's *The Caine Mutiny* (1954), and Sidney Lumet's *Stage Struck* (1958).

5. Kurosawa, in *Rashomon* (1950), shot Toshiro Mifune's run through the Japanese forest, tracking with his actor horizontally, from left to right. Mifune becomes a dappled vision across the forested frame.

6. Eisenschitz, *Nicholas Ray*, 223.

7. Eisenschitz, *Nicholas Ray*, 223. The teleplay freely adapts the passage from *A Tale of Two Cities*.

8. Eisenschitz, *Nicholas Ray*, 224. Neither the Association for Recorded Sound Collections nor UCLA's television archive has a copy of this episode, but I found it and watched it online. Oddly, the credits are shown in the middle of the episode.

9. The spelling "Seurat" is used in Weiner, "Interview with Ida Lupino." However, "Surratt" is used by most online sources, including *Encyclopaedia Britannica*, Wikipedia, and most importantly, the Library of Congress. "Surratt" is used in Lupino's directed episode for *On Trial*, "The Trial of Mary Surratt," as well as *Kraft Television Theater*'s "The Story of Mary Surratt" (March 23, 1955) and Robert Redford's *The Conspirator* (2010). In 2010, Robert Redford's Wildwood Productions released *The Conspirator*, directed by Redford and starring Robin Wright as Mary Surratt. This was Wright's biggest step back into acting after a long absence while she raised her children.

10. Weiner, "Interview with Ida Lupino," 176.

11. See Grisham and Grossman, *Ida Lupino, Director*, 162.

12. *Kraft Television Theatre* (NBC, 1947–1958) aired "The Story of Mary Surratt," directed by Richard Dunlap, on March 23, 1955, the year before Lupino's own directed study.

13. Gregg was a ubiquitous television actress who, interestingly enough, was one of the offscreen voices for Norman Bates's mummified mother in Hitchcock's *Psycho*. In 2023, I was finally able to view this episode, which currently is found only in the Library of Congress National Film Registry. This is a fully feminist narrative.

14. For the interrogation of women, see Ginzburg, *Clues, Myths*. Ginzburg's research

in archives in Modena, Italy, shows that during its sixteenth-century witch trials, powerful magistrates and cardinals bullied women of meager means who had been accused of witchcraft until the women, terrified of their captors, confessed. Ginzburg writes with empathy of this unjust aggression and condemns the subsequent murder of these women.

15. Grisham and Grossman, *Ida Lupino, Director*, 163.

16. Weiner, "Interview with Ida Lupino," 176.

17. Ivano was a true veteran who had worked in silent films with F. W. Murnau, Erich von Stroheim, Charles Vidor, and Josef von Sternberg.

18. Hal Roach Studios Production Budget, December 7, 1955, #9647, box 13, Hal Roach Collection, Cinematic Arts Library, University of Southern California, Los Angeles.

19. In *The Hitch-Hiker*, Musuraca introduces Talman's character in much the same way, with very low key and focused lighting.

20. Grisham and Grossman, *Ida Lupino, Director*, 128.

21. Lorre worked with Bertolt Brecht in Germany before starring in Lang's *M*. After Hitler came to power in Germany, Lorre moved to England, where he worked with Hitchcock in *The Man Who Knew Too Much* (1934). Lorre's sinister presence was established by his roles in *The Maltese Falcon* (1941) and *Casablanca* (1942). He worked often at Warner Bros., where, as the star of the Mr. Moto movies from 1937 to 1939, he played yet another foreign character, who was ostensibly Japanese but far less ominous.

22. The windowpanes in this shot recall the squares drawn on the the Farley home's garage door in *Hard, Fast and Beautiful*, which Florence (Sally Forrest) used for her early tennis practice.

23. Grisham and Grossman, *Ida Lupino, Director*, 133.

24. For example, Aldrich made *Whatever Happened to Baby Jane?* (1962) in nineteen days for $900,000 despite the ongoing feuding between his leads, aging divas Bette Davis and Joan Crawford, who both had made the move to television. Accounts of their on-set fights were told to me by Bill Aldrich, Bob's son. Bob also told me the budget for Baby Jane, as well as the nineteen-day timeline. *Baby Jane* was nominated for four academy awards.

25. René Micha, *Robert Aldrich* (Brussels: Club du Livre de Cinéma, 1957). Other volumes in the series are about Robert Bresson, John Huston, Jean Renoir, Vittorio De Sica, Luis Buñuel, and Marcel Carné.

26. Aldrich directed five episodes of *Four Star Playhouse*, three with Dick Powell and two with Charles Boyer. Production was at RKO Pictures. The executive producer for the series is listed as Don W. Sharpe; the associate producer was Warren Lewis.

27. John Bagni and Gwen Bagni wrote "The Bad Streak" and other *Four Star Playhouse* episodes. Gwen continued to write for the series after John died in 1954. She was nominated for an Emmy for Outstanding Writing for her work on the 1979 miniseries *Backstairs at the White House*.

28. Sanford (Sandy) Meisner was an acting guru from the 1950s through the 1970s who developed a method that used independent activity as a tool to help actors focus and thus ground their written characters. The other famous acting experts at the time were Stella Adler and Lee Strasberg, both of whom taught the Stanislavski technique, often called method acting, a term that is misused. Lupino did not subscribe to method acting, but I assume she disliked time-consuming self-indulgence, which is the common negative connotation of the method. Although Lupino didn't seem to direct performance using any specific method, her direction of actors was instinctively modern, realistic, truthful, and restrained. Lupino's performance in Aldrich's *The Big Knife* does seem to reflect both techniques. In that film, she was surrounded by Meisnerian and method actors: Jean Hagen, Wendell Corey, Shelley Winters, Rod Steiger, and Aldrich himself, a Meisner follower.

Lupino thought Aldrich's rehearsal methods were particularly outstanding because they produced deeply naturalistic results—that is, truth. Her performance was understated and distinct, yet it shows her particular and characteristic discipline and skill, and her own acting style fit seamlessly into the fabric of the film. Although not a method actress, she could certainly pass for one.

29. I was one of two female director-fellows at the American Film Institute at the time. To verify my notes and recollections, I consulted Robert Aldrich's taped transcript in the collection of the Louis B. Mayer Library, American Film Institute, Los Angeles.

30. Grisham and Grossman, *Ida Lupino, Director*, 134.

31. John Horn, *The Frame*, KCRW, 2021.

32. Grisham and Grossman, *Ida Lupino, Director*, 183–185. The authors examine this episode in some depth.

33. Henry Slesar, "A Crime for Mothers," *Alfred Hitchcock's Mystery Magazine* 5, no. 12 (December 1960). Slesar is credited with the story or teleplay for dozens of episodes on *Alfred Hitchcock Presents* and *The Alfred Hitchcock Hour*. See YouTube playlist "The Best of Alfred Hitchcock Presents," November 1, 2022, https://www.google.com/search?client=safari&rls=en&q=The+BEst+of+Alfred+Hitchcock+Presents&ie=UTF-8&oe=UTF-8.

34. Marshall D. Schechter, "Observations on Adopted Children," *Archives of General Psychiatry* 3, no. 1 (1960): 21–32.

35. Ellen Herman, "Timeline of Adoption History," Adoption History Project, updated February 24, 2012, https://pages.uoregon.edu/adoption/timeline.html.

36. Alfred Hitchcock, Harold Lloyd Master Seminar, AFI Conservatory, Los Angeles, February 3, 1970.

37. From Hitchcock's epilogue to the episode.

38. Jack Edmund Nolan, "Ida Lupino," *Films in Review* 16 (1965): 62. See Grisham and Grossman, *Ida Lupino, Director*, for an in-depth look at "The Masks."

39. "The Masks" has been reviewed as one of the top five *Twilight Zone* episodes. See "User Reviews," IMDb, last updated November 3, 2023, https://www.imdb.com/title/tt0734659/reviews?ref_=tt_ov_rt. Don Presnell and Marty McGee observe that "'The Masks' is one of the most enduring TZ episodes and is also one of the most historic. It is the only one of the 156 episodes to be directed by a woman. In addition, it marks the only time in the series that a person (male or female) both acted and directed in *The Twilight Zone*." Don Presnell and Marty McGee, *A Critical History of Television's* The Twilight Zone, *1959–1964* (Jefferson, NC: McFarland), 183.

40. The director for "Hear the Mellow Wedding Bells" is listed as Lupino in some publications and online sources, but Medford is credited in the episode itself. IMDb lists eighty directing credits for Medford for dozens of series and television movies, including *The Fugitive*, *Dynasty*, and *The Twilight Zone*. (Lupino directed more episodes overall than Medford, but Medford did direct "Wedding Bells.")

41. The schedule is given as "6 days/69 hours, Budget total $127,805." "Hear the Mellow Wedding Bells" (Director Don Medford), September 11, 1962, Schedule, p. 1, Prod. No. 6802; and Metro-Goldwyn-Mayer Inc. Television Production Budget, 9-13-62, Producer E. Jack Newman, script date 8-31-62, film type B&W, schedule, MGM Production Dept. (TV Shows) Collection, Cinematic Arts Library, University of Southern California, Los Angeles.

42. Ned Comstock, film historian and librarian, undated with a handwritten note, MGM Production Dept. (TV Shows) Collection, Cinematic Arts Library, University of Southern California, Los Angeles.

43. Sam Peckinpah often hired day players, whom he relied on and highly respected. Excellent examples can be seen in his film *The Wild Bunch* (1969). According to IMDB and

Peckinpah's and Lupino's wiki pages, Lupino hired Peckinpah to work on her *Mr. Adams and Eve* series when she found him living in a shack behind her property.

Chapter 9. Patterns and Strategies in Lupino's Television Directing

1. Becker, "Televising Film Stardom," 9. Becker draws on the discussion of "ordinariness" by Susan Murray in *Hitch Your Antenna to the Stars: Early Television and Broadcast Stardom* (New York: Routledge, 2005).

2. Hal Humphrey, "TV, the Great Rejuvenator," *Los Angeles Mirror*, September 9, 1954, 26. Also quoted in Becker, "Televising Film Stardom," 11.

3. Robert Johnson, "Mr. Duff and Ida," *TV Guide*, June 1–7, 1957, 18.

4. As of this writing, this episode is not available on the internet, but one can view it at the Paley Center, Beverly Hills, California.

5. Johnson, "Mr. Duff and Ida," 18.

6. Untitled script for *Mr. Adams and Eve*, episode production number 9618, August 17, 1955, folder 1–2, Ida Lupino Collection, Harry Ransom Center, University of Texas at Austin.

7. Dwight Whitney, "Guess Who's Coming to Dinner?" *TV Guide* 14, no. 4 (1966): 6. The two stars met the prime minister on November 14, 1967.

8. A successful film based on *The Untouchables* series was made in 1987 with Kevin Costner, Sean Connery, Andy Garcia, and Robert DeNiro, directed by Brian de Palma.

9. "Television: Mother Lupino," *Time*, February 8, 1963, http://content.time.com/time/subscriber/article/0,33009,829844,00.html.

10. Nolan, "Ida Lupino," 62.

11. A successful film based on the series was made in 1993 with Harrison Ford in the lead role.

12. Pippa Scott, telephone interview by author, December 12, 2019.

13. A good example is the music for the *Thriller* episode "Pigeons from Hell" (June 6, 1961), whose scoring makes predominant use of the string section.

14. Stephen King, *Danse Macabre* (New York: Everett House, 1981), 219.

15. Alan Warren, *This Is a Thriller: An Episode Guide, History and Analysis of the Classic 1960s Television Series* (Jefferson, NC: McFarland, 2004), 124. Warren includes Hitchcock's version of Cornell Woolrich's "Three O'Clock" in this category

16. Robert Middleton was in more than thirty films, including *The Big Combo* (1955) and *The Desperate Hours* (1955), and dozens of television episodes during his career of more than twenty-five years. He appeared primarily in westerns, detective shows, and crime dramas, but he also had comedic roles, including a recurring role as Jackie Gleason's boss on *The Honeymooners*.

17. Warren, *This Is a Thriller*, 123.

18. The IMDb website does not note many of Lupino's collaborative contributions.

19. Grisham and Grossman, *Ida Lupino, Director*, 135.

20. Jack Edmund Nolan, "Ida Lupino," *Films in Review* 16 (1965): 61–62.

Conclusion. Lupinian Collaboration, the New Auteurism

1. Pauline Kael, "The Current Cinema: Dames," review of *A Woman under the Influence*, *New Yorker*, December 9, 1974, 178. Rowlands earned an Oscar nomination for Best Actress in 1975; Cassavetes received a nomination for Best Director.

2. Muse Awards recognize "the vision and achievements of women who work in the entertainment industry." For a list of awardees, see "Past Muse Award Honorees," New York Women in Film and Television, https://www.nywift.org/muse/past-honorees/.

3. Gina Rowlands, interview for "Ida Lupino: Through the Lens."

4. Kristine McKenna, "Under a Woman's Influence," *Los Angeles Times*, May 3, 1992, F2. In a revealing error, McKenna attributed the quote to "the late Ida Lupino, whose work had a similar gritty realism." A correction appeared the next day acknowledging the mistake: "Lupino, 74, lives in Hollywood and is active and well, according to her spokesperson."

5. Hastie notes that the production company was "never to be." Hastie, *Bigamist,* 13.

6. Gehman and McFadden, "Golden Sex," B8.

7. Lupino, "Ida Lupino."

8. Luaine Lee, "Ida Lupino Still Grande Dame of the Cinema," *Chicago Tribune*, February 13, 1982. Lupino said she had completed a book about her life with the collaboration of Bernard Katz, called "Laugh Like Hell," and was looking for a publisher. Ginger Varney, who inteviewed Lupino in 1982, shed light on Lupino's autobiography title, commenting that for Lupino, there was "nothing more humiliating or embarrassing than the self-absorption of self-pity." Varney then quoted Lupino: "When the bastards think they have you done, kiddo, that's when you laugh like hell!" Varney, "Ida Lupino, Director."

9. David Everitt, "A Woman Forgotten and Scorned No More," *New York Times*, November 23, 1997, sec. 2, p. 34.

10. "Frances Farmer Biopic: Ida Lupino Directs, Fem-Finances Film," *Variety*, November 27, 1974, 7, Margaret Herrick Library, Academy of Motion Picture Arts and Sciences, Los Angeles. The title of Farmer's autobiography (which was largely written by Farmer's friend Jean Ratcliffe) was taken from an Emily Dickinson poem. Grisham and Grossman, *Ida Lupino, Director*, viii. This poem can be seen in the online Emily Dickinson Archive at https://www.edickinson.org/editions/1/image_sets/235394.

11. "Frances Farmer Biography Slated for Indy in '75," *Boxoffice*, December 9, 1974, NE-4.

12. Eric Estrin, "The Unraveling of Frances Farmer," *Washington Post*, January 23, 1983, https://www.washingtonpost.com/archive/lifestyle/style/1983/01/23/the-unraveling-of-frances-farmer/8b1160fd-9535-474b-84e7-8bc08be388a7/.

13. Lupino had an artist's need to show reality as ambiguous, without clear or easy choices. Her stories were liminal, real-life stories of wanderers who found hard luck and faced the most difficult choices. As Alexandre Astruc wrote, "The world of an artist is not the one that conditions him, but the one which he needs in order to create and to transform perpetually into something that will obsess him even more than that by which he is obsessed. The obsession of the artist is artistic creation." Alexandre Astruc, "What Is Mise en scène?," in *Cahiers du Cinéma*, vol. 1, *The 1950s*, ed. Hillier, 266–268, originally published as "Qu'est-ce que la mise-en-scène?," *Cahiers du Cinéma* 100 (October 1959).

14. Bart, "Lupino, the Dynamo." It's probable that Lupino was negotiating a three-picture deal that fell through.

15. American Film Institute, "The Trouble with Angels," *AFI Catalog of Feature Films: The First 100 Years, 1893–1993,* accessed January 9, 2024, https://catalog.afi.com/Catalog/moviedetails/22691.

16. Bart, "Lupino, the Dynamo." According to Bart, Bridget Duff, Lupino and Howard Duff's daughter, was to have a small role in the film, but her name does not appear in the credits. Bart also stated that Lupino and Duff were planning a children's book about a creature called a "Fleep," a cross between a flea and a fly. Lupino was to write and Duff, who was a cartoonist as well as an actor, would illustrate.

17. Bart, "Lupino, the Dynamo."

18. Bosley Crowther, "Angel in Trouble: Hayley Mills Sparkles in an Uneven Movie," *New York Times*, April 7, 1966, 45; and American Film Institute, "Trouble with Angels."

19. Dan Georgakas, "Ida Lupino: Doing It Her Way," *Cineaste* 25, no. 3 (2000): 35.

20. Listing the men in the picture as "The Outsiders" is an ironic comment on Lupino's usual female protagonists, most of whom are outcasts.

21. Ken Anderson, "The Trouble with Angels, 1966," *Dreams Are What Le Cinema Is For* (blog), October 9, 2014, https://lecinemadreams.blogspot.com/2014/10/the-trouble-with-angels-1966.html?m=1.

22. Grisham and Grossman, *Ida Lupino, Director*, 118.

23. Gypsy Rose Lee, footage taken behind the scenes of *The Trouble with Angels*, 1965–1966, M1281775, Home Movie Collection, Academy Film Archive, Academy of Motion Picture Arts and Sciences, Los Angeles. Lee made so many films between the mid-1940s and the mid-1960s that Erik Preminger, Lee and Otto Preminger's son, created a television show, *The Gypsy Rose Lee Show*, to air them. Lee seemed to enjoy being an actor filming other actors, writers, and directors; see Erik Preminger's documentary about his mother, *Gypsy Rose Lee's Home Movies* (1998; archive footage; IMDB). Rose Lee's papers can be accessed at the Billy Rose Theatre Division at The New York Public Library, T-MSS 1990-014.

24. Also shown in the the same footage are Binnie Barnes as Sister Celestine and Mary Wickes as Sister Clarissa. Jerry Goldsmith, who scored Lupino's *Thriller* episodes, was the music director, and Lionel Linden was the director of photography.

25. Parker, "Discovering Ida Lupino," 21.

26. Hayley Mills, interview by Randy Haberkamp, *Hollywood Home Movies: Treasures from the Academy Film Archive*, YouTube video, November 20, 2020, starting at 40:00, https://www.youtube.com/watch?v=C4DJEtjt82M&t=64s. This short video is an introduction to the Academy's Home Movie Collection. Lynne Kirste, special collections curator at the Academy of Motion Picture Arts and Sciences, also makes an appearance. She has curated many of the home movies filmed by actors, directors, and cinematographers that have found their way into the collection. Gypsy Rose Lee's movies are just a few among many.

27. "Director's Delight," undated pressbook for *The Trouble with Angeles*, 11, Pressbook Collection, Cinematic Arts Library, University of Southern California, Los Angeles.

28. Robert Ellis, "Ida Lupino Brings New Hope to Hollywood," *Negro Digest*, August 1950, 47.

29. Ellis, "Ida Lupino Brings New Hope," 48. It's likely that the financial backer had a connection to Howard Hughes.

30. R. L. Armstrong, "South of the Chocolate Mountains: Scattered Impressions of *The Hitch-Hiker*," *Bright Lights Film Journal*, August 1, 2002, https://brightlightsfilm.com/south-chocolate-mountains-scattered-impressions-hitch-hiker/#.YPsI0i2cbOQ.

31. Ellis, "Ida Lupino Brings New Hope," 49.

32. Edwin Schallert, "Ida Lupino Will Film 'Pachuco' at RKO, Bond Names Tommy Cook," *Los Angeles Times*, September 27, 1949, A7.

33. Maggie Hennefeld, "Film History," *Feminist Media Histories* 4, no. 2 (2018): 77.

34. Johnston, "Women's Cinema," 32.

35. Hennefeld, "Film History," 77.

36. Johnston, "Women's Cinema," 32; and Stewart, *Ida Lupino as Film Director*, 6.

37. Richard Brody, "Andrew Sarris and the 'A' Word," *New Yorker*, June 19, 2012, https://www.newyorker.com/culture/richard-brody/andrew-sarris-and-the-a-word.

38. Pauline Kael, "Circles and Squares," *Film Quarterly* 16, no. 3 (1963): 12–26; Barthes, "Death of the Author"; and Michel Foucault, "What Is an Author?" (1969), in *Language, Counter-Memory, Practice: Selected Essays and Interviews*, ed. Donald F. Bouchard, trans. Donald F. Bouchard and Sherry Simon (Ithaca, NY: Cornell University Press, 1977), 113–138. See also Sarris's reply to Kael. Andrew Sarris, "The Auteur Theory and the Perils of Pauline," *Film Quarterly* 16, no. 4 (1963): 26–33.

39. Sellors, *Film Authorship*, 127.
40. Everitt, "Woman Forgotten."
41. Everitt, "Woman Forgotten."
42. Thomson, *New Biographical Dictionary*, 605.
43. Varney, "Ida Lupino, Director."
44. Scorsese, "Ida Lupino."
45. Michael Mallory, who interviewed Lupino in 1994, lamented that she never received an Oscar. Michael Mallory, "There Is Nothing like a Dame! Ida Lupino," *Scarlet Street: The Magazine of Mystery and Horror*, no. 13 (1994): 45–51.
46. Robert Osborne, "Lupino Still WIN-ning Praises of the Industry," Rambling Reporter, *Hollywood Reporter*, November 17, 1993, 6, box 107, Personality Clippings File, Constance McCormick Collection, Cinematic Arts Library, University of Southern California, Los Angeles.
47. Osborne, "Lupino Still WIN-ning Praises of the Industry." For a list of Lupino's various Emmy nominations and other awards, see "Ida Lupino: Awards," IMDb, https://www.imdb.com/name/nm0526946/awards.
48. Lupino, "Me, Mother Directress."

BIBLIOGRAPHY

Archival Collections

Archive Research and Study Center. UCLA Film & Television Archive, University of California, Los Angeles.

Biblioteca Renzo Renzi della Cineteca di Bologna, Bologna, Italy.

Billy Rose Theatre Collection. New York Public Library.

Cinematic Arts Library, University of California, Los Angeles.

Constance McCormick Collection. University of Southern California, Los Angeles.

Hal Roach Collection. Cinematic Arts Library, University of Southern California, Los Angeles.

Home Movie Collection. Academy Film Archive, Academy of Motion Picture Arts and Sciences, Los Angeles.

Ida Lupino Collection. Harry Ransom Center, University of Texas, Austin.

Louis B. Mayer Library. American Film Institute, Los Angeles.

Margaret Herrick Library Digital Collection. Margaret Herrick Library, Academy of Motion Picture Arts and Sciences, Beverly Hills, CA.

Mary Pickford Center for Motion Picture Study. Academy of Motion Picture Arts and Sciences, Los Angeles.

MGM Production Dept. (TV Shows) Collection, Cinematic Arts Library, University of Southern California, Los Angeles.

Motion Picture Association of America Production Code Administration Records, 1927–1967. Collection 102. Margaret Herrick Library, Academy of Motion Picture Arts and Sciences, Los Angeles.

Museum of Modern Art (MoMA), New York.

O'Brian, Hugh. Papers, 1949–1973. Collection 257. Performing Arts Special Collections, Charles E. Young Research Library, University of California, Los Angeles.

Personality Clipping File Collection. Cinematic Arts Library, University of Southern California, Los Angeles.

Pressbook Collection. Cinematic Arts Library, University of Southern California, Los Angeles.

RKO Pictures, Scripts Collection, 003, Production Information Files, Box RKO–S-1592, Circulation N. UCLA Library Special Collections, University of California, Los Angeles.

RKO Radio Pictures Studio Records. Collection PASC 3. UCLA Library Special Collections, Charles E. Young Research Library, University of California, Los Angeles.

Sally Forrest Collection. In processing. UCLA Library Special Collections, Charles E. Young Research Library, University of California, Los Angeles.

TV Shows Collection. Cinematic Arts Library, University of Southern California, Los Angeles.

Published Sources

American Film Institute. "The Trouble with Angels." *AFI Catalog of Feature Films: The First 100 Years, 1893–1993*. Accessed January 9, 2024. https://catalog.afi.com/Catalog/moviedetails/22691.

Andersen, Thom. "Red Hollywood." In *Literature and the Visual Arts in Contemporary Society*, edited by Suzanne Ferguson and Barbara S. Groseclose, 142–196. Columbus: Ohio State University Press, 1985.

Anderson, Christopher. *Hollywood TV: The Studio System in the Fifties*. Austin: University of Texas Press, 1994.

Anderson, Ken. "The Trouble with Angels, 1966." *Dreams Are What Le Cinema Is For* (blog), October 9, 2014. https://lecinemadreams.blogspot.com/2014/10/the-trouble-with-angels-1966.html?m=1.

Andrew, Dudley, and Carole Cavanaugh. *Sansho Dayu (Sansho the Bailiff)*. London: British Film Institute, 2000.

Armstrong, R. L. "South of the Chocolate Mountains: Scattered Impressions of *The Hitch-Hiker*." *Bright Lights Film Journal*, August 1, 2002. https://brightlightsfilm.com/south-chocolate-mountains-scattered-impressions-hitch-hiker/#.YPsI0i2cbOQ.

Arnold, Sarah. *Gender and Early Television Mapping Women's Role in Emerging US and British Media, 1850-1950* (London: Bloomsbury Academic, 2021).

Astruc, Alexandre. "What Is *Mise en scène?*" In Hillier, *Cahiers du Cinéma*, vol. 1, *The 1950s*, 266–268. First published as "Qu'est-ce que la mise-en-scène?," *Cahiers du Cinéma* 100 (October 1959).

Balio, Tino. *Grand Design: Hollywood as a Modern Business Enterprise, 1930–1939*. Berkeley: University of California Press, 1993.

Banks, Miranda, Vicki Mayer, and John T. Caldwell. *Production Studies: Cultural Studies of Media Industries*. New York: Routledge, 2009.

Barnouw, Eric. *Tube of Plenty: The Evolution of American Television*. 2nd rev. ed. New York: Oxford University Press, 1990.

Bart, Peter. "Lupino, the Dynamo." *New York Times*, March 7, 1965, X7.

Barthes, Roland. "The Death of the Author" (1967). In *Image, Music, Text*, translated by Stephen Heath, 142–148. London: Fontana, 1977.

Baudrillard, Jean. *Le système des objects*. Paris: Gallimard, 1968.

Becker, Christine. "An Industrial History of Established Hollywood Film Actors on Fifties Prime Time Television." PhD diss., University of Wisconsin–Madison, 2001.

Becker, Christine. *It's the Pictures That Got Small: Hollywood Film Stars on 1950s Television*. Middletown, CT: Wesleyan University Press, 2008.

Becker, Christine. "Televising Film Stardom in the 1950s." *Framework: The Journal of Cinema and Media* 46, no. 2 (2005): 5–21.

Berenstein, Rhona J. "Acting Live: TV Performance, Intimacy, and Immediacy (1945–1955)." In *Reality Squared: Televisual Discourse on the Real*, edited by James Friedman, 25–49. New Brunswick, NJ: Rutgers University Press, 2002.

Bergstrom, Janet. "Lost in Translation? Listening to the Hitchcock-Truffaut Interview." In *A Companion to Alfred Hitchcock*, edited by Thomas Leitch and Leland Poague, 387–404. Malden, MA: Blackwell, 2011.

Bergstrom, Janet. "Murnau in America: Chronicle of Lost Films." *Film History* 14, nos. 3–4 (2002): 430–460.

Bergstrom, Janet. "The Mystery of The Blue Gardenia." In *Shades of Noir: A Reader*, edited by Joan Copjec, 97–120. London: Verso, 1993.

Berke, Annie. *Their Own Best Creations: Women Writers in Postwar Television*. Oakland: University of California Press, 2022.

Blinn, Johna. "Ida Lupino's Scrambled Egg Act." *Los Angeles Times*, April 17, 1975, H28.

Blinn, Johna. "Oneiric Cinema: 'The Woman on the Beach.'" *Film History* 11, no. 1 (1999): 114–125.

Bonnaud, Frédéric. "Radical Kindness." Translated by Jonathan Robbins. *Film Comment* 48, no. 2 (2012): 22–25.

Borde, Raymond, and Etienne Chaumeton. *Panorama du film noir americain, 1941–1953.* Paris: Editions du Minuit, 1955.

Bordwell, David. *Reinventing Hollywood: How 1940s Filmmakers Changed Movie Storytelling*. Chicago: University of Chicago Press, 2017.

Brody, Richard. "Andrew Sarris and the 'A' Word." *New Yorker*, June 19, 2012. https://www.newyorker.com/culture/richard-brody/andrew-sarris-and-the-a-word.

Brody, Richard. "Not Wanted." Movies. *New Yorker*, June 20, 2016, 17. https://www.newyorker.com/goings-on-about-town/movies/not-wanted.

Brooks, Peter. *The Melodramatic Imagination: Balzac, Henry James, Melodrama, and the Mode of Excess.* New Haven, CT: Yale University Press, 1976.

Brooks, Tim, and Earl Marsh. *The Complete Directory to Prime Time Network and Cable TV Shows, 1946–Present.* New York: Ballantine, 1995.

Bruno, Giuliana. *Streetwalking on a Ruined Map: Cultural Theory and the City Films of Elvira Notari.* Princeton, NJ: Princeton University Press, 1993.

Brunsdon, Charlotte, and Lynn Spigel. *Feminist Television Criticism: A Reader.* London: McGraw-Hill Education, 2007.

Bubbeo, Daniel. *The Women of Warner Brothers: The Lives and Careers of Fifteen Leading Ladies, with Filmographies for Each.* Jefferson, NC: McFarland, 2002.

Caldwell, John Thornton. "Industrial Auteur Theory (Above the Line/Creative)." In *Production Culture: Industrial Reflexivity and Critical Practice in Film and Television*, 197–231. Durham, NC: Duke University Press, 2008.

Calvino, Italo. *Six Memos for the Next Millennium.* Cambridge, MA: Harvard University Press, 1988.

Carman, Emily. *Independent Stardom: Freelance Women in the Hollywood Studio System.* Austin: University of Texas, 2016.

Charles, John. "Ernie Kovacs: Biography." Turner Classic Movies. Accessed January 9, 2024. https://www.tcm.com/tcmdb/person/105013%7C48853/Ernie-Kovacs#biography.

Chung, Hye Seung. *Hollywood Asian: Philip Ahn and the Politics of Cross-Ethnic Performance.* Philadelphia: Temple University Press, 2006.

Collins, Jim, Hilary Radner, and Ava Preacher Collins, eds. *Film Theory Goes to the Movies.* London: Routledge, 1993.

Cook, Pam. *The Cinema Book.* 3rd ed. London: BFI, 2007.

Cook, Pam. "*Outrage* (1950)." In Kuhn, *Queen of the 'B's*, 57-72.

Cook, Pam. "The Place of Women in the Cinema of Raoul Walsh." In *Issues in Feminist Film Criticism*, edited by Patricia Erens, 19–27. Bloomington: Indiana University Press, 1990.

Coppola, Francis Ford. "Playboy Interview: Francis Ford Coppola." Interview by William Murray. In *Francis Ford Coppola: Interviews*, edited by Gene D. Phillips and Rodney Hill, 17–43. Jackson: University of Mississippi Press, 2004.

Cosgrove, Ben. "'I'm Gonna Live by the Gun and Roam': Portrait of an American Spree Killer." *Life*, April 1, 2014. http://time.com/3879488/billy-cockeyed-cook-portrait-of-an-american-spree-killer/.

Cotten, Joseph. "Orson and Me." *New York Daily News*, October 13, 1985.

Crowther, Bosley. "Angel in Trouble: Hayley Mills Sparkles in an Uneven Movie," *New York Times*, April 7, 1966, 45.

Cushing, Lincoln. "Kabat-Kaiser: Improving Quality of Life through Rehabilitation." Kaiser Permanente. June 14, 2017. https://about.kaiserpermanente.org/who-we-are/our-history/kabat-kaiser-improving-quality-of-life-through-rehabilitation.

Dargis, Manohla. "Revisiting a Film from Ida Lupino, Hollywood Star Turned Director." Review of *Never Fear*. *New York Times*, January 24, 2019.

Davis, Mike. *City of Quartz: Excavating the Future in Los Angeles*. New York: Verso, 1990.

Desjardins, Mary R. *Recycled Stars: Female Film Stardom in the Age of Television and Video*. Durham, NC: Duke University Press, 2015.

"Director's Cut: Samuel Fuller and the French Connection." *New Yorker*, November 17, 2002. https://www.newyorker.com/magazine/2002/11/25/directors-cut.

Dixon, Wheeler Winston. *Lost in the Fifties: Recovering Phantom Hollywood*. Carbondale: Southern Illinois University Press, 2005.

Dixon, Wheeler Winston. "Lupino, Ida." *Great Directors* 50. Senses of Cinema. April 2009. https://www.sensesofcinema.com/2009/great-directors/ida-lupino.

Donati, William. *Ida Lupino: A Biography*. Lexington: University Press of Kentucky, 1996.

du Kruif, Paul. "Many Will Rise and Walk." *Reader's Digest*, February 1946.

Durgnat, Raymond. "Paint It Black: The Family Tree of Film Noir." *Cinema*, nos. 6–7 (1970): 49–56.

Dyer, Richard. *Heavenly Bodies: Film Stars and Society*. New York: Routledge, 2004.

Eggener, Keith. "Good Neighbors Make Glass Houses: Design Dialogues in Mexico City and Southern California, c. 1940–1960." In *Found in Translation: Design in California and Mexico, 1915–1985*, edited by Wendy Kaplan, 260–280. Los Angeles: Los Angeles County Museum of Art, 2017.

Eisenschitz, Bernard. *Nicholas Ray: An American Journey*. Minneapolis: University of Minnesota Press, 1996.

Ellis, Robert. "Ida Lupino Brings New Hope to Hollywood." *Negro Digest*, August 1950, 47–49.

Enelow, Shonni. "The Greatest Love of All." *Film Comment* 54, no. 3 (2018): 56–61.

Estrin, Eric. "The Unraveling of Frances Farmer." *Washington Post*, January 23, 1983. https://www.washingtonpost.com/archive/lifestyle/style/1983/01/23/the-unraveling-of-frances-farmer/8b1160fd-9535–474b-84e7–8bc08be388a7.

Everitt, David. "A Woman Forgotten and Scorned No More." *New York Times*, November 23, 1997, sec. 2, p. 34.

"Feature Reviews: *The Hitch-Hiker*." *Boxoffice*, January 17, 1953.

Federici, Silvia. *Wages against Housework*. Bristol, UK: Power of Women Collective and Falling Wall Press, 1975.

"Film Reviews." Review of *The Hitch-Hiker*. *Variety*, January 21, 1953.

Finler, Joel W. *The Hollywood Story*. 3rd ed. London: Wallflower, 2003.

Foster, Gwendolyn Audrey. *Women Film Directors: An International Bio-Critical Dictionary*. Westport, CT: Greenwood, 1995.

Foucault, Michel. "What Is an Author?" (1969). In *Language, Counter-Memory, Practice: Selected Essays and Interviews*, edited by Donald F. Bouchard, translated by Donald F. Bouchard and Sherry Simon, 113–138. Ithaca, NY: Cornell University Press, 1977.

"Frances Farmer Biography Slated for Indy in '75." *Boxoffice*, December 9, 1974, NE-4.

Freyche, M.-J., A. M.-M. Payne, and C. Lederrey. "Poliomyelitis in 1953." *Bulletin of the World Health Organization* 12 (1955): 595–649. https://www.ncbi.nlm.nih.gov/pmc/articles/PMC2542300/pdf/bullwho00548-0107.pdf.

Gehman, Richard, and Michael McFadden. "The Golden Sex: They Use Beauty, Brains to Produce TV." *Los Angeles Herald Examiner*, May 14, 1963, B1, B8.

Georgakas, Dan. "Ida Lupino: Doing It Her Way." *Cineaste* 25, no. 3 (2000): 32–36.
Geraghty, Christine. "Re-examining Stardom: Questions of Texts, Bodies and Performance." In *Stardom and Celebrity: A Reader*, edited by Sean Redmond and Su Holmes, 98–110. Los Angeles: Sage, 2007.
Gilmore, James N., and Sidney Gottlieb, eds. *Orson Welles in Focus*. Bloomington: Indiana University Press, 2018.
Ginzburg, Carlo. *The Cheese and the Worms: The Cosmos of a Sixteenth-Century Miller*. Translated by John Tedeschi and Anne C. Tedeschi. Baltimore: Johns Hopkins University Press, 1980. First published as *Il formaggio e i vermi: Il cosmo di un mugnaio del'500* (Torino: Giulio Einaudi, 1976).
Ginzburg, Carlo. *Clues, Myths, and the Historical Method*. Translated by John Tedeschi and Anne C. Tedeschi. Baltimore: Johns Hopkins University Press, 1989. First published as *Miti, emblemi, spie: Morfologia e storia* (Torino: Giulio Einaudi, 1986).
Greven, David. "Ida Lupino's American Psycho: *The Hitch-Hiker* (1953)." *Bright Lights Film Journal*. February 27, 2014. https://brightlightsfilm.com/ida-lupinos-american-psycho-hitch-hiker-1953/#.YATTty1h3OR.
Grisham, Therese, and Julie Grossman. *Ida Lupino, Director: Her Art and Resilience in Times of Transition*. New Brunswick, NJ: Rutgers University Press, 2017.
Hadžihalilović, Lucile. Interview by Nicolas Rapold. In Laura Kern, "The Miracle of Life," *Film Comment* 52, no. 3 (May–June 2016): 34–39.
Haid, Raul. "Kiss Me Deadly (Robert Aldrich, 1955)." Senses of Cinema, March 2019. https://www.sensesofcinema.com/2019/cteq/kiss-me-deadly-robert-aldrich-1955.
Hannsberry, Karen Burroughs. *Femme Noir: Bad Girls of Film*. Vol. 1, *Introduction: Bacall to Lupino*. Jefferson, NC: McFarland, 1998.
Haskell, Molly. *From Reverence to Rape: The Treatment of Women in the Movies*. Harmondsworth: Penguin, 1974.
Hastie, Amelie. *The Bigamist*. New York: Palgrave MacMillan, 2009.
Hastie, Amelie. *Cupboards of Curiosity: Women, Recollection, and Film History*. Durham, NC: Duke University Press, 2007.
Hastie, Amelie. "The Trouble with Lupino." *Cinema Comparative Cinema* 4, no. 8 (2016): 50–55.
Heck-Rabi, Louise. *Women Filmmakers: A Critical Reception*. Metuchen, NJ: Scarecrow, 1984.
Hennefeld, Maggie. "Film History." *Feminist Media Histories* 4, no. 2 (2018): 77–83.
Henry, Michael. "Ida Lupino: Parce que le coeur n'est pas de marbre." *Positif: Revue mensuelle de cinéma*, no. 540 (2006): 64.
Herman, Ellen. "Timeline of Adoption History." Adoption History Project. Last updated February 24, 2012. https://pages.uoregon.edu/adoption/timeline.html/.
HHT [Howard Thompson]. Review of *The Bigamist* at the Astor. *New York Times*, December 26, 1953, 10.
Hill, Erin. *Never Done: A History of Women's Work in Media Production*. New Brunswick, NJ: Rutgers University Press, 2016.
Hillier, Jim, ed. *Cahiers du Cinéma*. Vol. 1, *The 1950s: Neo-Realism, Hollywood, New Wave*. Translated by Liz Heron. Cambridge, MA: Harvard University Press, 1985.
Hillier, Jim, ed. *Cahiers du Cinéma*. Vol. 2, *The 1960s (1960–1968): New Wave, New Cinema, Reevaluating Hollywood*. Cambridge, MA: Harvard University Press, 1986.
Hilmes, Michele. "Is Archiving a Feminist Issue? Historical Research and the Past, Present, and Future of Television Studies." *Cinema Journal* 47, no. 3 (2008): 152–158.
Hirsch, Foster. *The Dark Side of the Screen*. New York: A. S. Barnes, 1981.

Hirsch, Joshua. "Film Gris: Reconsidered." *Journal of Popular Film* 34, no. 2 (2006): 82–93.

Hoberman, J. [James Lewis]. "Ida Lupino, a Woman of Spine on Both Sides of the Lens." *New York Times*, November 24, 2016. https://www.nytimes.com/2016/11/24/movies/ida-lupino-a-woman-of-spine-on-both-sides-of-the-lens.html.

Hopper, Hedda. "Ida Lupino Pushes Hunt for Talent: Ability Rather Than Names to Be Sought by Actress-Producer." *Los Angeles Times*, September 4, 1949, D1.

Horne, Gerald. *Class Struggle in Hollywood, 1930–1950: Moguls, Mobsters, Stars, Reds, and Trade Unionists*. Austin: University of Texas Press, 2001.

"The Hosts: Open House on TV." *TV Guide*, February 4–10, 1956, 21.

Huber, Christoph. "Mother of All of Us: Ida Lupino, the Filmaker." *Cinema Scope*, no. 65 (2015). https://cinema-scope.com/features/mother-of-all-of-us-ida-lupino-the-filmaker/.

Humphrey, Hal. "TV, the Great Rejuvenator." *Los Angeles Mirror*, September 9, 1954, 26.

Hurd, Mary G. *Women Directors and Their Films*. Westport, CN: Praeger, 2007.

Hutchinson, Thomas H. *Here Is Television: Your Window to the World*. New York: Hastings House, 1948.

"Ida Lupino: Through the Lens," produced and directed by Torrie Rosenzweig, written by Gidion Phillips, narrated by Peter Graves. *Biography*, A&E, March 24, 1998.

Isenberg, Noah. *Detour*. London: Palgrave McMillan, 2008.

Johnson, Robert. "Mr. Duff and Ida." *TV Guide*, June 1–7, 1957, 18.

Johnston, Claire. "Women's Cinema as Counter-Cinema" (1979). In *Feminist Film Theory: A Reader*, edited by Sue Thornham, 31–40. New York: New York University Press, 1999.

Jones, J. R. *The Lives of Robert Ryan*. Middletown, CT: Wesleyan University Press, 2015.

Kael, Pauline. "Circles and Squares." *Film Quarterly* 16, no. 3 (1963): 12–26.

Kael, Pauline. "The Current Cinema: Dames." Review of *A Woman under the Influence*. *New Yorker*, December 9, 1974, 171–178.

Kaplan, E. Ann, ed. *Women in Film Noir*. London: British Film Institute, 1998.

Kay, Karyn, and Gerald Peary, eds. *Women and the Cinema: A Critical Anthology*. New York: E. P. Dutton, 1977.

Kazan, Elia. *Kazan on Directing*. New York: Vintage Books, 2010.

Kearney, Mary Celeste, and James M. Moran. "Ida Lupino as Director of Television." In Kuhn, *Queen of the 'B's*, 137–150.

Kelly, Gabrielle, and Cheryl Robson. *Celluloid Ceiling: Women Film Directors Breaking Through*. London: Supernova, 2014.

King, Stephen. *Danse Macabre*. New York: Everett House, 1981.

King, Susan. "A Very Independent Streak." *Los Angeles Times*, October 15, 2002. https://www.latimes.com/archives/la-xpm-2002-oct-15-et-king15-story.htm.

Klinger, Barbara. *Melodrama and Meaning: History, Culture, and the Films of Douglas Sirk*. Indianapolis: Indiana University Press, 1994.

Koszarski, Richard. *Hollywood Directors, 1941–1976*. New York: Oxford University Press, 1977.

Kuhn, Annette. "Introduction: Intestinal Fortitude." In Kuhn, *Queen of the 'B's*, 1–12.

Kuhn, Annette, ed. *Queen of the 'B's: Ida Lupino behind the Camera*. Westport, CT: Greenwood, 1995.

Lane, Lupino. *How to Become a Comedian*. 3rd ed. London: F. Muller, 1946.

Lee, Luaine. "Lupino Still Grande Dame of the Cinema." *Chicago Tribune*, February 13, 1982, 33.

Levitin, Jacqueline, Judith Plessis, and Valerie Raoul. *Women Filmmakers: Refocusing*. New York: Routledge, 2003.

Losey, Joseph, and Michel Ciment. *Conversations with Losey*. London: Methuen, 1985.

Lupino, Ida. "Ida Lupino: Just Plain Mother to Camera Brood." *Los Angeles Times*, June 18, 1967, C7.

Lupino, Ida. "Interview with Ida Lupino, Los Angeles, September 1974." By Patrick McGilligan and Debra Weiner. In Patrick McGilligan, *Film Crazy: Interviews with Hollywood Legends*, 219–29. New York: St. Martin's, 2014.

Lupino, Ida. "Me, Mother Directress." *Action* 2, no. 3 (1967): 14–15.

Lupino, Ida, and Mary Ann Anderson. *Ida Lupino: Beyond the Camera*. Albany, GA: Bear-Manor Media, 2011.

Maland, Charles J. "'Film Gris': Crime, Critique and Cold War Culture in 1951." *Film Criticism* 26, no. 3 (2002): 1–30.

Mallory, Michael. "There Is Nothing like a Dame! Ida Lupino." *Scarlet Street: The Magazine of Mystery and Horror*, no. 13 (1994): 45–51.

Mamber, Stephen. "The Television Films of Alfred Hitchcock." *Cinema* 7, no. 1 (1971): 2–7.

Mann, Denise, and Lynn Spigel, eds. "Television and the Female Consumer." Special issue, *Camera Obscura: A Journal of Feminism and Film Theory* 16 (1988).

Martin, Angela. "Refocusing Authorship in Women's Filmmaking." In *Women Filmmakers: Refocusing*, edited by Jacqueline Levitin, Judith Plessis, and Valerie Raoul, 29–34. New York: Routledge, 2003.

Mathews, Tom Dewe. "The English Jean Harlow." *Guardian*, April 22, 2002. https://www.theguardian.com/film/2002/apr/22/artsfeatures2.

Mayer, Vicki. *Below the Line: Producers and Production Studies in the New Television Economy*. Durham, NC: Duke University Press, 2011.

Mayne, Judith. *Directed by Dorothy Arzner*. Bloomington: Indiana University Press, 1944.

McCarthy, Todd. Introduction to *Painting with Light*, by John Alton. 1949. Reprint, Berkeley: University of California Press, 2013.

McGilligan, Patrick. *Film Crazy: Interviews with Hollywood Legends*. New York: St. Martin's, 2014.

McHugh, Kathleen Anne. *American Domesticity: From How-to Manual to Hollywood Melodrama*. Oxford: Oxford University Press, 1999.

McHugh, Kathleen Anne. "Miranda July and the New 21st Century Indie." In *Indie Reframed: Women's Filmmaking and Contemporary American Independent Cinema*, edited by Linda Badley, Claire Perkins, and Michele Schreiber, 239–253. Edinburgh: Edinburgh University Press, 2016.

McKenna, Kristine. "Under a Woman's Influence." *Los Angeles Times*, May 3, 1992, F2.

Micha, René. *Robert Aldrich*. Brussels: Club du Livre de Cinéma, 1957.

Miklitsch, Robert, ed. *Kiss the Blood off My Hands: On Classic Film Noir*. Urbana: University of Illinois Press, 2014.

Miller, Frank. "*The Hitch-Hiker*." Turner Classic Movies, June 28, 2004. https://www.tcm.com/tcmdb/title/78138/the-hitch-hiker#articles-reviews?articleId=78324.

Miller, Jack. "Lean and Mean: 2 Films by Ida Lupino." *A Place for Film* (blog). Indiana University Blogs, February 8, 2021. https://blogs.iu.edu/aplaceforfilm/author/jarymill/.

Mills, Hayley. Interview by Randy Haberkamp. *Hollywood Home Movies: Treasures from the Academy Film Archive*. YouTube video, starting at 40:00. https://www.youtube.com/watch?v=C4DJEtjt82M&t=64s.

Miyao, Daisuke. *The Aesthetic of Shadow: Lighting and Japanese Cinema*. Durham, NC: Duke University Press, 2011.

Montañez Smukler, Maya. "Working Girls: The History of Women Directors in 1970s Hollywood." PhD diss., University of California, Los Angeles, 2014.

Morra, Anne. "Ida Lupino." In *Modern Women: Women Artists at the Museum of Modern Art*, edited by Alexandra Schwartz, 234–237. New York: Museum of Modern Art, 2010.

Moss, Marilyn Ann. *The Oxford Handbook of Japanese Cinema*. Oxford: Oxford University Press, 2014.

Moss, Marilyn Ann. "The Tough and Tender Sides of a *Mad Dog* Classic." *Cineaste* 36, no. 2 (2011): 6–11.

Mourlet, Michel. "In Defense of Violence." In *Cahiers du Cinéma*, vol. 2, *The 1960s (1960–1968): New Wave, New Cinema, Reevaluating Hollywood*, edited by Jim Hillier, translated by David Wilson, 132–134. Cambridge, MA: Harvard University Press, 1986. First published as "Apologie de la violence," *Cahiers du Cinéma* 107 (1960).

Murray, Susan. *Hitch Your Antenna to the Stars: Early Television and Broadcast Stardom*. New York: Routledge, 2005.

Naremore, James. "American Film Noir: The History of an Idea." *Film Quarterly* 49, no. 2 (1996): 12–28.

Naremore, James. Foreword to *Orson Welles in Focus: Texts and Contexts*, edited by James N. Gilmore and Sidney Gottlieb, vii–x. Bloomington: Indiana University Press, 2018.

Naremore, James. *More Than Night: Film Noir in Its Contexts*. Berkeley: University of California Press, 1998.

Newcomb, Horace, and Paul M. Hirsch. "Television as a Cultural Forum." In *Television: The Critical View*, edited by Horace Newcomb, 561–573. Oxford: Oxford University Press, 1987.

Nolan, Jack Edmund. "Ida Lupino." *Films in Review* 16 (1965): 61–62.

Noriega, Chon A., Mari Carmen Ramirez, and Pilar Tompkins Rivas. *Home—So Different, So Appealing*. Los Angeles: UCLA Chicano Studies Research Center Press, 2018. Exhibition catalog.

O'Dell, Cary. "'The Hitch-Hiker': National Film Registry #10." *Now See Hear!* (blog). Library of Congress Blogs, November 22, 2018. https://blogs.loc.gov/now-see-hear/2018/11/the-hitch-hiker-national-film-registry-10.

Odens, Peter. "The Billy Cook Murders." *Calexico Chronicle*, August 18, 1991.

O'Rawe, Catherine. "Gender, Genre and Stardom: Fatality in Italian Neorealist Cinema." In *The Femmes Fatale: Images, Histories, Context*, edited by Helen Hanson and Christine O'Rawe, 127–42. London: Palgrave Macmillan, 2010.

Osborne, Robert. "Lupino Still WIN-ning Praises of the Industry." Rambling Reporter. *Hollywood Reporter*, November 17, 1993.

Parish, James Robert, and Don E. Stanke. *The Forties Gals*. Westport, CT: Arlington House, 1980.

Parker, Barry M. "Newsreel: Lost Lupino." *American Film*, June 1, 1981, 14.

Parker, Francine. "Discovering Ida Lupino," *Action* 6–8 (1973): 19–23.

Parsons, Louella, and Harriet Parsons. "Ida Lupino, Rarest of the Rare." *New York Journal-American*, December 5, 1965.

Paulson, Michael. "Giving a Hand to Parents in Theatre." *New York Times*, November 10, 2018, AR6.

Pinkerton, Nick. "Changing the Narrative." Review of David Bordwell's *Reinventing Hollywood*. *Film Comment* 53, no. 5 (2017): 78.

Powdermaker, Hortense. *Hollywood, the Dream Factory: An Anthropologist Looks at the Movie-Makers*. Boston: Little Brown, 1950.

"Preserving the Silver Screen." *Library of Congress Information Bulletin* 58, no. 12 (December 1999). https://www.loc.gov/loc/lcib/9912/nfb.html.

Presnell, Don and Marty McGee. *A Critical History of Television's* The Twilight Zone, *1959–1964*. Jefferson, NC: McFarland.

Quart, Barbara Koenig. *Women Directors: The Emergence of a New Cinema*. New York: Praeger, 1988.

Rabinovitz, Lauren. "*The Hitch-Hiker* (1953)." In Kuhn, *Queen of the 'B's*, 90–102.

Richie, Donald. *The Films of Akira Kurosawa*. Berkeley: University of California Press, 1998.

Rickey, Carrie. "Lupino Noir." *Village Voice*, October 29–November 4, 1980, 43–45.

"Rider on the Storm." *Sword and Scale* (blog), December 21, 2015. https://www.swordandscale.com/rider-on-the-storm.

Rivette, Jacques. "Notes on a Revolution." In Hillier, *Cahiers du Cinéma*, vol. 1, *The 1950s*, 93–97. First published as "Notes sur une revolution," *Cahiers du Cinéma* 54 (1955): 18–19.

Rivette, Jacques. "On Imagination." In Hillier, *Cahiers du Cinéma*, vol. 1, *The 1950s*, 104–106. First published as "De l'invention," *Cahiers du Cinéma* 27 (1953).

Roberts, Richard M. "Lupino Lane, Music Hall Comedian." *Classic Images* (October 1996): 22–25.

Rosen, Marjorie. *Popcorn Venus: Women, Movies, and the American Dream*. New York: Avon, 1973.

Ross, Kristin. *Fast Cars, Clean Bodies: Decolonization and the Reordering of French Culture*. Cambridge, MA: MIT Press, 1995.

Rossellini, Isabella. *Some of Me*. New York: Random House, 1997.

Rule, Vera. "Obituary: Joseph Cotten." *Guardian*, February 8, 1994.

Saks, Sol. Interview by Bill Freiberger. Television Academy. May 21, 2009. https://interviews.televisionacademy.com/interviews/sol-saks#interview-clips.

Sarris, Andrew. *The American Cinema: Directors and Directions, 1929–1968*. Boston: Da Capo, 1996.

Sarris, Andrew. "The Auteur Theory and the Perils of Pauline." *Film Quarterly* 16, no. 4 (1963): 26–33.

Schallert, Edwin. "Ida Lupino Will Film 'Pachuco' at RKO, Bond Names Tommy Cook." *Los Angeles Times*, September 27, 1949, A7.

Schatz, Thomas. *Boom and Bust: American Cinema in the 1940s*. History of the American Cinema, edited by Charles Harpole, vol. 6. Berkeley: University of California Press, 1999.

Schatz, Thomas. *The Genius of the System: Hollywood Filmmaking in the Studio Era*. New York: Pantheon, 1988.

Schechter, Marshall D. "Observations on Adopted Children." *Archives of General Psychiatry* 3, no. 1 (1960): 21–32.

Scheib, Ronnie. "Ida Lupino: Auteuress (1980)." *Screening the Past*. http://www.screeningthepast.com/issue-41-ronnie-scheib-dossier/ida-lupino-auteuress/. First published in *Film Comment* 16, no. 1 (February 1980): 54–64, 80.

Scheib, Ronnie. "*Never Fear* (1950)." In Kuhn, *Queen of the 'B's*, 40–56.

Scheib, Ronnie. "Round Table: Ronnie Scheib." *Screening the Past*. November 2016. http://www.screeningthepast.com/2016/11/round- table_ronnie-scheib/. First published in *Metro*, no. 109 (1997): 3–12.

Schickel, Richard. *Conversations with Scorsese*. New York: Alfred A. Knopf, 2011.

Schrader, Paul. "Notes on Film Noir." In *Film Genre Reader*, edited by Barry Keith Grant, 167–182. Austin: University of Texas Press, 1986.

Scorsese, Martin. "Ida Lupino: Behind the Camera, a Feminist." *New York Times Magazine*, December 31, 1995, sec. 6, p. 43.

Scorsese, Martin. "Three Portraits in the Form of a Homage: Ida Lupino, John Cassavetes,

Glauber Rocha." In *Projections 7: Film-makers on Film-making in Association with Cahiers du Cinéma*, edited by John Boorman and Walter Donohue, 87–93. London: Faber and Faber, 1997.
Scorsese, Martin, and Francis Ford Coppola. "A Conversation with Martin Scorsese and Francis Ford Coppola." Interview by Geoffrey Gilmore. *USSB Hollywood Insiders*, 1997. YouTube video, July 24, 2013. https://www.youtube.com/watch?v=uJE3Zqb9zXY.
Sellors, C. Paul. *Film Authorship: Auteurs and Other Myths*. New York: Wallflower, 2010.
Shore, Dinah. *The Celebrity Cookbook*. Los Angeles: Price Stern Sloan, 1966.
Silver, Alain, and Elizabeth Ward, eds., *Film Noir: An Encyclopedia of the American Style*. New York: Abrams, 1993.
Silver, Charles. "An Auturist History of Film." Museum of Modern Art, November 6, 2012. https://www.moma.org/explore/inside_out/2012/11/06/ida-lupinos-never-fear-the-younglovers/.
Slesar, Henry. "A Crime for Mothers." *Alfred Hitchcock's Mystery Magazine* 5, no. 12 (December 1960).
Smith, Cecil. "Dainty Ida Takes Up Whip as Director of Westerns." TV Scene. *Daily News*, c. 1959–1960.
Smith, Imogen Sara. "The Lost Land." *Film Comment* 55, no. 1 (2019): 48–53.
Smyth, J. E. *Nobody's Girl Friday: The Women Who Ran Hollywood*. Oxford: Oxford University Press, 2018.
Sobchack, Vivian Carol. "*Detour*: Driving in a Back Projection." In *Kiss the Blood off My Hands: On Classic Film Noir*, edited by Robert Miklitsch, 113–129. Urbana: University of Illinois Press, 2014.
Sobchack, Vivian Carol. "Scary Women: Cinema, Surgery, and Special Effects." In *Carnal Thoughts: Embodiment and Moving Image Culture*, 36–52. Berkeley: University of California Press, 2004.
Sontag, Susan. *On Women*. Edited by David Rieff. New York: Picador, 2023.
Spencer, Kathleen L. *Art and Politics in "Have Gun—Will Travel": The 1950s Television Western as Ethical Drama*. Jefferson, NC: McFarland, 2014.
Spicer, Andrew. *Film Noir*. London: Taylor and Francis, 2002.
Spigel, Lynn. *Make Room for TV: Television and the Family Ideal in Postwar America*. Chicago: University of Chicago Press, 2013.
Spigel, Lynn. *Welcome to the Dreamhouse: Popular Media and Postwar Suburbs*. Durham, NC: Duke University Press, 2001.
Stacey, Jackie. *Stargazing: Hollywood Cinema and Female Spectatorship*. New York: Routledge, 1994.
Stein, Ruthe. "How Ida Lupino Broke into Man's World of Directing." *San Francisco Chronicle*, November 11, 2015, 7.
Stein, Ruthe. "Mother Directs: Ida Lupino behind the Camera." Eat Drink Films. November 11, 2015. http://eatdrinkfilms.com/2015/11/19/mother-directs-ida-lupino-behind-the-camera/.
Steinberg, Cobbett. *TV Facts*. New York: Facts on File, 1980.
Stewart, Lucy Ann Liggett. *Ida Lupino as Film Director, 1949–1953: An Auteur Approach*. New York: Arno, 1980.
Summer, Anita. "What Did You Spend Money on When You First Felt Rich?" *Cosmopolitan* 182, no. 1 (1977): 94, 96, 98.
Tasker, Yvonne, and Suzanne Leonard, eds. *Fifty Hollywood Directors*. London: Routledge, 2015.
Taubin, Amy. "Why Settle for Less?" *Film Comment* 54, no. 4 (2018): 58-60.
Thomas, John D. "Shelf Life." *Village Voice*, October 21, 1997, 90.
Thompson, Kristin, and David Bordwell. "Side Effects and Safe Haven: Out of the Past."

Observations on Film Art (blog), March 24, 2013. https://www.davidbordwell.net/blog/2013/03/24/side-effects-and-safe-haven-out-of-the-past/.

Thomson, David. *The New Biographical Dictionary of Film*. 5th ed. New York: Alfred A. Knopf, 2010.

Truffaut, François. *The Films in My Life*. New York: Simon and Schuster, 1985.

Truffaut, François. "A Wonderful Certainty." In Hillier, *Cahiers du Cinéma*, vol. 1, *The 1950s*, 93–97. First published as Robert Lachenay [François Truffaut], "L'admirable certitude," *Cahiers du Cinéma* 46 (1955).

Vallance, Tom. "Sally Forrest: Performer Who Made Her Name as a Dancer, but Found Real Fame in Ida Lupino's Taboo-Busting Films." *Guardian*, April 7, 2015. https://www.independent.co.uk/news/people/news/sally-forrest-performer-who-made-her-name-dancer-found-real-fame-ida-lupino-s-taboo-busting-films-a107826.html.

Varney, Ginger. "Ida Lupino, Director." *LA Weekly*, November 12–18, 1982, 10, 12.

Velez, Jorge. "John Alton Documentary." YouTube video, December 12, 2013. https://www.youtube.com/watch?v=zJYXAxLeXM4.

Vermilye, Jerry. *Ida Lupino*. New York: Pyramid, 1977.

Waldman, Diane. "*Not Wanted* (1949)." In Kuhn, *Queen of the 'B's*, 13–39.

Walker, Janet. *Couching Resistance: Women, Film, and Psychoanalytic Psychiatry*. Minneapolis: University of Minnesota Press, 1993.

Warren, Alan. *This Is a Thriller: An Episode Guide, History and Analysis of the Classic 1960s Television Series*. Jefferson, NC: McFarland, 2004.

"Wearing Mother's Clothes." *TV Guide*, May 14–20, 1960, 8–9.

Weinberger, Stephen. "Joe Breen's Oscar." *Film History* 17, no. 4 (2005): 380–391.

Weiner, Debra. "Interview with Ida Lupino." In *Women and the Cinema: A Critical Anthology*, edited by Karyn Kay and Gerald Peary, 169–178. New York: Dutton, 1977.

Wexman, Virginia Wright, ed. *Film and Authorship*. New Brunswick, NJ: Rutgers University Press, 2003.

White, James Dillon. *Born to Star: The Lupino Lane Story*. Melbourne: Heinemann, 1957.

Whitney, Dwight. "Ida Lupino, Director." *TV Guide*, October 8–14, 1966, 14–16.

Whyte, William H. *The Organization Man: The Book That Defined a Generation*. Philadelphia: University of Pennsylvania Press, 2002. First published 1956 by Simon and Schuster (New York).

Wittern-Keller, Laura. *Freedom of the Screen: Legal Challenges to State Censorship, 1915–1981*. Lexington: University of Kentucky Press, 2008.

Wollen, Peter. "The Auteur Theory: Michael Curtiz, and *Casablanca*." In *Authorship and Film*, edited by David A. Gerstner and Janet Staiger, 61–76. New York: Routledge, 2003.

"Women Directing for Television." Presentation as part of *She Made It: Women Creating Television and Radio*, Museum of Television and Radio, Los Angeles and New York, January 13–February 16, 2006.

Wood, Robin. *Hitchcock's Films Revisited*. Rev. ed. New York: Columbia University Press, 1989.

Wood, Robin. *Howard Hawks*. Detroit: Wayne State University Press, 2006.

Wylie, Philip. *Generation of Vipers*. New York: Rinehart, 1955.

Yecies, Brian, and Aegyung Shim. "The Rise of the Female Writer-Director and the Changing Face of Korean Cinema." Chap. 9 in *The Changing Face of Korean Cinema, 1960–2015*. London: Routledge, 2015.

Yoo, Hyon Joo, ed. *South Korean Film: Critical and Primary Sources*. Vol. 3. New York: Bloomsbury Academic, 2021.

Zox-Weaver, Annalisa. *Women Modernists and Fascism*. New York: Cambridge University Press, 2011.

Zylstra, Frieda. "Ida Lupino Likes Role in Kitchen." *Chicago Daily Tribune*, April 11, 1958, 38.

ILLUSTRATION CREDITS

iv RKO Radio Pictures Studio Records, UCLA Library Special Collections, Charles E. Young Research Library, University of California, Los Angeles
2 Archive Research and Study Center, UCLA Film & Television Archive, University of California, Los Angeles
4 Ida Lupino Collection, Harry Ransom Center, University of Texas at Austin
5 Ida Lupino Collection, Harry Ransom Center, University of Texas at Austin
7 From A&E documentary, 1998; original at Biblioteca Renzo Renzi Della Cineteca di Bologna
8 Ida Lupino Collection Box 1-2, Harry Ransom Center, University of Texas at Austin
9 Ida Lupino Collection, Harry Ransom Center, University of Texas at Austin
13 Sally Forrest Collection, UCLA Library Special Collections, Charles E. Young Research Library, University of California, Los Angeles
18 Archive Research and Study Center, UCLA Film & Television Archive, University of California, Los Angeles
22 Archive Research and Study Center, UCLA Film & Television Archive, University of California, Los Angeles
37 From film booklet inside Park Nam-ok's DVD film set *Landscape after the War*
39 Ida Lupino Collection, Box 2, Harry Ransom Center, University of Texas at Austin
42 Author's collection
48 Sally Forrest Collection, UCLA Library Special Collections, Charles E. Young Research Library, University of California, Los Angeles
58 Sally Forrest Collection, UCLA Library Special Collections, Charles E. Young Research Library, University of California, Los Angeles
68 Archive Research and Study Center, UCLA Film & Television Archive, University of California, Los Angeles
69 Archive Research and Study Center, UCLA Film & Television Archive, University of California, Los Angeles
72 Archive Research and Study Center, UCLA Film & Television Archive, University of California, Los Angeles
74 Sally Forrest Collection, UCLA Library Special Collections, Charles E. Young Research Library, University of California, Los Angeles
80 Sally Forrest Collection, UCLA Library Special Collections, Charles E. Young Research Library, University of California, Los Angeles
88 Sally Forrest Collection, UCLA Library Special Collections, Charles E. Young Research Library, University of California, Los Angeles
90 Sally Forrest Collection, UCLA Library Special Collections, Charles E. Young Research Library, University of California, Los Angeles
94 RKO Radio Pictures Studio Records, Collection PASC 3. UCLA Library Special Collections, Charles E. Young Research Library, University of Califorina, Los Angeles

99 Archive Research and Study Center, UCLA Film & Television Archive, University of California, Los Angeles
108 Archive Research and Study Center, UCLA Film & Television Archive, University of California, Los Angeles
108 Archive Research and Study Center, UCLA Film & Television Archive, University of California, Los Angeles
118 Ida Lupino Collection, Cinematic Arts Library, University of Southern California, Los Angeles
127 Archive Research and Study Center, UCLA Film & Television Archive, University of California, Los Angeles
136 TV Shows Collection, Cinematic Arts Library, University of Southern California, Los Angeles
141 From DVD *Golden Age of Television*, Volume 14; author's collection
144 From DVD *Alfred Hitchcock Presents,* Season 6, Episode 16, airdate January 24, 1961; author's collection
157 From DVD *The Untouchables*, Season 4, Volume 2, airdate March 5, 1963; author's collection
159 From DVD *The Fugitive*, Season 1, Episode 16, airdate January 14, 1964; author's collection
163 From *Thriller,* Season 2, Episode 2, airdate September 26, 1961; author's collection
177 Personality Clipping File Collection, Cinematic Arts Library, University of Southern California, Los Angeles

INDEX

Page numbers in italics indicate an illustration.

Alexandra Seros was born in sunny Southern California among the orange groves and open roads of the San Fernando Valley (while, just a mile away, Ida Lupino was acting and directing in the canyons of Chatsworth and foothills of the Santa Monica Mountains). Seros is a screenwriter and filmmaker known for her extensive collaborations with industry producers, directors, and writers, including Chris Moore, Jonathan Demme, Don DeLillo, Lianne Halfon, and Mike DeLuca. She has written original and adapted screenplays for every major studio and is a member of both the Screen Actors Guild (SAG) and the Writers Guild of America (WGA). As an AFI Director Fellow and a UCLA PhD graduate in film and media studies, Seros has been a mentor at Sundance and at UCLA in its Graduate Screenwriting Program. She is a founding member of Extera Public Charter Schools, providing education to underserved communities. Seros has also created scholarships for Latino students doing graduate work through the University of California educational system. She is a member of the UCLA Film & Television Archive Board. Seros has produced the restoration of "No. 5 Checked Out" (1956), Lupino's first cowritten teleplay. She has one son, Bruno Seros-Ulloa.